Intelligence

—— for ——

Homeland
Security

Intelligence
for
Homeland
Security

AN INTRODUCTION

Jeffrey Douglas Dailey
James Robert Phelps

LYNNE
RIENNER
PUBLISHERS

BOULDER
LONDON

Published in the United States of America in 2021 by
Lynne Rienner Publishers, Inc.
1800 30th Street, Boulder, Colorado 80301
www.rienner.com

and in the United Kingdom by
Lynne Rienner Publishers, Inc.
Gray's Inn House, 127 Clerkenwell Road, London EC1 5DB
www.eurospanbookstore.com/rienner

Library of Congress Cataloging-in-Publication Data
Names: Dailey, Jeffrey D., author. | Phelps, James R., author.
Title: Intelligence for homeland security : an introduction / Jeffrey
    Douglas Dailey and James Robert Phelps.
Description: Boulder, Colorado : Lynne Rienner Publishers, Inc, [2021] |
    Includes bibliographical references and index. | Summary: "Explains the
    role of the intelligence community in the context of homeland
    security"— Provided by publisher.
Identifiers: LCCN 2021016152 | ISBN 9781626379633 (Hardcover : alk. paper)
    | ISBN 9781626379640 (Paperback : alk. paper)
Subjects: LCSH: Intelligence service—United States. | Internal
    security—United States. | National security—United States. |
    Terrorism—Prevention—Government policy—United States.
Classification: LCC JK468.I6 D327 2021 | DDC 327.1273—dc23
LC record available at https://lccn.loc.gov/2021016152

British Cataloguing in Publication Data
A Cataloguing in Publication record for this book
is available from the British Library.

Printed and bound in the United States of America

The paper used in this publication meets the requirements
of the American National Standard for Permanence of
Paper for Printed Library Materials Z39.48-1992.

5 4 3 2 1

Contents

Tables and Figures

Tables

Figures

Acknowledgments

I would very much like to thank several people for getting this book to the actual finish line. One is my coauthor, James Phelps, who supported the effort with his best. I would not have tackled the project without him. I also owe more than I can say to my close friend Debbie Wilkinson, who proofread every chapter too many times to count.

I thank my editor, Marie-Claire Antoine, who has provided both friendly support and guidance for what turned out to be longer than expected. Her editorial expertise is exceeded only by her patience.

And, last, the views expressed in this book are solely those of the authors and do not reflect the views or opinions of any US government agency or other institution.

—Jeffrey Douglas Dailey

1

Protecting
the Homeland

There have been a number of intelligence successes and failures since 9/11 that deal with the issue of homeland security. The killing of Osama bin Laden was a success. The abandonment of Iraq in 2011 was a failure. When the last of the US troops were pulled out of Iraq, the Iraqi army and government were incapable of maintaining order or preventing the rise of the Islamic State of Iraq and Syria (ISIS) and the establishment of a caliphate that spread across northern Syria and Iraq and resulted in widespread destruction and death. Because of the great upheavals caused by the Arab Spring, this outcome was easily predicted by those who understood and studied the dynamics of the Islamic world; the US government and those following homeland security certainly did not. The result in the United States was an increase in domestic terrorist attacks by individuals who claimed allegiance to ISIS, such as the Pulse Nightclub shootings in Orlando, Florida; the San Bernardino, California, shootings; the attack on the Curtis Caldwell Center in Garland, Texas; and others.

More recently, in the United States and around the world, countries have experienced devastating loss of life and economic loss due to the advent of SARS-CoV-2 (aka the novel coronavirus or Covid-19) that originated in Wuhan, China, in 2019. Events and actions by the Chinese government in the fall of 2019 should have set off warning bells in the US national security and intelligence community, but it appears that they did not. The lack of diligence on the part of the World Health

Organization (WHO) and the Chinese government's delay or cover-up of truthful information regarding the human-to-human spread of the virus resulted in its being transported to countries around the world, with devastating results. There are different public opinions as to whether the virus originated from animals or from a lab that conducts research on dangerous diseases in the Wuhan Institute of Virology. US intelligence officials have not yet determined whether the outbreak began through contact with infected animals or if it was a result of a laboratory accident in Wuhan, but either way, China did nothing to contain the spread of the disease or to warn the rest of the world about what was coming their way. Even if Covid-19's spread was the result of an accident, the question remains of why US intelligence failed to provide advance warning to the Department of Homeland Security (DHS), the Centers for Disease Control and Prevention (CDC), the National Institutes of Health (NIH), and President Trump before the beginning of 2020 and the first case made it to the United States.

Often answers to historical events only come in retrospect. Today, there remain more questions than answers. Trust in the CDC in Atlanta, Georgia, although not a part of Homeland Security, is at an all-time low. Being a part of Health and Human Services (HHS), the CDC had no authority to communicate directly with or share its information through DHS agencies such as the Federal Emergency Management Agency (FEMA). Intelligence agencies clearly failed to share information that might have prompted action as soon as the world became aware of the virus outbreak in Wuhan as early as November 2019, or when it was being discussed in online medical social media groups in December 2019.

This book is about the current state of domestic intelligence within the country, generally, and specifically within the agency officially charged with protecting the United States from all threats: the Department of Homeland Security. There exist several agencies at the federal level that are charged directly with that responsibility, including both the Federal Bureau of Investigation (FBI) and the Central Intelligence Agency (CIA), as well as many others at all levels that indirectly collect information necessary to the country's safety. This book covers all agencies, particularly at the federal level, that obtain information relevant to any threat to the United States. Our discussion includes to whom (and under what conditions) the information/intelligence is sent, and who should receive it, in a homeland security intelligence system that (at some point, hopefully) works in a timely and efficient manner. The book is designed to teach students who are interested in what works and what does not work in terms of domestic intelligence related to direct and indirect threats to the United States, at least at the present time within the homeland security enterprise and the intelligence community's ability to support it.

Setting the Stage

From the end of World War II until the fall of the Soviet Union in the early 1990s, the US government considered the primary threat to America to be Communist Soviet Union (and, of course, to a somewhat lesser extent Communist China). The Cold War enemy was well known, as were its capabilities. Its intentions were somewhat unknown, and for this the United States had the CIA and other intelligence agencies to keep the nation safe. Or, at least, to allow the illusion that US citizens were safe.

From about 1982 until 2001, the war on drugs gave the United States a new enemy to think about: drug cartels and smugglers. Several former US presidents told the nation that the number one menace to America was illegal drugs. As for the terrorist threat, prior to the attacks on September 11, 2001, the focus of the government and the intelligence community was primarily the threat from state-supported terrorism, not groups like al-Qaeda and ISIS. The United States was worried that nations such as North Korea, Libya, Iraq, and Iran were giving aid and support to people who wanted to do it harm. And, of course, the mainstays of the Cold War, Russia and China, were still around and worrisome to a greater or lesser extent depending on the situation and circumstances.

On February 26, 1993, the World Trade Center in New York City was attacked by a terrorist group with links to a local radical mosque. Members of the group drove a rental van with approximately 1,200 pounds of explosives to an underground parking garage at the base of the Twin Towers. The explosion killed six people and injured over a thousand. This attack, however, did not focus the attention of the nation on the threat from international terrorist groups, to include al-Qaeda and similar nonstate actors. It is hard to comprehend why the 1993 attack on the World Trade Center didn't direct the focus of the intelligence community, FBI, CIA, and other federal agencies to the threat posed by international terrorism. Perhaps it was the swift apprehension of the perpetrators followed by their conviction and incarceration that gave a false sense of security. It took the eventual attack on 9/11 to alert the government, the intelligence community, and law enforcement to the threat posed by Osama bin Laden and his followers.

The *Final Report of the National Commission on Terrorist Attacks upon the United States* (also known as the Kean/Hamilton Commission and the 9/11 Commission) was issued on July 23, 2004. Basically, the 9/11 Commission faulted the intelligence community for failing to connect the dots; for the absence of big-picture, long-range strategic intelligence; and for a lack of imagination. The report specifically noted the lack of a National Intelligence Estimate (NIE) on the terrorist threat between 1998 and 2001 and implied that if an NIE on terrorism had been produced, it might have helped the intelligence community and FBI to prevent the 9/11 attack. The 9/11 Commission lays most of the blame for the failure of 9/11 on the intelligence community and on the lack of a strategic warning about groups such as al-Qaeda.

From both a historical and a societal perspective, it is imperative to understand what changes were brought about within this country and worldwide as a result of 9/11. The United States was not the same country it had been on September 10, 2001. US culture also changed, much as it did on December 7, 1941, after the attack on Pearl Harbor, only without any established goal or measure of conclusion for Americans to achieve.

On October 11, 2001, as he announced the upcoming invasion of Afghanistan, President Bush declared a war on terror, also known as the global war on terrorism, against all those who seek to export terror anywhere they might be. This resulted in a war that is still ongoing in Afghanistan, then in Iraq, followed by the deployment of US forces to fight terrorism in the Philippines and Africa. The war on terror was a multidimensional campaign that involved major wars and covert operations in Yemen and elsewhere, and a semiglobal program of killing suspected terrorists or capturing them for imprisonment at Guantanamo Bay or rendition to other undisclosed sites. Instead of having specific enemies to target and defeat, the United States faced an elusive, dispersed, evolving enemy that spanned continents, ethnicities, languages, political motivations, religions, and cultures.

Domestically the war on terror resulted in new antiterror legislation (the USA PATRIOT Act), a new security agency (DHS), new surveillance programs by the National Security Agency and the FBI, and increased security measures at airports, borders, and public events.

By the end of Bush's second term, public opinion had turned negative concerning aspects of his handling of the Iraq War and some other national security concerns, including the indefinite detention without trial of accused enemy combatants at Guantanamo Bay, the use of torture against those detainees in an effort to extract intelligence, and the use of unmanned aerial vehicles (UAVs) to target and kill suspected enemies in countries not directly associated with combat areas in Iraq and Afghanistan. Barack Obama, a critic of Bush's foreign policy, won the presidency in 2008, and the expression "war on terrorism" quickly disappeared from official communications. In a 2013 speech, Obama stated that the vaguely defined global war on terror would be replaced by more focused actions against hostile groups. With that said, though, there were foreign policy continuities between the two administrations, including using UAVs for targeted killings, deploying special operations forces, and utilizing US security agencies for wide-ranging surveillance of US citizens.

The war on terror became unlike any war the United States had fought in the past: "There's no specific battlefield and the enemy isn't an army."[1] Political theorist Richard Jackson used a slightly more expansive definition when he described the war on terror as "simultaneously a set of actual practices—wars, covert operations, agencies, and institutions—and an accompanying series of assumptions, beliefs, justifications, and narratives—it is an entire language or discourse."[2] To attempt to define it is to understand that, for all practical (governmental agency) purposes, this general fluidity is designed to provide government agencies with the most flexibility and funding necessary to meet elusive goals. This artificial government-established paradigm allows agencies the latitude to act without adherence to previously court-upheld restraints regarding surveillance. The so-called war on terror has fundamentally, and for all current intents and purposes, seemingly reversed the inherent foundation of the Bill of Rights: that individuals are *assumed innocent* until proven guilty. The new paradigm is that *all* are presumed guilty until evidence (or surveillance) indicates subjectively or objectively that they are low-level threats and, therefore, of little immediate concern to the reputations of the government agencies that surveil them. Absolutely no one inside or outside the government—elected, appointed, or civil service—seems to be completely sure what the evidentiary level is to indicate a suspect or citizen is a viable threat that needs to be addressed.

In 2020, an ongoing global disease caused by severe acute respiratory syndrome coronavirus-2 (SARS-CoV-2) became the Covid-19 pandemic, also known as the coronavirus pandemic. According to the WHO, the disease is primarily spread between people by direct, indirect, or close contact with infected people via mouth or nose secretions.

Authorities worldwide have responded by attempting to implement travel restrictions, lockdowns, workplace controls, and facility closures and by limiting the number of people who can gather for any given event or activity. The pandemic has resulted in global social and economic disruption. It has also led to global widespread supply shortages. Lasting damage was done to the US population and economy.

On January 21, 2020, the first known case of Covid-19 in the United States was announced in Snohomish County, Washington, in a thirty-five-year-old man who had visited family in Wuhan, China. At that point the DHS and the CDC should have requested a shutdown of all incoming international travel from China and set a quarantine of all people who came into contact with this individual. This did not happen. There was no DHS Pandemic Response Plan to implement. There was no validated and tested CDC plan for any type of pandemic. Individual states, counties, cities, and agencies tried to prevent the spread of the disease on their own, often applying flu pandemic response plans in the process. This didn't work for the prevention of Covid-19 and resulted in a significant number of deaths among patients in nursing homes for the elderly. From January 2020 to March 2021 there were over 29 million cases diagnosed in the United States by positive tests with over 533,000 deaths from the disease according to the CDC website. Over 119 million cases were reported worldwide by Johns Hopkins University with over 2 million deaths at mid-March 2021. The jury is still out on whether the recent pandemic experience will result in improved medical intelligence and a cohesive pandemic response plan.

Defining Terrorism

Every country that has been subjected to terrorism has defined it in a unique way. Even terrorism experts such as Bruce Hoffman and David Whittaker proffer differing definitions. In fact, in the United States, there are many competing definitions of what constitutes terrorism, based on the philosophies of different agencies. Martin consolidates several definitions of terrorism and produces a composite American definition:

> Premeditated and unlawful acts in which groups or agents of some principal engage in a threatened or actual use of force or violence against human or property targets. These groups or agents engage in this behavior intending the purposeful intimidation of governments or people to affect policy or behavior with an underlying political objective.[3]

Supreme Court Justice Potter Stewart once wrote that "hard-core pornography" was hard to define, "but I know it when I see it."[4] So it is with terrorism. There may not be an internationally accepted and consolidated definition of what does and does not constitute terrorism, but you probably know it when you see it (hopefully, not directly as a witness). The reason such a bold statement can be made is that terrorism is not an ideology, form of warfare, or sociological construct. It is a military tactic often employed by small reactionary groups against much larger, better equipped and trained military forces and their associated governments and populations. Anybody at any time can plan and carry out an act of terrorism. Why? Because the ultimate purpose of terrorism is to cause the targeted community to be terrified that they might also be subjected to similar unjustified, indiscriminate, violent acts. If the recipient population becomes terrified that they too may be the victims of such an attack, then the terrorist tactic has succeeded.

The phrase "one person's terrorist may be another person's freedom fighter" has become commonplace. Semantically speaking, the terms *terrorist* and *extremist* are value-laden statements about actions and actors. Consider the events that led to the separation of the United States from Great Britain in the late 1700s. Did the Boston Tea Party participants, on December 16, 1773, represent extremism to the British loyalists or government? What issue regarding parliamentary representation became the alleged proximate cause for the symbolic actions taken by the colonists? Were the actions damaging to the British government and the monopolistic East India Company upon their refusal to return the tea to the company docks overseas? Why would the colonists object to the Tea Act and its associated taxes? What were the Coercive Acts passed by the British parliament in 1774, and what was the ultimate result? These are the kinds of questions that must be asked when looking into the subjects of extremism and terrorism.

Terrorists justify their causes as noble. Yet, ultimately, what is and is not terrorism is a matter of perception. That perception is driven by politics, religion, culture, upbringing, and any number of other considerations. The Declaration of Independence is essentially a revolt against perceived tyranny in the eyes of its authors and signatories, and yet the British government viewed it as a statement of treason against the Crown. Also, from the perspective of the British, the Boston Tea Party, Stamp Act Revolt, and other colonial offenses were seen as acts of open rebellion against lawful authority. This concept, the idea that perception colors interpretation, is the single greatest reason that terrorism has been so difficult to define.

The Palestinians and British view the Haganah, Irgun, and Lehi paramilitary forces as terrorists while the Jews living in Israel see them as heroes and martyrs without whom there would be no Jewish nation today. Members of the National Liberation Front (FLN) of Algeria saw themselves as revolutionaries and are seen today by the Algerian people as heroes and martyrs while the Harkis, which supported French forces during the Algerian revolt, are seen as traitors. The French obviously have a different perspective of the FLN and the Harkis. Yet the French dissident paramilitary Organisation Armée Secrète is viewed exactly oppositely by both sides. Which are terrorists? Nationalists? Revolutionaries? Heroes? It is a matter of perspective that will always depend on whether you are on the side that won or the side that lost. Thus, today there is still a great deal of disagreement worldwide as to how terrorism should be defined.

Types of Terrorism

Before moving into the issue of intelligence for homeland security, it is important to establish a common basis and comprehension of the categories of terrorism. Generally, there are four typologies of terrorism: state-sponsored, dissident, religious, and international. From the perspective of homeland security, the concept of criminal terrorism should be considered here as well. Table 1.1 shows a consolidated list of terrorism typologies.

Why create a typology of criminal terrorism? The simple answer is that DHS agencies deal with a wide range of activities: from apprehending Mexican drug cartels and human traffickers to crimes involving counterfeiting and child pornography; from searching for weapons of mass destruction while concurrently expediting normal trade between other countries and the United States to providing maritime and aviation security. All of these are activities may be used by criminals to advance their illicit business enterprises, but they are not actually encompassed by other definitions of terrorism. As such, the terroristic violence used by these criminal enterprises is also being addressed by DHS agents.

Defining Homeland Security

The concept of homeland security is amorphous at best. While the term was used prior to the 9/11 attacks, it didn't enter into the national vocabulary until afterward. The subsequent creation of a Department of

Table 1.1 Types of Terrorism

Type	Description	Examples
State-sponsored	Terrorism "from above" committed by governments against perceived enemies (usually internal)	Al-Anfal campaign against the Kurds Killing fields of the Khmer Rouge
Dissident	Terrorism "from below" committed by nonstate movements and groups against governments, ethnonational groups, religious groups, and many other perceived enemies	Red Brigades FARC
Religious	Terrorism motivated by an absolute belief that an otherworldly power has sanctioned it	Aum Shinrikyo Army of God
Criminal	Terrorism motivated by sheer profit, or some amalgam of profit and politics	Los Zetas cartel Tamil Tigers
International	Terrorism that spills over on the world's stage	al-Qaeda ISIS

Source: James R. Phelps, Jeffrey Dailey, and Monica Koenigsberg, *Border Security,* 2nd ed. (Durham, NC: Carolina Academic Press, 2018).

Homeland Security, with its associated cabinet secretary position, led to a period of time during which the new agency has had to learn and grow, consolidating functions of different components and realigning responsibilities elsewhere. Ultimately, this is an ongoing process for the organization and the nation.

Defining homeland security is difficult as it incorporates so much that a single focused definition is virtually impossible. More than a decade after the formation of DHS, the agency's educators at the Center for Homeland Defense and Security, a component of the Naval Postgraduate School in Monterey, California, could not produce a comprehensive or accepted definition. This poses a problem not only for DHS but for the nation as a whole.

The solution may be to stop thinking of homeland security from the perspective of national security. There is a misconception that homeland security and national security are synonymous terms. Concurrent with this view is that the intelligence for each would be the same with the same focus and outcomes. Neither of these perceptions could be further from the truth. While the concepts frequently overlap in their specific areas of focus, they are not the same. USLegal.com notes that

National security is a corporate term covering both national defense and foreign relations of the U.S. It refers to the protection of a nation from attack or other danger by holding adequate armed forces and guarding state secrets. The term national security encompasses within it economic security, monetary security, energy security, environmental security, military security, political security and security of energy and natural resources. Specifically, national security means a circumstance that exists as a result of a military or defense advantage over any foreign nation or group of nations, or a friendly foreign relations position, or a defense position capable of successfully protesting hostile or destructive action.[5]

USLegal.com goes on to cite *Cole v. Young*, where the US Supreme Court observed that the term *national security* is used in a definite and limited sense relating only to those activities directly concerned with the nation's safety and not relating to the general welfare.[6]

The National Strategy for Homeland Security (2007) defines the concept as "a concerted national effort to prevent terrorist attacks within the United States, reduce America's vulnerability to terrorism, and minimize the damage and recover from attacks that do occur."[7] This is the definition of *homeland security* we use for the purposes of this text. The national strategy is intended to guide, organize, and unify efforts to secure the homeland through use of a common framework to accomplish four goals:

- prevent and disrupt terrorist attacks;
- protect the American people, critical infrastructure, and key resources;
- respond to and recover from incidents that come to fruition; and
- continually strengthen the foundations of homeland security to ensure long-term success.[8]

Fundamental to the above goals is the concept of risk reduction, where "we accept that risk—a function of threats, vulnerabilities, and consequences—is a permanent condition [requiring application of] a risk-based framework across all homeland security efforts in order to identify and assess potential hazards."[9]

Another concept that is key to the success of the homeland security endeavor is the recognition and acceptance that citizens, communities, the private sector, and faith-based and nonprofit organizations all perform a central role in the process in addition to those federal agencies specifically tasked with securing the homeland. Thus, the government institutes such programs as Ready.gov and See Something, Say Something. What is interesting among all of the homeland security management options is that there is no required function of intelligence.[10]

For the first few years after 9/11, terrorism was at the heart of both of the definitions, but over time that changed. The definition of *homeland security* was broadened to include other national threats, in addition to terrorism:

- a unified national effort to prevent and deter terrorist attacks, protect and respond to hazards, and to secure the nation's borders.[11]
- a seamless coordination among federal, state, and local governments to prevent, protect against, and respond to threats and natural disasters.[12]
- a concerted national effort to ensure a homeland that is safe, secure, and resilient against terrorism and other hazards where American interests, aspirations, and ways of life can thrive.[13]

With the maturation of the DHS in 2010, the definition of homeland security took on an institutional flavor. That is, homeland security became everything that DHS is responsible for and includes specific areas of responsibility (bureaucratic turf) of the major DHS subcomponents, including the Coast Guard, Immigration and Customs, and others: preventing terrorism, responding to and recovering from natural disasters, enforcing customs and collecting customs revenue, administering legal immigration services, and maintaining the safety and stewardship of the nation's waterways and marine transportation system, as well as other legacy missions of the various components of DHS.[14]

In 2011, in the National Strategy for Counterterrorism, the White House simply defined homeland security as "defensive efforts to counter terrorist threats."[15] And, in 2012, DHS defined it in its strategic plan as efforts "to ensure a homeland that is safe, secure, and resilient against terrorism and other hazards."[16]

Then for the 2014 Quadrennial Homeland Security Review, homeland security became a concerted national effort that involves a widely distributed and diverse group of federal, state, local, tribal, nongovernmental, territorial, and private-sector partners as well as individuals, families, and communities.[17]

As Christopher Bellavita noted in June 2008, the problem with defining homeland security resides in the fact that there are seven areas of focus that all, based on an individual's perspective, drive the definition:

1. Terrorism: this includes actions by federal, state, local, tribal, and territorial actors to address all sources of terrorism, to prevent such acts or at least minimize the damage from terrorist attacks.

2. All hazards: the approach must include man-made and natural disasters of all types, not just terrorism.

3. Terrorism and catastrophes: the conceptual goal is to prevent when possible, respond when prevention fails, and recover from events that are terroristic or catastrophic natural disasters. (Hurricane Katrina in 2005 was a catastrophe for the city of New Orleans.)

4. Jurisdictional hazards: Every jurisdiction has a different measure of what threats and hazards are going to be significant to that location, so the level of preparation and response needs to be proportionate, thus each jurisdiction has to prepare for what is appropriate to its region of the country. Inland states usually have less to fear from hurricanes than coastal ones, for example.

5. Meta hazards: These are social threats that can disrupt the long-term stability of the way of life people expect to experience. The massive homeless populations in Los Angeles County and the city of San Francisco are examples of how a social issue can impact a community's way of life.

6. National security: here the perspective is to address national-level threats to sovereignty, territorial integrity, the entirety of the domestic population (such as the threat posed by Covid-19), and the national-level critical infrastructure.

7. Security above all: This is the ultimate threat to the country. Consider that when security takes priority above everything else, then everything else (civil liberties) can be infringed upon at will by government in the name of providing security for all.[18]

So, what is homeland security? That raises another question: Is DHS *securing* the homeland or *defending* the homeland? Homeland defense is easily defined and can be best stated as the military protection of US territory, sovereignty, domestic population, and critical infrastructure against external threats and aggression. If that's the case, then isn't homeland security the effort extended by all government agencies at all levels to protect the United States, its population, and critical infrastructure from all hazards, natural or man-made? The efforts to address and protect against all hazards, both natural and man-made, result in wholly different means of intelligence gathering for different purposes and outcomes.

Homeland security differs from national security in that national security is addressed by foreign policy as implemented by the US State Department, US Department of Defense, and US Commerce Department (trade relations) as well as the Environmental Protection Agency. Homeland security is a matter of internal protection against terrorism such that terrorist attacks and their effects are minimized, and recovery is swift and assured. Thus, homeland security falls under the responsibility of the DHS, US Department of Energy, US Department of Justice, and US Commerce Department (data collection and analysis including by the National Oceanic and Atmospheric Administration). Other government agencies provide concurrent support and overlapping responsibilities associated with both national and homeland security.

Defining Intelligence

There are many definitions of intelligence. Mark Lowenthal defines it as "the process by which specific types of information important to national security are requested, collected, analyzed, and provided to policy makers; the products of that process; the safeguarding of these processes and this information by counterintelligence activities; and the carrying out of operations as requested by lawful authorities."[19] A solid, practical definition, although somewhat generic, since it includes a process, a product, safeguarding, and operations. A phrase such as "information important to national security" can really mean anything, at any time, under any circumstances. And, of course, as circumstances change, over time, then "needs" change, too. And intelligence is time-dependent, as well. What is valuable right now, or today, may not be tomorrow, or next week, or next month. As of 2004 and the Intelligence Reform and Terrorism Prevention Act (IRTPA), all intelligence is defined as national intelligence, and there exist three subsets: foreign, domestic, and homeland security. Foreign intelligence is fairly straightforward, but the delineation between domestic and homeland security intelligence is sometimes blurred.

There are various types of intelligence, at least in terms of types of collection. These include HUMINT (human intelligence), OSINT (open-source intelligence), GEOINT (geospatial intelligence), SIGINT (signals intelligence), image intelligence (IMINT), and MASINT (measurement and signatures intelligence). This book covers the above types of intelligence, as they relate to homeland security intelligence.

Defining Homeland Security Intelligence

Homeland security intelligence is what this book is about. A consolidated definition of homeland security intelligence is presented from multiple statements in the DHS's 2012 strategic plan: homeland security intelligence (as a product) is any relevant, timely information related to efforts to ensure a homeland that is safe, secure, and resilient against terrorism and other threats. The focus is on relevant, timely, practical intelligence related to assisting those responsible for America's safety, including first responders.

The information-sharing environment, formalized in IRTPA in December 2004, was intended to ensure that not only was terrorism-related intelligence to be shared widely and acted upon federally and locally, but that the sharing of "all relevant and appropriate information throughout [all] levels of government and with private and non-profit sectors and our foreign partners on the full range of homeland security issues" was essential to ensuring the four goals of the national strategy functioned as the American people expected.[20] Of course, events in Parkland (2018), Orlando (2016), San Bernardino (2015), Charleston (2015), and Boston (2013), among many others, demonstrate that this most important aspect of successful homeland security, the sharing of pertinent intelligence from federal to local and community-based organizations, has been woefully inadequate.

Structure of the Book

The materials are presented in a series of chapters related to specific concepts appropriate for extensive discussion and analysis. We begin with foundational materials so that subsequent concepts can be tied to a common understanding of the origins and lexicon of the topics. In Chapter 2 we take a look at the origins of homeland security and its relationship to domestic terrorism, including abolitionist John Brown and the raid at Harpers Ferry, the creation and rise of the Ku Klux Klan, and the labor riots at the beginning of the twentieth century. In Chapter 3 we examine the two attacks on the Twin Towers in New York City, almost a decade apart, and the recommendations of the 9/11 Commission Report, including the creation of the DHS, along with a look at the Tsarnaev brothers and the Boston Marathon bombing. In Chapter 4 we explain the role of the intelligence community in the context of national security. We then examine the roles played by homeland security agencies in Chapter 5 and that of other federal agencies in Chapter 6 before addressing the issue of counterintelligence in Chapter 7. In Chapter 8 we present a detailed analysis of domestic threats and how they impact national and homeland security. This is followed by an examination and investigation of the differences between homeland, national, and practical intelligence in Chapter 9, and how different agencies use different terms for similar concepts. An example of a functioning intelligence system within the DHS is examined in detail in Chapter 10, where we discuss FEMA planning, response, recovery, and mitigation as if it were a functioning intelligence agency. We conclude with Chapter 11 and our proposal of what we see as essential for bringing homeland security intelligence into the twenty-first century.

Notes

1. Guy Raz, "Defining the War on Terror," NPR, November 1, 2006.
2. R. Jackson, *Writing the War on Terrorism: Language, Politics and Counter-Terrorism* (Manchester, UK: Manchester University Press, 2005).
3. C. A. Martin, *Understanding Terrorism: Challenges, Perspectives, and Issues* (Los Angeles: Sage, 2009), p. 44.
4. *Jacobellis v. Ohio*, 378 US 184 (1964), https://www.law.cornell.edu/supreme court/text/378/184.
5. USLegal.com, https://definitions.uslegal.com/n/national-security/ (accessed June 12, 2018).
6. Ibid.
7. US Department of Homeland Security (DHS), *National Strategy for Homeland Security*, October 2007, https://www.dhs.gov/national-strategy-homeland -security-october-2007.
8. Ibid.
9. Ibid., p. 41.
10. Ibid., p. 44.
11. DHS, *U.S. Department of Homeland Security Strategic Plan, Fiscal Years 2008–2013*.
12. White House, National Security Strategy, 2010.
13. DHS, *Quadrennial Homeland Security Review*, 2010.
14. Department of Homeland Security, 2010.
15. White House, *National Strategy for Counterterrorism*, 2011.
16. DHS, *National Strategy for Homeland Security*, 2012.
17. DHS, *Quadrennial Homeland Security Review*, 2014.
18. Christopher Bellavita, "Changing Homeland Security: What Is Homeland Security?" *Homeland Security Affairs* 4, article 1 (June 2008), https://www.hsaj .org/articles/118.
19. Mark M. Lowenthal, *Intelligence: From Secrets to Policy,* 7th ed. (Thousand Oaks, CA: Sage, 2017), p. 10.
20. DHS, National Strategy for Homeland Security, October 2007, https://www .dhs.gov/national-strategy-homeland-security-october-2007.

2

The Origins of the Homeland Security Enterprise

We begin this chapter with an examination of the history of domestic terrorism in the United States, the origins of the Department of Homeland Security, and the purported failures of intelligence agencies and the FBI to identify or interdict the 9/11 hijackers. We also explore the rise of racial extremism following the Civil War and conclude with a look at right-wing radicalism.

Defining Terrorism and Domestic Terrorism

Important to comprehending the discussion of terrorism and domestic terrorism is a common basis for use of these terms. Title 22, Chapter 38 of the United States Code defines terrorism as "premeditated, politically motivated violence perpetrated against noncombatant targets by subnational groups or clandestine agents."[1] And the US Code of Federal Regulations defines terrorism as "the unlawful use of force and violence against persons or property to intimidate or coerce a government, the civilian population, or any segment thereof, in furtherance of political or social objectives."[2] The US Code of Federal Regulations definition is noticeably broader than the US Code definition: "political or social objectives" can cover a lot of ground, obviously, and mean different things to different people, at different times.

The FBI defines domestic terrorism as "violent, criminal acts committed by individuals and/or groups to further ideological goals stemming from domestic influences, such as those of a political, religious, social, racial, or environmental nature."[3] Although this appears to be a remarkably wide definition, the USA PATRIOT Act expanded it even further, to "an act dangerous to human life that is a violation of the criminal laws of a state or the United States, if the act appears to be intended to: (i) intimidate or coerce a civilian population; (ii) influence the policy of a government by intimidation or coercion; or (iii) to affect the conduct of a government by mass destruction, assassination or kidnapping."[4]

All of the above fit virtually every riot or semimajor public disturbance that has occurred in the United States at any point in time. There are usually reasons for riots. But let us begin with the definition: *Merriam-Webster's Collegiate Dictionary* defines a riot as "a violent public disorder; *specif.* a tumultuous disturbance of the public peace by three or more persons assembled together and acting with a common intent."[5] So, making the possibly dangerous assumption that a "common intent" can be superimposed on, or commingled (legal term) with the aforementioned USA PATRIOT Act definition, which includes acts that are intended to "intimidate or coerce a civilian population," then it can be said with some justification that riots in general that occur or have occurred in US lands can be considered acts of domestic terrorism, at least according to the USA PATRIOT Act, since, essentially, riots attempt or have attempted in the past, at the very least, to "intimidate" other sections of the American public.

It should be mentioned that a riot is distinguishable from either a lawful assembly or an unlawful assembly: Lawful assembly is guaranteed by the First Amendment to the US Constitution, which prohibits the government from limiting the right of the people "peaceably to assemble," and which, according to the Supreme Court, also includes the right to espouse varied viewpoints. Assembly becomes unlawful when persons (assumption here is more than, say, two people) come together to commit a possible crime involving force or a noncriminal act likely to upset or terrify the public. When the three or more persons assembled together commit a "tumultuous disturbance of the public peace" (according to *Merriam-Webster*), then you have a riot. Whatever a "tumultuous disturbance of the public peace" is. Actual riots were (or are) seemingly linked to some sort of grievance or complaint and were/are usually done to lodge a protest about something (allegedly) of extreme interest to those complaining or rioting or committing tumultuous disturbances of some sort. In the past, riots have been expressions of frustration by the oppressed or dispossessed, or they might have been directly related to hate or prejudice.

History of Domestic Terrorism in America

Domestic terrorism did not begin on September 11, 2001, as many Americans believe. It began much earlier in this country. The starting date could arguably be considered the Boston Massacre on March 5, 1770.

The people of the United States have a long history of rioting when protesting, going back to the March 5, 1770, event in Boston protesting the Townshend Acts imposed by the British on the colonies. After colonials repeatedly threw snowballs and taunted the British soldiers, the soldiers, feeling themselves in serious danger, fired their muskets, killing three colonials on the spot and wounding eight others. This was the beginning of American domestic terrorism (from the perspective of the British), and similar protests (or you may want to call them riots) would happen, with similar responses by the government with use of force, for the next 250 years.

Perhaps the best example of a domestic terrorist (individual or group) can be presented in the case of John Brown.

John Brown

During his life and after his hanging John Brown was known by many names: "traitor, patriot, thief, murderer, hero, martyr, and more."[6] No matter the term used, the one that describes him best is *uncompromising*. John Brown demonstrated American patriotism through an uncompromising commitment to the religious and political ideals on which the United States of America was founded—to the point of dying for them. Brown's attack on the federal armory at Harpers Ferry on October 17, 1859, became the spark that drove the Confederate States to secede to protect their way of life, including the slavery their economy was built upon.

John Brown "believed in 'righteous violence,' the willingness to kill and die for a higher good."[7] As Albert Marrin writes in *A Volcano Beneath the Snow*,

> To many, [John Brown] was (and is) a good man, a hero, a freedom
> fighter, a saint. More, he was a martyr who willingly gave his life, and
> the lives of three of his sons, to free those in bondage. Yet to many
> others, Brown was (and is) "the Father of American Terrorism," a liar,
> a criminal, a fanatic who would have destroyed a nation to achieve his
> ends.[8]

The story of American domestic terrorism begins with John Brown, but
it is not where it ends.

A Product of His Upbringing

John Brown's strict Calvinist upbringing and a firm belief in the opening words of the Declaration of Independence and Constitution helped
to solidify his conviction that the United States and slavery were incom-
patible.[9] In November 1834, Brown was already proposing to friends
the need for abolition and formal education for blacks. However, the
idea didn't take hold in his rural New York environs. A year later he
would move his family to Ohio, start a new business, and become a land
speculator around the newly approved Pennsylvania-Ohio Canal.

Two events in 1837 would turn Brown from investor to crusader.
The Panic of 1837 crashed the US economy. President Andrew Jackson's move away from state- and bank-issued currency and a mandate
that the US government would only accept silver and gold specie (currency) for payment of debts and sale of federal lands created an instan-
taneous cessation of cash flow throughout the nation. Nine-tenths of the
country's manufacturing and factories closed. Two-thirds of clerks and
salesmen lost their jobs. For seven years, depression, joblessness, and
low wages and prices would control the economy. Land speculators like
Brown found themselves holding large sections of land on money bor-
rowed from banks, friends, and investors, yet nobody had the requisite
gold or silver necessary to purchase the land and allow him to meet payment requirements to his creditors.

Then, on November 7, 1837, the Presbyterian minister Elijah Love-
joy was murdered by proslavery forces for publishing abolitionist
papers. The case was given national coverage and discussed at length in
communities across the Northern states. At an abolitionist prayer meeting in Hudson, Ohio, John Brown openly concluded the meeting by
stating for all to hear that he pledged his life to fighting slavery with
increasing hostility.

By 1842 Brown was bankrupt and completely destitute. He had lost
his three youngest sons to illness and reached a point where he had no

more ties to prevent a move to radicalization and violent acts toward slavery and its adherents.[10]

The Road to Harpers Ferry

Between the Panic of 1837 and his death in 1859, "John Brown managed not only to free himself of the pervasive and supposedly scientifically respectable white supremacism of his time but also to develop personal relationships with black people that were to be sustained, intimate, trusting, and egalitarian."[11]

After the brutal caning of Senator Charles Sumner (Massachusetts) by Representative Preston Smith Brooks (South Carolina) on the floor of the US Senate in May 1856, and the attack on the Free State community of Lawrence, Kansas, by proslavery militia from Missouri, John Brown told those who would listen, "Something is going to be done now. We must show by actual work that there are two sides to this thing, and that they cannot go on with impunity."[12] In making such a statement, and arranging for his sons and their families to move to Kansas, Brown and his family started on the path toward violent action to end slavery.

Frederick Douglass, an ex-slave and staunch Northern abolitionist and public agitator, found Brown's declaration that "No political action will ever abolish the system of slavery. It will have to go out in blood. Those men who hold slaves have even forfeited their right to live"[13] to be the clearest and most alarming declaration ever heard from an abolitionist. It was clear that Brown fully intended to bring about the end of slavery, by force.

Over the next three years Brown would act on his deeply held principles in Kansas, New York, Canada, and ultimately Virginia. As noted in a pocket book published shortly after his execution, "It was Brown's idea that he was divinely appointed to bring American slavery to a sudden and violent end."[14] Brown had become the leader of the ultra-abolitionist movement.

Upon hearing the *Dred Scott v. Sandford* pronouncement from the Supreme Court in March 1857, John Brown started his move to liberate the slaves of the South through violent means. Brown knew that the Northern abolitionists would never countenance open warfare on the South, nor would they fund, supply, or arm activities that might take place in the Southern slaveholding states. This forced Brown to manipulate and cajole the financiers of his exploits in Kansas to continue their funding after the state had been accepted into the Union as a free state.

He used this funding to purchase Sharps rifles and revolvers, to travel to and recruit ex-slaves in Canada, and to relocate an armed force to a farm just north of the railroad community of Harpers Ferry, Virginia, in the months leading up to October 16, 1859.

Harpers Ferry

The town of Harpers Ferry sits at the confluence of the Potomac and Shenandoah Rivers, on the border between Virginia (later West Virginia) and Maryland. It is the hub of the B&O Railroad where the line splits, between routes to Charleston/Winchester and Martinsburg/Cumberland, and Baltimore to the east. Maryland and Virginia were slave states, while just to the north, Pennsylvania was a free state.

Brown, two of his sons, and Jeremiah Anderson rented a farm from the Widow Kennedy in Sharpsburg, Maryland, on July 4, 1859. Here they set up operations to conceal their real purpose; they brought one of Brown's daughters-in-law and one of his daughters to join them and continue the pretense of establishing a farm. Shipments of weapons and people were sent to Chambersburg, about forty miles to the north in Pennsylvania, in preparation for the raid on Harpers Ferry and subsequent raids into Virginia to free slaves and incite a slave rebellion.

The morning of October 16, 1859, a Sunday, prayers were held, final arrivals were inducted into the new constitutional government that John Brown had created to justify the coming attacks, military commissions were formally made of the participants, and final plans were put in place. At 8 p.m. the group proceeded to Harpers Ferry, walking in pairs, widely separated, and keeping as quiet as possible. By 10:30 that night, the attack was under way. By midnight, the band of nineteen men had control of the federal arms manufacturing facilities and storage depot with about 100,000 rifles. They also controlled the railroads and river bridges, and had cut the telegraph lines to town. A war of liberation had been "launched by a white man leading a small interracial band, striking an industrial mountain town where slaves were scarce."[15] Brown dispatched a wagonload of men into the Shenandoah Valley to begin their work of liberating slaves on Virginia plantations. Unfortunately, having already been discovered by security guards working the B&O Railroad bridge, the war to liberate Southern slaves rapidly devolved into a frenzy of shooting where the first to die was Heyward Shepherd, a free Black baggage master at the Harpers Ferry depot.

Warnings by outriders from Harpers Ferry resulted in the gathering of about 150 armed men, some trained militia, in Charlestown, who proceeded to move toward the captured arsenal. By noon on October 17 the counterattack was under way. Once the gunmen occupied the high levels of the three-story buildings in town, coupled with the loss of their only supply and access route from Maryland, the Brown raiders were essentially cut off and subjected to gunfire from above, a veritable shooting gallery.

Within hours of the news reaching Washington, DC, Colonel Robert E. Lee, summoned by Lieutenant James Ewell Brown Stuart (often known as Jeb Stuart), was called to duty, given command of ninety US Marines from the Navy Yard in the capital, and on his way to Harpers Ferry to take charge of the situation and confront Brown's forces. These future secessionist generals arrived in Sandy Hook, Maryland, across the river from Harpers Ferry before midnight, and the end of John Brown's insurrection followed the next day.

John Brown's attack on Harpers Ferry lasted thirty-two hours and culminated in a five-minute attack by the US Marines under the leadership of Colonel Robert E. Lee. Two days later, under the protection of Virginia's governor, Brown and his handful of surviving men were moved to Charlestown where they were jailed and ultimately tried for their crimes, not against the federal government facility but the people and Commonwealth of Virginia. On October 31, two attorneys from the Northern states arrived to take over Brown's defense from the appointed Southern public defenders; however, it mattered little. The judge refused to allow them to recall prosecution or defense witnesses, and the case quickly moved to closing arguments. By 1:30 on the afternoon of October 31, closing arguments were completed and the jurors withdrew for deliberations. Forty-five minutes later they returned with a unanimous, but not unexpected, decision—guilty on all three counts (treason, murder, and insurrection).

Offered an opportunity to speak to the court before he was sentenced, Brown essentially admitted his guilt and declared the righteousness of his cause; he said he never intended murder or treason, only to provide slaves with the opportunity to be free, by their own actions or with the help of him and his compatriots. He called on the South to recognize its hypocrisy as a Christian community that did not treat others as they would want to be treated themselves and, according to a multitude of sources, closed with a declaration of martyrdom.

The judge sentenced Brown to death by hanging.

John Brown's assault on the federal armory at Harpers Ferry was a military failure. Not a single Southern slave was freed because of the attack, and those offered their freedom by Brown surrendered after the attack was suppressed. Yet within five years all the slaves held by Confederate States would be freed by Union troops who remembered Brown in their campfire and marching songs. The lyrics of "John Brown's Body" are an example of the conversion of an act of terrorism into the martyrdom of the perpetrator.

Not only did Brown influence the Black Civil Rights activists, he was lauded as an example and hero by late twentieth-century domestic terrorists such as Timothy McVeigh and Paul Hill. However, long before them, another much more devious and secretive group arose that has committed acts of terror against people based on their ethnicity and religion all across the United States: the Ku Klux Klan.

Rise of the KKK

The original Ku Klux Klan (KKK), a reactionary organization to the Confederate States' loss of the Civil War, modeled its behavior on the radical, uncompromising ideology of Southern chivalry and the need to protect Southern womanhood—to the point of extreme violence after the Civil War ended, and again fifty years later. For 100 years Brown's legacy led to racial segregation and Jim Crow laws, and when the Civil Rights movements of the 1960s and 1970s came into being it was the radical political groups, such as the Black Panther Party, that called for followers to emulate the dedication and violence demonstrated by Brown in the previous century.

With the end of slavery, reunification of the country, and military occupation of the former Confederacy, a wholly new form of domestic terrorism arose that is still with us today. By 1881, postwar Reconstruction had given way to a resurgent White supremacy. Former Confederate soldiers and sympathizers were regaining power across the South, and many Whites in Jefferson County, Missouri, wanted to join in this restoration of the old regime.

Who comprised this first Klan and why they acted as they did can be found only in the earliest versions of its history, all written by strongly sympathetic racist Southerners. These early publications are clearly biased in their presentations and must be read as such. However, subsequent versions of the history of the Ku Klux Klan would be much better documented and publicized, with less bias.

Mrs. S. E. F. Rose writes in *The Ku Klux Klan or Invisible Empire*, a work largely comprised of an earlier publication by professor of history Walter L. Fleming at Louisiana State University, the original "Klans were formed in all the Southern States, and their membership reached large numbers, estimated at half a million"[16] with the "purpose of protecting the homes and women of the South."[17] Rose describes the Klansmen as heroes and their works as glorious deeds. Her book received the endorsement of the Daughters of the Confederacy in 1913 and the Sons of Confederate Veterans in 1914 with recommendations it be placed in schools and libraries throughout the southern states. (This author remembers having read Rose's book in a Texas high school in the 1970s.)

With the Civil War ended, Southern agriculture devastated, railroad transportation nearly wrecked, and the emancipation of slaves having essentially resulted in four million nonworking hungry mouths crowding the towns and cities expecting aid from Union soldiers, the term *chaos* was rightly applied to the overall postwar condition in the states that had seceded from the Union. This situation was compounded by the arrival of carpetbaggers—Northern adventurers and Union Army camp followers who supported Reconstruction and were portrayed by those opposed to Lincoln's Republican party as corrupt profiteers who took advantage of the financial and political instability in the devastated postwar South.

The Reconstruction era government of the Southern states consisted of carpetbaggers, homemade Yankees (scalawags, often described "as despicable traitors to the South"),[18] and the recently freed and enfranchised former slaves. The remaining loyal Whites referred to this imposed government as the "Black and Tan Government."[19]

Six Confederate soldiers who returned to Tennessee after the war ended found the conditions facing them and their fellow Southerners to be difficult to accept after once being lords of their own lives, homes, and property. When they arrived in Pulaski, Giles County, in the winter of 1865–1866, they formed a fraternal organization for themselves and others. As the political situation precluded them from holding public office, voting, having government jobs, or receiving any benefits resulting from their service, they chose to band together in a secret order to deliver "the South from a bondage worse than death."[20] These Confederate veterans gave their organization the name Ku Klux, a play on the Greek *ku-klos,* meaning circle. They added Klan for symmetry and mystery. This was the birth of the Ku Klux Klan.

The original six members were Frank O. McCord (first Grand Cyclops), James R. Crowe (Grand Turk), Richard R. Reed, John B.

Kennedy, John C. Lester, and Calvin Jones. Per a letter from Kennedy to Mrs. Rose in March 1909, the mission of the KKK was as follows:

> To protect the weak and oppressed during the dark days of Reconstruction. To protect the women of the South, who were the loveliest, most noble and best women in the world. . . . They are proud they were Ku Klux, and could give aid to these dear Southern women again during the Reconstruction period, for it was a dark and distressing era in our beloved Southland.[21]

The group grew relatively quickly, and organization size reached the point of calling for a nationally recognized leader (see Figure 2.1). By the fall of 1866 former Confederate general Nathan Bedford Forrest was selected by the membership. He took the oath of office and became the Grand Wizard of the Invisible Empire—an organization that spanned fourteen states from Virginia to Texas.

As a social organization that was prohibited from meeting by the military forces occupying the former Confederate States, the members wore costumes and rode at night to get to their meeting locations. Along the way they soon realized that their costumes had a deleterious effect on the freedmen who saw the hooded and caped figures as representations of their dead masters, and on scalawags and carpetbaggers who saw the riders as an organized threat. These night riders in their hoods and cloaks would frequently call out freed slaves who they had determined to be guilty of some sort of wrongdoing and issue punishments in the form of severe whippings. The intent was to frighten the wrongdoer into proper behavior. Such wrong behavior could be perceived as acting beyond their accepted place in society, failing to give way to White people on a sidewalk, or speaking improperly to a White woman. It is difficult to ascertain how many of these events can be attributed to the members of the KKK, or to other organizations that concurrently arose, including the White Camelia, which was larger and more active than the Klan. However, the actors were more easily represented by the press and by memory as Klansmen. When the KKK was clearly identified as the perpetrator, it was often because the victim had offered what was considered violent resistance to the riders.

In February 1869, General Forrest, Grand Wizard of the KKK, issued a proclamation directing the short-lived order be disbanded. Anti-KKK legislation passed by Congress in 1872 allowed "federal troops to suppress the hooded order forcibly even though the Klansmen's goal of returning white, conservative rule to the Southern states

Figure 2.1 The Original KKK, 1865–1869

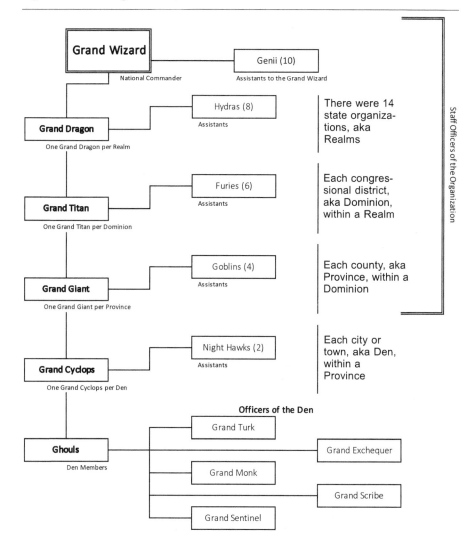

Credit: James Phelps, 2017, drawn from W. L. Fleming's appendixes to D. L. Wilson and J. C. Lester, *Ku Klux Klan: Its Origins, Growth and Disbandment* (New York: Neale Publishing, 1884).

was realized during that"[22] first decade following the Civil War. This ended the original Klan, but not the fear its members and presence engendered among the freedmen who remained in the South.

The Second Klan

At the end of World War I a new Ku Klux Klan arose to combat the perceived foreign influence and corruption of Americanism brought by large numbers of Catholic immigrants. It concurrently would find the prohibitionist movement a fertile ground to recruit members to defend the family against immorality. This new Klan saw a rapid rise and expansion to nearly every state, then suffered an almost immediate membership collapse followed by decades of struggle before being forced to dissolve after World War II. In the end, it did not go away, but retained some members and organizations well through the end of the twentieth century.

Thomas Pegram, in *One Hundred Percent American*, writes, "The 1920s Klan . . . was a massive social movement that helped to shape our collective past. . . . It attracted several million members and exercised substantial influence in many American communities."[23] Yet, by 1930 KKK membership had dropped to "as few as thirty-seven thousand."[24] This rapid rise and sudden collapse can be attributed to the changing society that followed World War I, Prohibition, and the onset of the Great Depression.

The second KKK was primarily a Protestant, White, anti-Catholic, anti-Semitic, fraternal organization with social mores and standards applied to and enforced among its community members. They established and enforced, in particular, their own version of legal and moral standards against "Catholics; bootleggers and other prohibition law violators; unfaithful husbands; sexually adventurous women; indiscreet, successful, or assertive blacks, Jews, or immigrants; even corrupt or unresponsive public officials."[25] The KKK had political committees and worked to control public school boards, to decide who would run for or be elected to state and local attorney general positions, and to elect "law and order" mayors.

This version of the KKK lasted only ten years, essentially dissolving by mid-1925. While known for its vigilantism, intimidation, and devotion to White supremacy, the 1920s KKK was, according to Pegram, "both a product and a reflection of the distinctive patterns of postwar America" yet with "few direct ties between the national popular movement of the 1920s and its regionally restricted, night-riding predecessor," which "was an explicitly political terrorist organization committed to driving Republican policies and newly enfranchised blacks from the public life of the South."[26]

New Klan, New Purpose

Inaugurated on Stone Mountain, outside Atlanta, Georgia, in 1915, the second Klan languished in only a few towns in Georgia and Alabama during World War I, until they stumbled on the bright idea of hiring the Southern Publicity Association (SPA) in 1920. SPA used professional salesmen to extoll the fraternal and virtuous nature of the new KKK. They created a new position within the organization for professional recruiters or Kleagles. These Kleagles could keep $4 of the $10 initiation fee from each new member they enrolled. Thus, the recruiters were paid based on their success as recruiters.

This new Klan advertised itself as the fighting brother of Masonry, and Kleagles often visited Masonic lodges, the Elks, Odd Fellows, and other men's clubs in their search for recruits. The advertising and process SPA employed worked. The new Klan grew from fewer than 2,000 members in 1920 to become a super lodge of White, Anglo-Saxon Protestantism with over 20 million members nationally, including over 94,000 Protestant ministers, before its mid-decade collapse in the 1920s.

By the end of 1921 there were large and politically strong Klaverns "in Texas, Oklahoma, Arkansas, and Louisiana, and it then spread to Colorado (a Klan stronghold), Kansas, and Missouri."[27] It grew to include chapters in California, Oregon, Indiana, Ohio, Illinois, Pennsylvania, New York, New Jersey, and the upper Midwest, Northeast, and many other states.

1920s Klan Violence

Particularly notable were the moral applications by the KKK, especially when it involved internal family disputes that were outside the bounds of conventional criminal procedures and the Protestant church couldn't take any action. Whether it was "instructing" a son for beating his father, administering therapeutic beatings to a philandering husband, or applying hot tar to fathers who left their children hungry and wives neglected, those who did not conform to the dictates of ideal family life were more likely to suffer punishment at the hands of their Klan peers than outsiders. In nearly every instance mentioned, the Klan consulted the aggrieved family members before taking any action.[28] Thus, the 1920s Klan stepped in and provided a moral solution to problems where there was no extant legal basis for action by the state or ethical precursor by the church.

Regardless of the fraternal and social image portrayed to new members and the media, the 1920s KKK was fundamentally violent, dangerous, and aberrant. Murders, whippings, and brandings and submitting local moral transgressors to tar and feathers or even castration were not unknown. But the KKK had limits. This Klan tended not to participate in lynch mobs. From 1922 to 1924, the most active years of the second Klan, the national lynching toll actually declined, and as Pegram writes, "In the taut, racially sensitive atmosphere of the postwar years, anti-black violence by the Klan did not exceed that committed by white society in general."[29] Moreover, as with any secret political society confronting a cultural dilemma, violence was the natural consequence, but existed primarily in the southern and southwestern realms. Pegram notes that, "even in the violent heartland of hooded moral regulation, the greatest waves of night riding and vigilantism had been curbed by the close of 1923."[30] In fact, even when they were not responsible for specific violence, the Klan's publicists tied the acts to KKK objectives so that reality and myth tended to blend.

Maintaining the Color Barrier

Even with an anti-Black focus among Klaverns, it wasn't the KKK but collective White violence that resulted in the destruction of Black settlements in Florida. Yet, in Oklahoma a team of masked Klansmen "abducted a black Tulsa activist, charged him with registering black voters and addressing a white woman impertinently, then beat and whipped him, cut off his ear, and urged him to leave the state, which he refused to do."[31] This Oklahoma act is a depiction of the lengths seen nationally by Klansmen when it came to ensuring segregation and racial separatism. Sustaining this separation of the races was by far the greatest concern and focus of the 1920s Klan, clearly placing it within the broad national consensus to prevent miscegenation, which would pollute the White blood line and civilization. What anti-Black activity the Klan employed aimed to prevent exercise of enfranchisement at the polling centers and to preclude any crossing of the racial barriers to social interaction. At one point the original salesman of the 1920s Klan, William Clarke of the SPA, called for the sterilization of male Black children.

So important was the protection of the color barrier, Klansmen across the South and Southwest would resort to beating, whipping, and even castrating offenders. And not just Black offenders, but in at least one case a White male was castrated for crossing the color barrier. Yet the public outcry over this type of vigilantism would lead national Klan leaders to call on the state and local leaders to rein in their members and restrict Klan activities to the political arena. Outrage over the violation of the color barrier was not always the primary focus of Klansmen— they often meted out similar punishments for those involved in pimping, bootlegging, and treating Blacks as equal with Whites, regardless of the offender's race. It wasn't just the Klan that carried out this vigilantism, but within the generally accepted mores of the era, the Klan's violence is what made them different from all the others.

Anti-Catholicism Trumps Racism

The other interesting component of the 1920s KKK was its focus on anti-Catholicism. Seemingly at cross-purposes, at times efforts were made to enlist Black Protestants in the anti-Catholic cause by enrolling them into Klan auxiliaries. Pegram writes of the "Loyal Legion of Lincoln and the Ritualistic Benevolent Society for American Born Citizens of African Blood and Protestant Faith"[32] as examples of Klan attempts to build anti-Catholic solidarity across the usually impermeable racial lines. The Klan even recruited large numbers of socialists into the Milwaukee den to promote anti-Catholicism.

The Catholics did not sit still for Klan attacks. Often the anti-Klan violence was strongest from the Catholics. Klan printing presses were bombed. Klan marches and gatherings were targeted by stone throwers. Full-scale anti-Klan Catholic-led riots happened in Ohio and Massachusetts. This resulted in driving away the moderate, fraternal-minded Klan members who had no desire to stand with and suffer physically in the face of what was essentially an ongoing war in some parts of the country.

Death, Taxes, and the Klan

The 1924 National Origins Act brought an end to open entry to the United States and essentially ended the fear of Catholicism and immigrants as the basis for the renewed Klan. The advent of Prohibition and onset of the Great Depression would nearly wipe out the organization except for entrenched groups of racists.

Other issues leading to the sudden decline and collapse of the 1920s Klan were problems with morality and abuses of power among those at the highest levels of state and national Klan leadership. An organization that advertised and recruited based on fraternity, sobriety, sexual morality, and the sacred nature of the family could not sustain itself when the hypocrisy of the leadership was made public.

The Klan declined in power and membership considerably in 1926, and that decline continued through the end of the decade. By the onset of the Great Depression the conditions that existed across the country, typically in working-class communities, was such that membership in a social and fraternal society simply could not be sustained. The Klan simply disappeared, nearly overnight, except in some southern states where racism was the primary motivation for membership. By 1944, in severe financial trouble and facing unpayable federal tax obligations, "the hooded order formally [dissolved], to be replaced in a new postwar period by a loose combination of Klans that were more clearly subversive, violent, and outside the shifting mainstream of American belief and behavior that had been the experience of the vast, troubled, and evanescent popular movement of the 1920s."[33]

The KKK still exists today as a race- and religion-based domestic terrorist group, however, in a much weaker and less organized form. The philosophy of the KKK can be found as the underpinning of White supremacist movements such as the Skinheads, Christian Identity, National Alliance, The Order, Phineas Priesthood, Volksfront, White Aryan Resistance, Aryan Brotherhood/Nation, Hammerskins, and others. The authors wish to advise readers that the list provided by the Southern Poverty Law Center is problematic as it includes every right-leaning political organization or group and all Christian churches that oppose abortion, nearly all of which are correctly organized with established political organizations.[34]

On an international basis, similar White supremacist groups with domestic terrorism activities within their own countries can be found in Argentina, Australia, Belgium, Bosnia and Herzegovina, Brazil, Canada, Catalonia, Chile, France, Germany, Greece, Iran, the Netherlands, New Zealand, Norway, Poland, Portugal, Romania, Russia, South Africa, Spain, Sweden, Serbia, Turkey, the United Kingdom, and Uruguay (not an all-inclusive list).

The Anarchists

There were other sources of domestic terrorism in the United States between the era of John Brown and the start of the Great Depression. Primary among these were the labor movements of the last decades of the nineteenth century and the first of the twentieth. As industrialism deepened and demand for miners and factory workers exploded, so too did the dynamite. Wherever workers protested, the strikebreakers, local police, National Guard, and even federal troops would ensure the event became bloody. The workers would reply in kind. Thousands would perish across the United States, and around the world, during this period of anarchistic violence.

When the Federation of Organized Trades and Labor Unions resolved that limiting the workday to eight hours was essential, the failure of industry and government to meet their demands led to a general strike across the nation on May 1, 1886. Almost half a million workers walked off the job in over 1,400 strikes.

Four days later, as Vivian Gornick describes in her work on the life of anarchist Emma Goldman, at a rally in Chicago's Haymarket Square in support of the strikers, at the end of the peaceful protest as evening approached, a pipe bomb was tossed into a police line, killing seven officers.[35] The police opened fire on the crowd and killed eleven demonstrators. Eight of the labor leaders were charged with the crime, and their trial took nearly a year and a half. Four would be hanged.

Among the movement's leaders, such as Jane Addams, Bill Heywood, and Eugene Debs, there was despair of the possibility of peaceful social change and a call for "propaganda by the deed."[36] So strong was the call for violence to correct the social ills of the day that a US president would die at the hands of anarchists.

Death of a President

Emma Goldman's speeches were invigorating, sometimes bringing deep philosophical changes to those who heard her calls for an end of all government. In May 1901 one such listener with Goldman's words ringing in his ears related, "Her doctrine that all rulers should be exterminated was what set me to thinking so that my head nearly split with the pain. Miss Goldman's words went right through me, and when I left the lecture I had made up my mind that I would have to do something heroic for the cause I loved."[37] After three close opportunities that were spoiled by either his hesitation or the sudden movement of the crowds, Leon Czolgosz finally found himself face to face with William McKinley at 4 p.m. on September 6, 1901, the third and final day of the president's visit to the Pan-American Exposition near Buffalo, New York. Two shots from a .32 caliber revolver, sounding much like firecrackers, struck President McKinley in the chest and abdomen at point-blank range. Within minutes McKinley would be in surgery at the exposition's medical clinic. One bullet had struck a button and bounced off the president's sternum, simply falling out of the wound as attendants undressed him. The second bullet passed through his stomach and was lodged somewhere deeper in his body. The attending surgeons couldn't find it and were leery of using the new x-ray machine on display at the exposition.

Though it looked at first like the president would recover, that would not be the case as gangrene infected the wounds in his stomach and his pancreas, resulting in the sudden decline of his condition on September 13. At 2:15 a.m. on September 14, 1901, President McKinley died, leaving the country in the hands of Theodore Roosevelt.

In the early years of the twentieth century justice was sure, and punishment was swift. On October 29, 1901, Leon Czolgosz, his legs weak and rubbery, was half dragged and half carried to New York's electric chair, where the guards completed their task of strapping him in and connecting the electrodes to his head and leg. As they slipped a leather mask—with holes cut for his nose and mouth—over his head, he cried out, "I killed the President for the good of the laboring people, the good people. I am not sorry for my crime but I am sorry I can't see my father."[38]

Battles for the Rights of Labor

Throughout the twentieth century the anarchists committed acts of terror. Yet the working men and their families fighting for better working conditions would also be victims of terrorism—at the hands of strikebreakers, corporate militia, and government troops. Of significant importance to the labor union movement, but mostly forgotten to classroom history, was the assault on the camp of striking coal miners in Ludlow, Colorado, where over 1,000 people had lived in canvas tents with plank floors and wooden walls for over eight months.

Strikebreaking militia arrived the morning of April 20, 1914, and issued an ultimatum. The men, sensing violence was about to start, sent their wives and children running from the camp toward the hills and prairie. When shooting started, those who had not yet left, or who refused to leave, pulled up floorboards to hide or sheltered in basements constructed under the tents. By sunset the resisting strikers had been subdued, but the militia had become a mob, rampaging and looting the camp, setting fire to tents and other structures that remained standing after dousing the canvas with oil. Those in the maternity bunker found the fire above pulling their remaining oxygen from the pit and the floorboards above too hot to touch. The next day the militia would continue burning everything left at the camp and looting whatever was salvageable. As Jones writes, "It was almost midday when rescue workers finally searched the maternity ward. Beneath the charred remains of the tent, they discovered the bodies of two young mothers and their eleven children, all of whom had suffocated."[39]

As domestic terrorists, the anarchists were not limited to the United States but led revolutions across Europe; they brought about World War I, the end of the czar in Russia, and the rise of the Soviet Union. Many anarchist organizations still exist today. They are well established and can be found on every continent except Antarctica, and across Oceania and the South Pacific. Some of these include the Union of Russian Workers (United States and Canada); Workers' Solidarity Alliance, the Curious George Brigade, Bash Back!, Anarchist People of Color, and Unconventional Action (United States); Casa del Obrero Mundial and the Zapatista Army of National Liberation (Mexico); Brazilian Workers Confederation, Uruguayan Anarchist Federation, and Mujeres Creando (South America); Anarchists Against the Wall and the Black Laundry (Israel); Al Badil Al Taharouri (Lebanon); Anarchist Communist Initiative, Anarchist Communist Youth Association of Narva, Free Union, Free Workers' Union, Action Directe, Bonnot Gang, Black Star, Conspiracy of Fire Nuclei, Informal Anarchist Federation, Italian Anarchist Federation, Italian Syndicalist Union, Orang Alternative, Workers' Initiative, Black Guards, Chernoe Znamia, Narodnaya Volya, Acrates, Solidaridad Obrera, Lund's Anarchist Group, Jura Federation, Nabat, Class War, Queer Mutiny, and Movement Against the Monarchy (Europe including Russia); and the Melbourne Anarchist Club, Mutiny Collective, and Radical Youth (Australasia and Oceania).

Clearly, the anarchist and labor terrorist organizations, whether working domestically or internationally, have not disappeared into the past.

Race Riots

In a nation where its Civil War was begun and fought in a purported attempt to "free the slaves," race riots have been endemic. Shortly after the Civil War, as Black Codes were enacted in the South in an effort to maintain some social control over the recently freed African Americans, riots broke out in Memphis and in New Orleans. Twelve churches in Memphis were burned, forty-six African Americans were killed, and an additional seventy were wounded. In New Orleans thirty-five were killed, with over a hundred wounded.

Ethnicity and racial bigotry have also been the catalyst for riots in this country. Although Chinese immigrants had greatly assisted in the building of the transcontinental railroad, after failing to cash in during the 1849 California Gold Rush, some Americans were convinced in the 1870s that immigrants were stealing their jobs. In 1885 in Wyoming, White coal miners, enraged that Chinese workers were willing to work for less than their unionized White American counterparts, engaged with two Chinese workers and beat one to death. Later that day, on September 2, the riot escalated, and a White mob descended on Rock Springs' Chinatown, burning it to the ground and killing twenty-eight Chinese.

Many riots have occurred that related directly to labor unrest and resentment toward management. General strikes by railroad workers in 1877 culminated in a riot in Pittsburgh on July 21, with shots being fired by both rioters and the Pennsylvania National Guard. When the shooting was over, forty members of the mob and five Guardsmen were dead.

The list of race-related riots in the United States is long. They happened all across the country in every state (and territory). Whether it was the anti-Chinese riot in Rock Springs, Wyoming Territory (1885); the White Democrats overthrowing the elected government of Wilmington, North Carolina (1898); riots in ten cities in 1967; the 2015 Baltimore, Maryland, riots following the death of Freddie Gray; or the 2020 riots after the death of George Floyd, this continuing part of US history is bloody, destructive, and divisive. It has happened under both Republican and Democratic presidents, for reasons of law, interracial marriage, voting rights, perceived and actual police abuse, and the result of alleged racial disparity in the people being drafted and sent to war. This internal problem has been with the people of North America since 1770; that violence has targeted slaves and slaveholders and anti-slavery Blacks and Whites, Germans, Italians, Mexicans, Latinos, Chinese, Japanese, Filipinos, Cubans, Puerto Ricans, North Africans, Arabs, and Koreans. The only commonality among all these riots is that what nearly always started as a peaceful assembly of the populace to address grievances to the government ended up with burning, looting, homicide, and violent police or even military responses to restore order.

Such riots will continue into the future, and it is important to look at the failure of intelligence (both local and federal) to address the potential that protests could erupt into violent conflict between the state and the populace. The recent death of George Floyd while in custody of the Minneapolis Police on Memorial Day 2020 prompted many race riots across the country.

Timothy McVeigh and Other Political Violence

The April 19, 1995, bombing of the Alfred P. Murrah Federal Building in Oklahoma City marked a remarkable and new change in US domestic terrorism. This was the point where race and religion were removed from the previous mix of causes for violence, and the focus was shifted toward what some perceived to be an abusive, totalitarian, and socialist-leaning federal government.

Timothy McVeigh and Terry Nichols constructed a 5,000-pound ammonium nitrate nitromethane explosive device in the back of a rented Ryder truck. McVeigh then drove the truck to Oklahoma City where he parked in front of the federal building at 9 a.m. His two-minute home-made fuse detonated the device that destroyed the structure, killing 168 people, including 19 children in a daycare center on the second floor. Another 684 people were injured in the blast.

Following the actions of the federal government at Ruby Ridge in 1992 and the siege of the Branch Davidian compound at Waco in 1993, McVeigh became strongly antigovernment in his beliefs and practices, particularly focusing on the Bureau of Alcohol, Tobacco, Firearms and Explosives (ATF) and its (perceived) egregious acts against the citizens of the United States under the direction of Attorney General Janet Reno. McVeigh actively wrote letters to newspapers, elected representatives, and gun show customers while selling pro–gun rights, pro–Second Amendment, and patriot literature and bumper stickers, which indicated a clear and focused attention on the ever-increasing movement toward a totalitarian police state that subjugated US citizens under a socialist regime. He focused on the concept that it was the Declaration of Independence to which patriots should maintain allegiance as the Constitution was corrupted by the self-serving political class and being used as a tool against the people rather than as a protection for actions enshrined in the Bill of Rights.

Timothy McVeigh was arrested for traffic and firearms violations near Perry, Oklahoma, shortly after the bombing. Just prior to being released on bail he was identified as a suspect in the bombing and held pending subsequent charges. On August 10, 1995, he was indicted on eleven federal counts, including conspiracy to use a weapon of mass destruction, use of a weapon of mass destruction, and eight counts of first-degree murder (the eight federal agents killed in the bombing), among other charges. A jury found him guilty on all eleven charges on June 2, 1997, and he was sentenced to death eleven days later.

McVeigh was the first federal prisoner to be executed since Victor Feguer in 1963. The execution took place on June 11, 2001, at the federal penitentiary in Terre Haute, Indiana. His remains were cremated and delivered to his attorney for disposition.

It is important to note that Timothy McVeigh was not anti-American. Nor was he uneducated, undereducated, or of low intellect. The prison psychiatrist concluded that McVeigh had an IQ of 126. McVeigh served honorably in the US Army, earned the Bronze Star among other awards during the liberation of Kuwait, and received an honorable discharge at the end of his service. He viewed his actions in Oklahoma as morally equivalent to what the US military carried out against Iraq and other countries. He argued that the federal government was hypocritical in its application of standards and laws and that it targeted those who acted (or spoke) against them. He wrote that the federal government and its agents, in particular the ATF, were the true barbarians.

McVeigh's accomplices were also charged with multiple crimes. Terry Nichols was convicted and sentenced to life in prison by a federal court. Michael and Lori Fortier had foreknowledge of the attack; Michael pleaded guilty and was sentenced to twelve years in prison in exchange for testimony against McVeigh and Nichols and immunity for Lori. He was released early and transferred to the witness protection program.

Jim Geraghty writes in *National Review* that politics "gives [Americans] an enemy, a target and focus for all of their worst impulses and feelings. Very few of us can completely escape the temptation to feel hate, contempt, disdain, and a desire for someone else. Politics gives us a target and an excuse."[40] This is the next phase of anarchist and antigovernment violence in the United States. It can be seen in people driving vehicles through crowds as was done in Nice, Berlin, Barcelona, London, and Toronto. It happens with random knife attacks in subways and on buses. It may show up in the mail from bombers in Austin, Texas. Shooters will walk into corporate headquarters and exact revenge as one did at YouTube. And there will be more mass shootings, such as the one in Las Vegas where law enforcement still has no perceived motive.

Conclusion

Timothy McVeigh was a beginning for modern right-wing terrorism in the United States. The Anti-Defamation League's report on right-wing terrorism between July 1993 and March 2017, *A Dark and Constant Rage: 25 Years of Right-Wing Terrorism in the United States,* states that more than 800 people were killed or injured in 150 terrorist acts committed, attempted, or plotted by right-wing extremists.[41] These attacks surged during the mid- to late-1990s and again in 2009. Sixty-four incidents were carried out by White supremacists. Sixty-three were conducted by antigovernment groups such as militias and sovereign citizens.[42] While the study is clearly focused only on right-wing terrorism, it goes on to warn that authorities need to be wary not only of the extreme political right but also of the extreme left. James Hodgkinson, a sixty-six-year-old White male, opened fire on the Republican congressional caucus baseball team during a practice session on June 14, 2017. As David Usborne writes in *The Independent*, "the more the middle-ground of political discourse in America crumbles and disappears, the more the propensity towards hatred and a willingness to commit—or provoke—violence grows. That this is happening at both ends of the ideological spectrum at once only makes it more scary."[43]

This shift toward violent expression of political thought is problematic as it raises the question for law enforcement of whom to target for intelligence gathering. After the 9/11 attacks significant efforts were made in many US cities to involve leaders in the Muslim community and mosques to report on their constituents with radical beliefs. For example, today there are weekly meetings between Houston police intelligence officers and the clerics in mosques citywide. How will homeland security enter into a similar intelligence-gathering effort without making the same errors as the FBI during the 1960s and the ATF during the 1980s–1990s?

Notes

1. United States Code, Title 22, Chapter 38 §2656f.
2. 28 Code of Federal Regulations §0.85.
3. FBI, "Domestic Terrorism," https://www.fbi.gov/investigate/terrorism (accessed February 25, 2021).
4. USA PATRIOT Act, Pub. L. No. 107-52, Section 802.
5. *Merriam-Webster's Collegiate Dictionary*, 11th ed. (Springfield, MA: Merriam-Webster, Inc., 2004), p. 1075.

6. Evan Carton, *Patriotic Treason* (New York: Simon and Schuster, 2006), p. ix.

7. Albert Marrin, *A Volcano Beneath the Snow: John Brown's War Against Slavery* (New York: Alfred A. Knopf, 2014), p. 4.

8. Ibid.

9. Carton, *Patriotic Treason*, p. 30.

10. Ibid., pp. 83–84.

11. Ibid., p. 93.

12. Ibid., p. 185.

13. Thomas Fleming, *American Chronicles* (Boston: New Word City, 2016), p. 62.

14. Robert De Witt, *The Life, Trial and Execution of Capt. John Brown: Being a Full Account of the Attempted Insurrection at Harper's Ferry, VA* (Charleston: Bibliolife DBA, 2011), p. 8.

15. Tony Horwitz, *Midnight Rising: John Brown and the Raid That Sparked the Civil War* (New York: Henry Holt, 2011), p. 131.

16. S. E. F. Rose, *The Ku Klux Klan or Invisible Empire* (New Orleans: L. Graham Co., 1914), p. 3.

17. Ibid., p. 13.

18. Ibid., p. 124.

19. Ibid.

20. Ibid.

21. Ibid., p. 174.

22. Thomas Pegram, *One Hundred Percent American: The Rebirth and Decline of the Ku Klux Klan in the 1920s* (Chicago: Ivan R. Dee, 2011), p. 7.

23. Ibid., p. x.

24. Ibid., p. 20.

25. Ibid., p. 3.

26. Ibid., pp. 6–7.

27. Ibid., p. 10.

28. Ibid., p. 163.

29. Ibid., p. 60.

30. Ibid., p. 158.

31. Ibid., p. 62.

32. Ibid., p. 70.

33. Ibid., p. 20.

34. Southern Poverty Law Center, https://www.splcenter.org/hate-map (accessed November 14, 2020).

35. Vivian Gornick, *Emma Goldman: Revolution as a Way of Life* (New Haven: Yale University Press, 2011).

36. Ibid., p. 18.

37. Everett Marshall, *The Complete Life of William McKinley and the Story of His Assassination* (Chicago: Historical Press, 1901), p. 71.

38. Scott Miller, *The President and the Assassin: McKinley, Terror and Empire at the Dawn of the American Century* (New York: Random House, 2013), p. 330.

39. Thai Jones, "Why the Bloodiest Labor Battle in U.S. History Matters Today," *The Nation*, April 21, 2014, https://www.thenation.com/article/archive/why -bloodiest-labor-battle-us-history-matters-today/.

40. Jim Geraghty, "Politically Motivated Violence Is on the Rise," *National Review*, April 24, 2018.

41. Anti-Defamation League, *A Dark and Constant Rage: 25 Years of Right-Wing Terrorism in the United States* (New York: ADL, 2017).

42. Ibid.

43. David Usborne, "America Faces a New Wave of Homegrown Political Violence and Terrorism If Its Divisions Continue," *The Independent*, June 24, 2017.

3

The Creation
of the Department of
Homeland Security

The most extensive reorganization of our government in decades was the creation of the Department of Homeland Security (DHS), as a direct result of the attacks against the United States on September 11, 2001. Understanding why the DHS was created, which government agencies were absorbed into the DHS, and the difficult mission it has been tasked with accomplishing is essential to understanding the overall process of developing and acting on intelligence related to homeland security. However, it is important to set the stage for the events of 9/11 by looking at an earlier radical Islamic terrorist attack in the United States.

1993 Attack on the World Trade Center

The attack on the World Trade Center Twin Towers in New York City and the Pentagon in Alexandria, Virginia, in September 2001 was not the first attack by an Islamic terrorist group in the United States, nor even the first attack on the Twin Towers. On February 26, 1993, a large bomb was detonated beneath the World Trade Center on level B-2 of the underground garage. The resulting explosion killed six people and injured more than a thousand. The homemade truck bomb was intended to cause sufficient damage to drop one tower into the second, resulting in the destruction of both. The blast opened a hole within the structure from the third level of the basement to over seven stories up and into the complex. Had the bomb been correctly placed, next to the basement structural wall rather than just within the parking complex, it would have succeeded. The fact that there were only six fatalities was a miracle. The National Security Council was ordered by President Clinton to coordinate the response. The CIA's Counterterrorism Center queried its sources worldwide. The National Security Agency (NSA) located at Ft. Meade, Maryland, searched its databases for clues related to the attack. Control of the local investigation was coordinated by the FBI's New York field office, which set a pattern for future federal management of terrorist situations.

The 9/11 Commission Report stated that *four points* related to the 1993 bombing have significance for the 9/11 attacks. *First*, the bombing meant that the United States had a new, extremely dangerous enemy, one that had no limits in terms of rage or rationality. Anyone could be a target: young, old, civilian, military. The idea was simply to kill as many Americans as possible. The terrorist who actually planted the bomb, Ramzi Yousef, said later that he wanted to kill as many as 250,000 people.[1]

The US law enforcement system is efficient and effective, particularly in a reactive sense. The FBI and Justice Department did an excellent job searching for clues after the bombing. The FBI identified a part from a rental van that had been reported stolen the day before the bombing, in Jersey City. The man who had rented the van, Mohammed Salameh, continually called the rental office, attempting to get his rental deposit back ($400), and he was arrested at the office by the FBI on March 4, 1993, six days after the bombing had occurred. Shortly after Salameh was arrested, the FBI had two others in custody, including Nidal Ayyad, the person who had acquired the chemicals necessary to build the bomb, and the person who had mixed the chemicals together, Mahmoud Abouhalima.[2] So, the *second* primary feature relating to the 9/11 attacks was the relatively quick work of the FBI in investigating and arresting the primary authors of the 1993 attack.

The three central arrests in the bombing led the FBI to the Farouq mosque in Brooklyn. A primary figure related to the mosque was Sheikh Omar Abdel Rahman, an extremist Muslim cleric. Rahman, who was blind and known as the "Blind Sheikh," preached the extremist philosophy of Sayyid Qutb, a Muslim who had lived in the United States while attending college in Colorado in the 1950s. Born Egyptian and raised Muslim, Qutb memorized the Quran as a boy and later moved to Cairo to work as a teacher and writer. Because some of his writing was considered rebellious, his superiors arranged for him to travel to the United States to attend graduate school. Qutb enrolled at the Colorado State College of Education (now known as the University of Northern Colorado). Although his opinion of America and Americans was thought to be benign at first, he quickly decided that Americans and American culture were barbaric and dangerous to Old World values. He believed, after observing life in Greeley, Colorado, that Americans lacked basic virtues and were simplistic and barbarous. And, worse, because dreams actually could come true in a boundless land, America itself was dangerous. Qutb cut short his college career and returned to Egypt after the assassination of the founder of the Muslim Brotherhood, Hassan al-Banna. Over the next fifteen years Qutb refined his violent political theology based on his experiences in Colorado. He believed, and wrote, that the entire modern world, characterized and represented by America, was *jahiliyya*, a barbarous state that had existed prior to the Prophet Muhammad, and only the strict, unchanging, absolute law of the Prophet could redeem the uncivilized condition. Qutb called all true Muslims to a holy war against the modern world, and against America, which represented it, and which, according to Qutb, oppressed Muslims worldwide.

Qutb's extreme writings and beliefs led to his execution by the Egyptian government in 1966. His martyrdom accelerated the movement, unfortunately. His views and writings could be dismissed as the rantings of a madman, except for one thing: there is a direct link between Qutb and the architect of the 9/11 attacks. Qutb's brother Muhammad went into exile after his brother's execution and taught at King Abdul Aziz University. One of his students was Osama bin Laden.

According to an FBI informant, Rahman was planning to bomb major New York landmarks, including the Holland and Lincoln tunnels. Based on this, the FBI arrested Rahman and various confederates in the plot in June 1993. As a result of the FBI investigation and arrests, the US attorney for the Southern District of New York prosecuted and convicted multiple individuals, including Salameh, Ayyad, Rahman, and Abouhalima. This, unfortunately, created the incorrect impression that the current US law enforcement system was entirely capable and well-equipped to deal with terrorism. So, *third*, the use of the legal system to address the first Twin Towers bombing in 1993 resulted in the unintended effect of completely obscuring the need to examine the new threat against the United States, as well as the "real" ability of current US intelligence and law enforcement systems to prevent a similar attack on the World Trade Center, or some other critical infrastructure of the country. Because the symptoms were handled so successfully, in the minds of many citizens, there was no worry. Neither the president nor Congress nor the media felt the need to ask whether our current law enforcement and intelligence community structure was sufficient to deal with the real problem. The question would not be asked until 2001.

Law enforcement in this country is designed to investigate, determine if and when a crime was committed, collect any and all legal evidence relating to the crime, arrest the possible perpetrators if they can be found, present the evidence to a prosecutor, and, assuming enough viable evidence is available, convict the offender. This was done after the 1993 World Trade Center bombing. The process marked for the public the fact that the system worked. Just like on television shows every night, the case was solved, justice was done, and the offenders were put away. No one asked if the evidence suggested the events might mean that worse was to come. Therefore, *fourth* and perhaps worst in the list of points related to the 1993 World Trade Center bombing, no one suggested looking for clues to more general terrorist tactics, such as methods of entry and finance, and possible modes of operation within the country.

Additionally, the successful prosecution and convictions of the terrorists contributed to a widespread public underestimation of the capabilities of the new threat. The overarching image left in the public mind was that of an incredibly stupid Salameh calling the rental agency again and again, demanding the return of his $400 rental deposit on the truck used in the bombing. This led to one of the greatest intelligence failures of the modern era.

One hundred forty-one years, ten months, and five days after nineteen religiously motivated extra-national combatants conducted an assault on the US government with the intent of righting the terrible wrongs the government condoned (John Brown's attack on Harpers Ferry), another nineteen religiously motivated extra-national combatants conducted an assault much more devastating in its initial impact, resulting in a worldwide response to their acts of terrorism. The 9/11 hijackers may not have been domestic terrorists, but their attack and the continuing war on terror around the world continue to inspire large numbers of domestic terrorists in multiple countries.

Terrorism of all types has been with us for centuries. Currently, the form of terrorism the US government and associated major agencies focus upon is religious terrorism, generally ignored until the attacks of 9/11. The US government still does not overtly intervene in much state-sponsored and criminal terrorism. However, if there is some underlying political or economic benefit, the government may intervene, especially through rhetoric. As far as internal (domestic) dissident terrorism, it is generally treated as criminal behavior.

September 11, 2001

At 7:59 a.m. American Airlines Flight 11 departed Boston's Logan International Airport en route to Los Angeles with a crew of eleven and eighty-one passengers. Among those passengers were five Middle Eastern men who would hijack the aircraft. Fifteen minutes after Flight 11 departed, United Airlines Flight 175 also departed en route to Los Angeles with nine crew members and fifty-six passengers, among them five Middle Eastern men who would hijack this aircraft.

American Airlines Flight 77 departed Washington Dulles International Airport at 8:20 a.m. en route to Los Angeles with a crew of six and fifty-eight passengers, including five more Middle Eastern men who would turn out to be hijackers. Twenty-two minutes later United Airlines Flight 93 departed Newark International Airport en route to San Francisco with a crew of seven and thirty-seven passengers. Sitting with these San Francisco–bound passengers were four Middle Eastern men intending to hijack this aircraft. Four minutes later the first aircraft, American Airlines Flight 11, flew into the northern façade of the World Trade Center's North Tower; seventeen minutes after that United Airlines Flight 175 flew into the southern façade of the South Tower. Thirty-four minutes later American Airlines Flight 77 flew into the Pentagon, and about half an hour after that, United Airlines Flight 93 crashed near Shanksville, Pennsylvania, after the passengers revolted against the control of the four hijackers.

The entire attack, from the takeoff of the first aircraft to the crash of the last, was only two hours and four minutes. All four aircraft had relatively few passengers in relation to their carrying capacity, yet all had full fuel loads as they were transcontinental flights heading from the East Coast to the West Coast nonstop. This created manageable passenger and crew complements for a small number of hijackers to control while allowing for fully fueled flying bombs to be used against their assigned targets. The attacks resulted in the deaths of 2,996 people and the injuries of over 6,000 others including many first responders in New York City. People from over ninety countries died in the attacks. In addition to the collapse of two World Trade Center towers, World Trade Center buildings 3, 4, 5, 6, and 7 as well as St. Nicholas Greek Orthodox

Church and the Deutsche Bank Building were destroyed or damaged in the attacks. Fires at the World Trade Center site burned for 100 days before finally being extinguished.

The Pentagon suffered damage to the three outer rings, with the Navy wing being the most significantly affected. Importantly, the structure had been undergoing significant strengthening over the years prior to the attack, which contributed to responders' ability to prevent the spread of fires and contain the damage, resulting in reduced numbers of dead and injured.

The attacks were the brainchild of Khalid Sheikh Mohammed, a leader in the al-Qaeda terrorist network and close associate of Osama bin Laden. The ringleader of the attacks in the United States was Mohamed Atta, the only Egyptian national among the hijackers. Fifteen of his team were from Saudi Arabia, two from the United Arab Emirates, and another from Lebanon. All were men, Muslim, and of Arab lineage.

The 9/11 Commission Report

After the attacks on the United States on September 11, 2001, the US Congress, along with the president, created the National Commission on Terrorist Attacks upon the United States (Public Law 107-306, November 27, 2002). The Commission, by law, was directed to investigate "facts and circumstances relating to the terrorist attacks of September 11, 2001," including those relating to "intelligence agencies, law enforcement agencies, diplomacy, immigration issues and border control, the flow of assets to terrorist organizations, commercial aviation, the role of congressional oversight and resource allocation, and other areas determined relevant by the Commission."[3] The mandate was obviously sweeping. The Commission reviewed over 2.5 million pages of documents and interviewed more than 1,200 individuals in ten countries.

The Commission learned about an old enemy long known to many US agencies, including the CIA, NSA, FBI, and Defense Department, that is "sophisticated, patient, disciplined, and lethal," and whose purpose is to "rid the world of religious and political pluralism, the plebiscite, and equal rights for women. It makes no distinction between military and civilian targets."[4] Alarmingly, the Commission reported that the institutions charged with "protecting our borders, civil aviation, and national security did not understand how grave this threat could be, and did not adjust their policies, plans, and practices to deter or defeat it."[5] It described "fault lines" within our government, between foreign and domestic intelligence, and between and within agencies, which contributed to the failure to warn the country of the impending attacks.

Prior Intelligence

There were many separate indicators of the attack as early as 1999 that were available to US intelligence and law enforcement agencies. All four of the hijackers who would later act as pilots of the flying bombs were already in the United States in late 1999 on legal visas and were attending flight training (or refresher training) in Arizona in 2000. Their presence was noted by an FBI agent. According to Attorney General John Ashcroft in his testimony before the 9/11 Commission in April 2004, the "single greatest structural cause for the September 11th problem was the wall that segregated or separated criminal investigators and intelligence agents."[6] And as noted by senior counterterrorism official Richard Clarke, "There were failures in the organizations . . . failures to get information to the right place at the right time."[7] It was these multiple failures to share information and connect the dots that led to the significant recommendations of the 9/11 Commission to implement changes to the US intelligence and law enforcement agencies' methods and operations.

The FBI knew that potential terrorists were taking flight lessons in the United States but not paying attention to or even asking about take-offs and landings, focusing strictly on how to control large aircraft in flight. The CIA Counterterrorism Center knew that known terrorist Nawaf Hazmi was in the United States and had just attended a meeting of al-Qaeda terrorists in Kuala Lumpur, yet it was prohibited from sharing the information with the FBI. The CIA's daily intelligence brief to President George W. Bush on August 6, 2001, clearly stated that the FBI had information indicating "patterns of suspicious activity in this country consistent with preparations for hijackings or other types of attacks."[8] Just a few days later a Minnesota flight school alerted the FBI that Zacarias Moussaoui was asking very suspicious questions. When the FBI determined that Moussaoui was a radical who had traveled to Pakistan, and that the Immigration and Naturalization Service had arrested him for overstaying his French visa, their request for a warrant to search his laptop was denied by FBI headquarters due to what the administrators believed to be a lack of probable cause.

The signs of a major, well-planned attack were everywhere and in the hands of those agencies tasked with interdicting and investigating terrorism, in the years and days leading up to the 9/11 attacks. Yet it was a fundamental failure of imagination and self-imposed restrictions on intelligence sharing that precluded these agencies and their active agents from taking any preemptive action. More so, as is noted in the post-9/11 treatment by the FBI of Agent Coleen Rowley following her May 21, 2002, memo to then FBI director Robert Mueller concerning his misleading congressional testimony, the deeply inbred and ensconced trend within the FBI (and other intelligence agencies) to act out of self-protection and to preclude public embarrassment works against the very recommendations of the 9/11 Commission and efforts to interdict and prevent more recent terrorist acts against the United States.

Recommendations to Improve Intelligence Operations and Sharing

According to the 9/11 Commission Report,

> History has shown that even the most vigilant and expert agencies cannot always prevent determined, suicidal attackers from reaching a target. . . . But the American people are entitled to expect their government to do its very best. They should expect that officials will have realistic objectives, clear guidance, and effective organization. They are entitled to see some standards for performance so they can judge . . . whether the objectives are being met.[9]

One of the primary recommendations of the 9/11 Commission Report dealt directly with intelligence related to national security.

> Targeting travel is at least as powerful a weapon against terrorists as targeting their money. The United States should combine terrorist travel intelligence, operations, and law enforcement in a strategy to intercept terrorists, find terrorist travel facilitators, and constrain terrorist mobility. . . .
> The small terrorist travel intelligence collection and analysis program currently in place has produced disproportionately useful results. It should be expanded. Since officials at the borders encounter travelers and their documents first and investigate travel facilitators, they must work closely with intelligence officials.[10]

It is vital that constraining terrorist travel becomes a primary part of an overall counterterrorism strategy for this country. The 9/11 Commission

Report authors believe, absolutely correctly, that "better technology and training to detect terrorist travel documents are the most important immediate steps to reduce America's vulnerability to clandestine entry. Every stage of our border and immigration system should have as a part of its operations the detection of terrorist indicators on travel documents."[11] This is critical. Each agency that deals with or investigates possible terrorist activity should have online linkages with the intelligence community. Currently, documents considered fraudulent are simply returned to the travelers, who are denied entry without further investigation. This should and must change, immediately. If and when possibly fraudulent documents are found, by any agency, alerts should go "red" to all pertinent agencies, and an investigation into that traveler should commence. A particular agency should have primary jurisdiction and be responsible for pursuing and concluding the investigation, and issuing a report on completion. These should be reviewed periodically and scanned for possible patterns. DHS's Office of Information and Analysis should be allocated more resources to complete its mission as the primary bridge between immigration and border protection and other government antiterrorism organizations, including the intelligence community.

The report correctly noted that the national security infrastructure was "constructed to win the Cold War." The United States is confronted by a completely different enemy today. What won the Cold War cannot win our current one. The Commission argues for a system that is "quick, imaginative, and agile," and offers five specific recommendations to do this:

- Unifying strategic intelligence and operational planning against Islamic terrorists across the foreign-domestic divide with a National Counterterrorism Center;
- Unifying the intelligence community with a new national intelligence director;
- Unifying the many participants in the counterterrorism effort and their knowledge in a network-based information-sharing system that transcends traditional governmental boundaries;
- Unifying and strengthening congressional oversight to improve quality and accountability; and
- Strengthening the FBI and homeland defenders.[12]

One of the biggest problems with the investigation and information gathering surrounding the prelude to the 9/11 attacks was that no one agency was in charge of managing the case. No one person or agency was responsible for acquiring specific information from anywhere in the government, or for assigning responsibilities regarding collection of intelligence, tracking progress, and/or bringing possible obstacles up to the level of alerts to policymakers where they might be resolved. In the words of the Commission, "Responsibility and accountability were diffuse."[13] Since the 2001 attacks, the problem has not been resolved. Some of the symptoms have been fixed, more or less, but the basic problem remains, although modified. Prior to September 11, 2001, the CIA was the primary agency responsible for combatting al-Qaeda, with the FBI in a clearly supporting role. Today, the CIA is still primary, but the number of supporting agencies has multiplied. Three of the unified Defense Department commands have counterterrorism as a primary mission: Central Command, Special Operations Command, and Northern Command. The Department of Homeland Security has as its primary mission the security of our national borders, along with the analysis of domestic vulnerabilities. The National Security Council is now enjoined by a new presidential advisory group, the Homeland Security Council.

The Terrorist Threat Integration Center, created in May 2003 by executive order of President Bush, housed at the CIA, has the primary responsibility for analysis of terrorism. However, the CIA also houses another terrorism center, the Counterterrorism Center, which played a major role prior to the 9/11 attacks. Another major counterterrorism intelligence unit is in the Defense Intelligence Agency. Another is the Department of Homeland Security, and the FBI has its own Terrorist Screening Center. This is a major duplication of effort, requires many skilled analysts, and places strategic demands on single-source national intelligence assets such as the NSA. Figuratively, according to the Commission, the United States had too many cooks operating in too many different kitchens trying to cook the same turkey. And, possibly worse, all the cooks were reporting to the president, asking him to coordinate their efforts toward producing a really good meal.

What was needed, as the Commission noted, was an integration of all sources of intelligence focused on the same problem, in order to see the enemy as a whole, and to coordinate efforts to effectively and efficiently combat it. The Commission correctly argued that the Terrorist Threat Integration Center, while given the primary responsibility for fighting terrorism, had no oversight or operational authority and was not part of any other operational entity, aside from reporting to the director of central intelligence. This was an obvious problem, and the Commission recommended the creation of a National Counterterrorism Center (NCTC), modeled on the preexisting Terrorist Threat Integration Center. The Commission argued for a Counterterrorism Center that would house experts in joint operational planning and joint intelligence, staffed by personnel from various agencies, working together on the singular problem. The NCTC was created in August 2004 by Executive Order 13354, incorporating the Terrorist Threat Integration Center, which became the foundation of NCTC's authorities in the Intelligence Reform and Terrorism Prevention Act (IRTPA) of 2004. Through both the executive order of President Bush and the subsequent IRTPA, the NCTC became the nation's center for information sharing and strategic operational planning in support to the president. The primary idea was that the NCTC would assign operational responsibilities to lead agencies and then track implementation by various agencies in support of its primary mission—one quarterback, leading a competent team. Or, to stay with the prior analogy, a head chef, assigning secondary duties to line and prep cooks in planning and coordinating the meal.

During and after the Cold War, the intelligence community was not a seamless integrated effort, as it is not today. Each agency concentrated on what it did best, collecting its own information, and then supplying it to policymakers via detailed reports. The CIA, for example, focused on human intelligence collection (HUMINT), all-source collection of information, and advanced science and technology. The NSA concentrated on signal collection and analysis, which it does and has done very well for decades, and the National Geospatial-Intelligence Agency collected imagery information and performed analysis. The National Reconnaissance Office utilized space platforms for intelligence collection, and so on. During the Cold War, after it, and prior to the 9/11 attacks, each agency did what it does, focusing on their own areas of expertise, as they primarily do today.

Overall, the 9/11 Commission attributed the blame for the absence of a warning prior to the September 2001 attacks to an inability of all-source analysts to connect the dots, or assemble pertinent timely information from multiple sources and agencies in a manner sufficient to warn policymakers of a realistic present danger. The biggest cause of this, according to the Commission, was a human or systemic resistance to the sharing of pertinent information. Humans, in general, conceive of information as power, or as directly related to power, and intelligence agencies even more so. Agencies collect all the information they can, for several reasons. One, the more information they have, the more likely some of it will be important, either immediately or in the near future; two, what they have might not be readily apparent as important to them, but they are aware that it certainly could be important to another agency, at some point, and, therefore, possibly used as a bargaining chip; and, three, the more you have, the more you can justify obtaining money to store it. For thirty years or more intelligence agencies have collected much more than could be analyzed in a timely fashion. This was part of the problem prior to 9/11. The US government has access to a vast amount of information. When databases not usually thought of as intelligence, such as customs or immigration information, are included, the storehouse is immense. But the government has a weak system for processing and using what it has. In the 9/11 story, for example, sometimes information that could be accessed—like the undistributed NSA information that would have helped identify Nawaf al Hazmi in January 2000—has meaning. But someone had to ask for it. In that case, no one did. Or, as in the episodes described in Chapter 8, the information is distributed but in a compartmentalized channel. Or the information is available, and someone does ask, but it cannot be shared. What all these stories have in common is a system that requires a demonstrated "need to know" before sharing. This approach assumes it is possible to know, in advance, who will need to use the information. Such a system implicitly assumes that the risk of inadvertent disclosure outweighs the benefits of wider sharing. Those Cold War assumptions are no longer appropriate. The culture in which agencies feel they own the information they gathered at taxpayer expense must be replaced by a culture in which the agencies instead feel they have a duty to share the information—to repay the taxpayers' investment by making that information available.[14]

The lack of data sharing was one of the existing problems prior to the 9/11 attacks. Another major problem was the inability or unwillingness of policymakers to simply listen to their experts, regarding the extant danger of a new threat.

> White House leadership is also needed because the policy and legal issues are harder than the technical ones. The necessary technology already exists. What does not are the rules for acquiring, accessing, sharing, and using the vast stores of public and private data that may be available. When information sharing works, it is a powerful tool. Therefore, the sharing and uses of information must be guided by a set of practical policy guidelines that simultaneously empower and constrain officials, telling them clearly what is and is not permitted.[15]

Erik Dahl argues that the two most commonly accepted reasons for intelligence failures in general, and the 9/11 attack in particular, include the "signals to noise" ratio, along with the "failure to connect the dots," familiar to anyone who has scanned the 9/11 Commission Report or listened to a CNN report about the terrorist attacks that day.[16] The basis of the former is that extraneous noise prevents realization that meaningful signals exist, and the latter simply that analysts were not cognizant enough to discern pertinent and available warnings present prior to an attack. In other words, a "strategic warning" was available but not recognized because it did not note a specific date, place, and time. Dahl contends that this view is incorrect, however, and that the information relating to a prospective attack is general and nonspecific, allowing policymakers to possibly see smoke but no fire and preventing any conceivable action to prevent the attack.

Dahl proposes that, in order to achieve success, two critical factors must be available: intelligence must have access to clear, precise warnings about the possible threat (essentially a tactical-level warning, as opposed to a more general strategic-level alert), and also policymakers must be receptive to the idea. Without both, according to Dahl, a timely warning cannot be practically made—and accepted and acted upon— and the attack cannot be prevented.[17] This analysis, although interesting, has a major drawback in that it simplifies many of the warnings and findings of the 9/11 Commission, particularly involving tactical versus strategic intelligence alerts; for example, after the 1993 Twin Towers bombing, law enforcement, including the FBI, made short and effective work of the investigation, leading the public and administration to believe that existing federal agencies could handle any new or possible threat from al-Qaeda. In addition, the organizational structure of the FBI was centered around an "office of origin" system, which designated one field office to lead an entire investigation. The point is that, regardless of whether strategic or tactical information was available, the way the Justice Department views "evidence" (as necessary for a legal conviction in a court of law) along with the historical structure of the FBI and its jurisdiction effectively prevented a single person or agency from tracking possible known terrorists prior to the attack.

Reorganization of Agencies and Creation of the Department of Homeland Security

In response to the terrorist attacks on September 11, 2001, the George W. Bush administration concluded there was a need to increase communication between intelligence, security, and preparedness agencies. In order to achieve this goal, federal policing agencies underwent a massive reorganization and realignment into a single agency, the Department of Homeland Security.

On November 19, 2002, Congress passed the Homeland Security Act of 2002, creating a new cabinet-level agency. The DHS activated in early 2003 with a focus on preventing future terrorist attacks within the United States, reducing the country's vulnerability to terrorism, and minimizing damage that might occur as a result of a terrorist attack. Rather than creating a new agency from scratch, DHS combined several existing federal agencies into a "superagency."

Among the agencies gathered into the DHS are the US Secret Service, the Immigration and Naturalization Service, US Customs, the Federal Emergency Management Agency, the Transportation Security Administration, and the US Coast Guard. Agencies that were *not* included under the umbrella of DHS include the Federal Bureau of Investigation, the Department of Defense, and the Central Intelligence Agency.

The DHS continued to develop and reorganize over time. In 2005, DHS Secretary Chertoff announced a six-point agenda to focus on the best ways to address potential threats to the United States.

1. Increase overall preparedness, particularly for catastrophic events
2. Create better transportation security systems to move people and cargo more securely and efficiently
3. Strengthen border security and interior enforcement, and reform immigration processes
4. Enhance information sharing with our partners
5. Improve DHS financial management, human resource development, procurement and information technology
6. Realign the DHS organization to maximize mission performance.[18]

Initiatives undertaken by DHS to meet this agenda include the "If You See Something, Say Something" campaign, emphasizing the importance of reporting suspicious activity; continued deployment of personnel and resources to border states, including Predator unmanned aerial system (UAS) coverage along the entire Southwest border; the "Blue Campaign" to combat human trafficking; the "Stop. Think. Connect." national public cybersecurity awareness campaign; and finally, efforts in response to the BP oil spill, the earthquake in Haiti, and other natural disasters nationwide.

There were significant battles between Congress and the White House on what should and shouldn't be incorporated into the new agency. However, those extensive discussions were ultimately resolved with the reorganization in 2005, and it has undergone several subsequent modifications to adapt to lessons learned through years of operations.

DHS Structural Components

The Department of Homeland Security's six-point agenda included restructuring some aspects.[19]

> Supporting the agenda, the department proposed to realign the Department of Homeland Security to increase its ability to prepare [for], prevent, and respond to terrorist attacks and other emergencies. These changes are to better integrate the Department and give department employees better tools to accomplish their mission. This was organized around four general concepts.

Centralize and Improve Policy Development and Coordination.

A new Office of Policy was created to:

- be the primary Department-wide coordinator for policies, regulations, and other initiatives
- ensure consistency of policy and regulatory development across the department
- perform long-range strategic policy planning
- assume the policy coordination functions previously performed by the Border and Transportation Security (BTS) Directorate
- include Office of International Affairs, Office of Private Sector Liaison, Homeland Security Advisory Council, Office of Immigration Statistics, and the Senior Asylum Officer.

Strengthen Intelligence Functions and Information Sharing.

A new Office of Intelligence and Analysis was developed [to] ensure that information is:

- gathered from all relevant field operations and other parts of the intelligence community
- analyzed with a mission-oriented focus
- informative to senior decision-makers
- disseminated to the appropriate federal, state, local, and private sector partners
- led by a Chief Intelligence Officer reporting directly to the Secretary, this office will be comprised of analysts within the former Information Analysis directorate and draw on expertise of other department components with intelligence collection and analysis operations.

Improve Coordination and Efficiency of Operations.

A new Director of Operations Coordination was created to:

- conduct joint operations across all organizational elements
- coordinate incident management activities
- use all resources within the Department to translate intelligence and policy into immediate action
- The Homeland Security Operations Center, which serves as the nation's nerve center for information sharing and domestic incident management on a 24/7/365 basis, will be a critical part of this new office.

Enhance Coordination and Deployment of Preparedness Assets.

The Directorate for Preparedness was created to:

- consolidate preparedness assets from across the Department
- facilitate grants and oversee nationwide preparedness efforts supporting first responder training, citizen awareness, public health, infrastructure and cyber security and ensure proper steps are taken to protect high-risk targets
- focus on cyber security and telecommunications
- include a new Chief Medical Officer, responsible for carrying out the Department's responsibilities to coordinate the response to biological attacks
- Managed by an Under Secretary this Directorate will include infrastructure protection, assets of the Office of State and Local Government Coordination and Preparedness responsible for grants, training and exercises, the U.S. Fire Administration, and the Office of National Capitol Region Coordination.

Other Department Realignments.

- Improve National Response and Recovery Efforts by Focusing FEMA on Its Core Functions. FEMA reports directly to the Secretary of Homeland Security. In order to strengthen and enhance our Nation's ability to respond to and recover from manmade or natural disasters, FEMA will focus on its historic and vital mission of response and recovery.
- Integrate Federal Air Marshal Service (FAMS) into Broader Aviation Security Efforts. The Federal Air Marshal Service was moved from the Immigration and Customs Enforcement (ICE) bureau to the Transportation Security Administration to increase operational coordination and strengthen efforts to meet this common goal of aviation security.
- Merge Legislative and Intergovernmental Affairs. This new Office of Legislative and Intergovernmental Affairs merged certain functions among the Office of Legislative Affairs and the Office of State

and Local Government Coordination in order to streamline inter-governmental relations efforts and better share homeland security information with members of Congress as well as state and local officials.

- Assign Office of Security to Management Directorate. The Office of Security was moved to return oversight of that office to the Under Secretary for Management in order to better manage information systems, contractual activities, security accreditation, training and resources.

Timeline

The Homeland Security Act of 2002 (HSA) provides certain flexibility for the Secretary of Homeland Security to establish, consolidate, alter or discontinue organizational units within the Department. The mechanism for implementing these changes is a notification to Congress, required under section 872 of the HSA, allowing for the changes to take effect after 60 days.

Other proposed changes will require Congressional action. The Department will work with Congress to accomplish these shared goals.

Background

The agenda is based on conclusions drawn as a result of the Second Stage Review. The review, initiated by the Secretary, examined nearly every element of the Department of Homeland Security in order to recommend ways that DHS could better

- manage risk in terms of threat, vulnerability and consequence
- prioritize policies and operational missions according to this risk-based approach
- establish a series of preventive and protective steps that would increase security at multiple levels.

Eighteen action teams composed of 10–12 subject matter experts and hundreds of public and private partners at the federal, state, local, tribal and international levels examined a wide range of issues, including:

- Risk/Readiness
- Information and Intelligence Sharing
- Performance Metrics
- Law Enforcement Activities
- Listening to External Partners
- Supply Chain Security
- Internal Communications and DHS Culture
- Research, Technology & Detection

All of these elements led to the Department of Homeland Security that exists today.

DHS Components

The following information is taken from the DHS website and consolidated for easy consumption by the reader. The full list can be found at dhs.gov/operational-and-support-components.

The Directorate for National Protection and Programs works to advance the department's risk-reduction mission. This mission addresses both physical and virtual threats and their associated human elements.

"The Science and Technology Directorate is the primary research and development arm of the Department. It provides federal, state and local officials with the technology and capabilities to protect the homeland."

"The Management Directorate is responsible for budget, appropriations, expenditure of funds, accounting and finance; procurement; human resources" and other management functions."

The Office of Policy is the primary policy formulation and coordination component for the DHS.

The Office of Health Affairs coordinates all medical activities of the Department of Homeland Security to ensure appropriate preparation for and response to incidents having medical significance.

The Office of Intelligence and Analysis is responsible for using information and intelligence from multiple sources to identify and assess current and future threats to the United States.

The Office of Operations Coordination is responsible for monitoring the security of the United States on a daily basis and coordinating activities within the department and with governors, homeland security advisers, law enforcement partners, and critical infrastructure operators in all fifty states and more than fifty major urban areas nationwide.

"The Federal Law Enforcement Training Centers provides career-long training to law enforcement professionals."

The Domestic Nuclear Detection Office works to enhance the nuclear detection efforts of federal, state, territorial, tribal, and local governments, and the private sector and to ensure a coordinated response to such threats.

"The Transportation Security Administration (TSA) protects the nation's transportation systems to ensure freedom of movement for people and commerce."

"United States Customs and Border Protection (CBP) is one of the Department of Homeland Security's largest and most complex components, with a priority mission of keeping terrorists and their weapons out of the U.S. It also has a responsibility for securing and facilitating trade and travel while enforcing hundreds of U.S. regulations, including immigration and drug laws."

Citizenship and Immigration Services secures America's promise as a nation of immigrants by providing accurate and useful information to customers, granting immigration and citizenship benefits, promoting an awareness and understanding of citizenship, and ensuring the integrity of our immigration system.

"United States Immigration and Customs Enforcement (ICE) promotes homeland security and public safety through the criminal and civil enforcement of federal laws governing border control, customs, trade, and immigration."

"The United States Coast Guard is one of the five armed forces of the United States and the only military organization within the Department of Homeland Security. The Coast Guard protects the maritime economy and the environment, defends our maritime borders, and saves those in peril."

"The Federal Emergency Management Agency (FEMA) supports our citizens and first responders to ensure that as a nation we work together to build, sustain, and improve our capability to prepare for, protect against, respond to, recover from, and mitigate all hazards."

"The United States Secret Service (USSS) safeguards the nation's financial infrastructure and payment systems to preserve the integrity of the economy, and protects national leaders, visiting heads of state and government, designated sites, and National Special Security Events."

Office of the Director of National Intelligence

The 9/11 Commission reported that there existed a need for restructuring the intelligence community both prior to and after the 9/11 attacks, due to the following:

- *Structural barriers to performing joint intelligence work.* National intelligence is still organized around the collection disciplines of the home agencies, not the joint mission. . . . No one component holds all the relevant information. . . .
- *Lack of common standards and practices across the foreign-domestic divide.* The leadership of the intelligence community should be able

to pool information gathered overseas with information gathered in the United States. . . .

- *Divided management of national intelligence capabilities.* . . . Following the end of the Cold War [the CIA] has been less able to influence the use of the nation's imagery and signals intelligence capabilities in three national agencies housed within the Department of Defense: the National Security Agency, the National Geospatial-Intelligence Agency, and the National Reconnaissance Office. . . .
- *Weak capacity to set priorities and move resources.* The agencies are mainly organized around what they collect or the way they collect it. But the priorities for collection are national. As the DCI [Director of Central Intelligence] makes hard choices about moving resources, he or she must have the power to reach across agencies and reallocate effort.
- *Too many jobs.* The DCI now has at least three jobs. He is expected to run a particular agency, the CIA. He is expected to manage the loose confederation of agencies that is the intelligence community. He is expected to be the analyst in chief for the government, sifting evidence and directly briefing the President as his principal intelligence adviser. No recent DCI has been able to do all three effectively. . . .
- *Too complex and secret.* Over the decades, the agencies and the rules surrounding the intelligence community have accumulated to a depth that practically defies public comprehension. . . . Even the most basic information about how much money is actually allocated to or within the intelligence community and most of its key components is shrouded from public view.[20]

Based primarily on the above, the 9/11 Commission recommended the following: "The current position of Director of Central Intelligence should be replaced by a National Intelligence Director with two main areas of responsibility: (1) to oversee national intelligence centers on specific subjects of interest across the U.S. government and (2) to manage the national intelligence program and oversee the agencies that contribute to it."[21] The DCI was replaced by the creation of the Office of the Director of National Intelligence, authorized by the 2004 Intelligence Reform and Terrorism Prevention Act (IRTPA). (Note: the IRTPA will be covered in detail in a subsequent chapter.)

The Tsarnaev Brothers and Other Post-9/11 Terrorists

Dzhokhar and Tamerlan Tsarnaev are classic examples of post-9/11 terrorism in the United States, and the failure of intelligence agencies to investigate and act to interdict them in their planning is a key case study in the problems of homeland security intelligence.

Ethnic Chechens and Muslims by upbringing, Dzhokhar and his parents, Anzor and Zubeidat, immigrated to the United States in 2002 where they applied for political asylum and settled near Boston, Massachusetts. Dzhokhar's older brother Tamerlan and two sisters followed their parents and brother and immigrated in 2003. On April 15, 2013, Dzhokhar and Tamerlan set off two homemade bombs near the finish line of the Boston Marathon. Four days later Tamerlan was killed in a shootout with police and his younger brother taken into custody later that same day.

Dzhokhar was tried and convicted in federal court on thirty counts, including seventeen counts that were eligible for the death penalty. Following his conviction, he was sentenced to death in May 2014 by that federal jury for his role in the Boston Marathon bombing. Although only the third person in US history to be sentenced to death under federal charges for acts related to terrorism, his death penalty was overturned by a federal appeals court in July 2020. He remains in prison awaiting a new sentencing trial.

From the perspective of intelligence, the FBI was informed in 2011 by the Russian Federal Security Service (FSB) that older brother Tamerlan was a follower of radical Islam. His YouTube channel linked him to Salafis and Islamic videos, but the FBI, who interviewed Tamerlan and his family and conducted extensive database searches, found no evidence of any terrorism activity, domestic or foreign. Tamerlan made a trip to Dagestan in 2012 where he frequently attended a mosque known for its radical Islam and anti-American teachings. The FSB reported this to the FBI. The FSB also provided to the FBI transcripts of recorded conversations between Tamerlan and his mother in March 2011 that indicated the two discussed jihad (a struggle against the enemies of Islam) as evidence of possible extremism within the family. In March and November of 2011 the FSB asked the FBI (they also asked the CIA in September 2011) to look at Tamerlan Tsarnaev carefully as a potential radical Islamic terrorist.

While the FBI correctly placed both Tamerlan and his mother, Zubeidat, on a terrorism watch list about eighteen months before the Boston Marathon bombings, they later dropped both of them from the list and ceased observation, after a very short investigation. This was either poor and incomplete investigation and decisionmaking or complete incompetence, or both, at multiple levels.

There is strong evidence that Tamerlan was either involved in or the perpetrator of a triple homicide in Waltham, Massachusetts, on the evening of September 11, 2011, the tenth anniversary of the 9/11 attacks. All three victims had their throats slit from ear to ear with such force as to nearly decapitate them. At the time this was a classic example of al-Qaeda and ISIS executions across the Middle East and Central Asia.

In a 2009 story, "Domestic Terrorism in the Post-9/11 Era," the FBI states,

> We're not shy about applying our full suite of anti-terror tools and capabilities to threats of homegrown terrorism. That includes our time-tested investigative techniques such as the use of surveillance and informants as well as the new intelligence skills and information-sharing channels we've cultivated since 9/11. . . .
>
> • Our 103 Joint Terrorism Task Forces around the nation bring together our law enforcement and intelligence partners into a single team dedicated to addressing terror threats of all kinds.
> • Beyond these task forces, we talk constantly with our local, state, and federal [partners]—those who have a finger on the pulse of their communities and can tell us about the individuals or groups on their radar.[22]

There are no publicly available records that show the FBI or CIA ever informed local or state law enforcement that the Tsarnaev brothers were under investigation or that foreign intelligence had reported the family members as potential terrorists. As of this writing the FBI has not responded to multiple requests for comments on this subject.

Conclusion

Between September 11, 2001, and September 11, 2015, there have been an additional thirty-one attempted terrorist attacks on targets in the United States or by people in the United States planning attacks outside of the country that have been thwarted by law enforcement. Twenty-three of these were planned by lone wolves or a group consisting of two persons.

Utilizing our characterization of what constitutes a terrorist attack, there have been more than 200 people killed, including many of the perpetrators, between September 11, 2001, and February 16, 2018. The types of attack range from cyber to bombings, from shootings to knifings, and the use of hatchets to shoe bombs. The targets of the attacks ranged from school children to city police to military personnel to elected congressional representatives.

The motivations ranged from political to religious. The attacks were directed at abortion clinics and providers, police, federal government including military venues and personnel, schools, gays, general workplace targets, and university students. Perpetrators were from the extreme right wing and extreme left wing of major political parties, from anti-Semitic groups, anti-Islamic groups, White supremacist groups, and just general members of the population who targeted others for no known reasons. The single overriding commonality among all of the attacks is that with very few exceptions, all were planned and carried out by lone wolves or cells consisting of three or fewer persons. As the number of persons involved increased, the potential for identification and interdiction by law enforcement increased.

The problem of terrorism in the United States in the post-9/11 world, as well as the problem for those involved in gathering, evaluating, and prosecuting available intelligence was succinctly stated by Police Chief Jerry Garner of Greeley, Colorado, during a lecture to college students in a course on Current Trends in Terrorism and Counter Terrorism. Chief Garner said, "Once a suicide bomber has left his home, somebody is going to die." The essential underlying fact behind this statement is that it is the responsibility of local, state, and national law enforcement agencies to do everything possible to gather and prosecute intelligence so as to interdict the terrorist *before* they take that final step and start heading to their target.

The US intelligence community must try to contain two extant problems: one, identify actual or potential terrorist sanctuaries, with the eventual goal of disrupting their operations, and/or eliminating them (with the assistance of all elements of national power); and, two, ascertain some way to identify, contain, or control those people who are in this country illegally. This includes both those who cross the border illegally and those who simply remain in the United States beyond the expiration of their legal stay. If this cannot be accomplished within the intelligence community alone, then it must be done in conjunction with the Department of Homeland Security and local, state, tribal, and federal law enforcement agencies. But it must be done. Homeland security must begin with border security. The biggest problem for national security is the prevention of people who are the primary threat to this country from entering or remaining within.

Such a proactive effort to prevent and interdict terrorist attacks before they result in death, injury, and destruction necessitates a major change in thought processes. The United States can no longer look at the investigation as a means to collect evidence that supports future prosecution. Instead, homeland security intelligence must view the world from a proactive mentality where the intent of intelligence gathering is to stop the behavior before it happens rather than to criminally prosecute offenders after they've carried out their attacks.

Notes

1. United States v. Yousef, No. S12 93 CR 180 (KTD) (S.D. N.Y.), October 22, 1997 (transcript), p. 4694.
2. United States v. Salameh, 152 F.3d 88, 107-108 2d Cir. 1998.
3. National Commission on Terrorist Attacks upon the United States, *9/11 Commission Report* (New York: Norton, 2004), p. xv.
4. Ibid., p. xvi.
5. Ibid.
6. John Ashcroft, Testimony Before 9/11 Commission, April 2004.
7. Richard Clarke, *Against All Enemies: Inside America's War on Terror* (New York: Free Press, 2004), p. 238.
8. Presidential Daily Briefing, August 6, 2001 (declassified), https://fas.org/irp/cia/product/pdb080601.pdf.
9. *9/11 Commission Report,* p. 365.
10. Ibid., p. 385.
11. Ibid., p. 400.
12. Ibid.
13. Ibid.
14. Ibid., pp. 416–417.
15. Ibid., p. 419.
16. Erik J. Dahl, *Intelligence and Surprise Attack: Failure and Success from Pearl Harbor to 9/11 and Beyond* (Washington, DC: Georgetown University Press, 2013), pp. 7–8.
17. Ibid.
18. Department of Homeland Security, "Department Six-Point Agenda," https://www.dhs.gov/department-six-point-agenda.
19. This section comes from ibid.
20. *9/11 Commission Report*, pp. 408–410.
21. Ibid., p. 411.
22. Federal Bureau of Investigation, "Domestic Terrorism in the Post-9/11 Era," September 7, 2009, https://archives.fbi.gov/archives/news/stories/2009/september/domterror_090709.

4

The Role of the Intelligence Community

This chapter is aimed at understanding the key functions of intelligence and the intelligence community (IC) in the context of national security. It is also important to understand how the requirements of the intelligence cycle relate to what a decisionmaker or the consumer is requesting the intelligence analyst or team of analysts to research and assess and form judgments and recommendations about. These requirements may fall under any of the collection methods (OSINT, HUMINT, SIGINT, IMINT, MASINT). Also, the requirements put forth should be an adjunct to policymaking, not policymaking itself. Ideally, the decisionmaker will provide the analyst with a clear set of requirements when they request information so as to make the cycle flow easier. However, this is not always the case. Often requirements are too broad or not broad enough and it causes the analyst to make decisions on their own as to how to fill in the gaps in the requirements. It is always possible to search for the wrong information.

The United States has massive, overlapping homeland security and intelligence enterprises. Homeland security intelligence is at the nexus of both of these two and impacts most of the agencies in both structures. The organization and functions of both enterprises are examined. The chapter begins by looking at the various definitions of homeland security and examining the US strategy for achieving a secure homeland. Then it shifts to look at the specific homeland security missions as well as programs and responsibilities of homeland security actors at the federal, state, local, private, nongovernmental, and public levels.

Intelligence

Intelligence is timely, relevant, and (relatively and hopefully) not generic information. Specifically, it is information about an adversary that is useful in dealing with them. This was the sense of General George Washington's observation to one of his officers in July 1777: "The necessity of procuring good intelligence is apparent and need not be further urged."[1]

To call information *intelligence* implies the (possible) existence of an adversary. Usually, the adversary is the enemy. But war, as Carl von Clausewitz pointed out, is simply the continuation of politics by other means.[2] Conversely, diplomacy is a kind of nonviolent warfare; it may be unfashionable to say so, but in diplomacy all nations are adversaries, if only in the sense that no two of them share a total commonality of interest. Thus, the information one nation must have in its dealing with another is intelligence.

Much of what one nation would know about another is readily available in the latter's books, newspapers, government publications, and electronic media. But other information is closely held, less readily available, and only obtained through subtle and usually secret methods, such as espionage and code breaking.

Secret intelligence is as old as warfare and diplomacy. It has been said, with some reason, that it is the missing dimension of history. Both foreign policy in peacetime and command decisions in wartime are driven by intelligence, much of which has necessarily been obtained by secret means. Obviously, such sources and methods must be protected by a cloak of secrecy if they are to continue to supply needed intelligence. But even after the intelligence has long since ceased to be of anything but historical interest, governments tend to hold secret the means used to acquire it, as well as the information itself.

During the Revolutionary War, when Dr. Benjamin Franklin was our ambassador to the French court, his most trusted secretary was an agent of the British Secret Service, a penetration that allowed King George III to know all that passed between the Continental Congress and Versailles soon after the fact. The man's treachery went unsuspected until, a full century later, the British government made public some of its archives.

General Thomas Gage, a British governor of colonial Massachusetts, ran a network of agents that spied on the preparations of the patriots in Boston and the surrounding countryside before the battles of Lexington and Concord. Their existence was confirmed only when Gage's personal papers became public knowledge in the 1930s, and the identities of most of them are still unknown.

US intelligence has two broad functions—collection and analysis—and one relatively narrow one—covert action. One key role whose importance many people underestimate is the dissemination of intelligence to the right consumer at the right time, enabling judgments and intelligence estimates that contribute to the formulation of national security policy. An additional function—counterintelligence—is integral to the entire intelligence process. While the need for collection and analysis is generally understood and accepted, there is less acceptance of covert action as an appropriate intelligence function and less understanding and acceptance of the critical importance of counterintelligence.

The intelligence cycle is defined as the steps by which information is converted into intelligence and made available to specified consumers. According to "How Intelligence Works" on the IC career website,[3] there are five steps in the cycle: (1) planning—determination of intelligence requirements, preparation of a collection plan, issuance of orders and requests to information collection agencies, and a continuous check on the productivity of collection agencies; (2) collection—acquisition of information and the provision of this information to processing and/or production elements; (3) processing—conversion of collected information into a form suitable to the production of intelligence; (4) analysis—conversion of information into intelligence through the integration, analysis, evaluation, and interpretation of all source data and the preparation of intelligence products in support of known or anticipated user requirements; and (5) dissemination—conveyance of intelligence to users in a suitable form. Some IC agencies also use a sixth component: feedback. However, from the perspective of DHS, and the associated law enforcement agencies that provide intelligence to DHS, feedback is a function of after action reports—an item that is often neglected or ignored as law enforcement is rarely offered the time to conduct introspective analysis of their actions before being pushed into the next event.

Failure in any part of the intelligence cycle can lead to policy misdirection and collapse. Intelligence failure (a highly subjective term, both in definition and application) in the context of national security reflects the outcome of any inadequacies within the intelligence cycle, to include the failure to complete any of the steps within the cycle.

The US intelligence community is a cooperative federation of sixteen (seventeen, counting the Office of the Director of National Intelligence) individual US government agencies that work independently and together to perform intelligence activities considered necessary for the conduct of foreign relations and national security of the United States. Member organizations of the IC include intelligence agencies, military intelligence, and civilian intelligence and analysis offices within federal executive departments. The IC is led by the director of national intelligence, who reports to the president of the United States.

Among their varied responsibilities, the members of the community collect and produce foreign and domestic intelligence, contribute to military planning, and perform espionage, covert operations, and counterintelligence operations. The authorization of the IC, particularly the NSA, was increased significantly by Executive Order 12333, signed on December 4, 1981, by President Ronald Reagan. Specifically, section 1:12(b) authorizes the NSA to provide "such administrative and technical support activities . . . as are necessary to perform the functions described in sections (1) through (12) above, including procurement." This was taken as authorization for the NSA to conduct surveillance of US and foreign citizens, to include phone metadata.

Leadership

As commander in chief, the president leads the national security policy process by setting the agenda, coordinating the transformation of broad policy into concrete programs, and directing program implementation. At the White House, homeland security policy (as an integral part of the national security policy) is developed by an interagency organization—the National Security Council (NSC). The NSC consists of various levels of interagency officials who represent some of the agencies within the US government. At the top, the NSC is chaired by the president and includes a senior team. At minimum, that includes the vice president, secretary of state, secretary of defense, secretary of the treasury, and national security adviser. They are advised by the Joint Chiefs of Staff and the director of national intelligence. Each administration can add more seniors (and departments) to the table—such as the director of the Department of Homeland Security, the attorney general, the director of the FBI, and the director of the CIA.

Individual federal agencies are directed to carry out the various programs within the overall homeland security mission, but the secretary of DHS leads the federal agency responsible by statute for homeland security—preventing terrorism and managing risks to critical infrastructure, securing and managing the border, enforcing and administering immigration laws, safeguarding and securing cyberspace, and ensuring resilience to disasters. Governors of the states, mayors, and other elected officials lead homeland security efforts at the state and local levels. Private-sector companies have to take similar measures in developing their own internal security procedures.

Goal-Oriented Mission Structure

The federal government uses two taxonomies, or groups, to characterize homeland security missions. In the Quadrennial Homeland Security Review, the government talks about missions in terms of reaching specific goals. For instance, efforts to reach the goal of "preventing illegal immigration" are part of the mission to "enforce and administer our immigration laws." This approach is useful in terms of differentiating between newer goals, such as preventing terrorism and cyberattacks, and the more traditional ones, such as border protection. There are five major homeland security missions in this first taxonomy:

1. Mission 1: Preventing Terrorism and Enhancing Security
   Goal 1.1: Prevent terrorist attacks
   Goal 1.2: Prevent the unauthorized acquisition or use of chemical, biological, or radiological and nuclear materials and capabilities
   Goal 1.3: Manage risks to critical infrastructure, key leadership, and events
2. Mission 2: Securing and Managing Our Borders
   Goal 2.1: Effectively control US air, land, and sea borders
   Goal 2.2: Safeguard lawful trade and travel
   Goal 2.3: Disrupt and dismantle transnational criminal organizations
3. Mission 3: Enforcing and Administering Our Immigration Laws
   Goal 3.1: Strengthen and effectively administer the immigration system
   Goal 3.2: Prevent unlawful immigration
4. Mission 4: Safeguarding and Securing Cyberspace
   Goal 4.1: Create a safe, secure, and resilient cyber environment
   Goal 4.2: Promote cybersecurity knowledge and innovation
5. Mission 5: Ensuring Resilience to Disasters
   Goal 5.1: Mitigate hazards

Goal 5.2: Enhance preparedness
Goal 5.3: Ensure effective emergency response
Goal 5.4: Rapidly recover

Missions 1 and 4 (counterterrorism and cybersecurity) are designed to counter the newer threats, while missions 2 (border security), 3 (immigration control), and 5 (improved emergency response) are devoted to carrying out traditional government functions.

Functional Mission Structure

Presidential Policy Directive (PPD) 8: National Preparedness uses an alternative taxonomy to group the missions according to *function*, which is being used today as the official homeland security management paradigm: prevent, protect, mitigate, respond, and recover. PPD 8 assigns responsibility to the secretary of DHS to coordinate development of our national preparedness framework, which consists of five subframeworks that correspond to the missions:

1. Preventing, avoiding, or stopping a threatened or actual act of terrorism;
2. Protecting our citizens, residents, visitors, and assets against the greatest threats and hazards in a manner that allows our interests, aspirations, and way of life to thrive;
3. Mitigating the loss of life and property by lessening the impact of future disasters;
4. Responding quickly to save lives, protect property and the environment, and meet basic human needs in the aftermath of a catastrophic incident;
5. Recovering through a focus on the timely restoration, strengthening, and revitalization of infrastructure, housing, and a sustainable economy, as well as the health, social, cultural, historic, and environmental fabric of communities affected by a catastrophic incident.

The president, the NSC, and the assistant to the president for homeland security and counterterrorism formulate national-level policy and then assign a federal agency (DHS, for all domestic actions) to pull together the disparate agencies that will implement that policy. The president has designated the secretary of DHS to develop the national preparedness program, but leadership in implementing policy is a distributed responsibility. State and local governments take the lead in implementing response and recovery programs within their jurisdictions. The federal government, the states, and the private sector each lead part of the effort in implementing protection programs. The federal government leads all prevention programs.

The federal government is the only US actor actively pursuing terrorism *prevention* outside the United States, primarily through our military, diplomatic, covert action, and law enforcement operations. The FBI, under the authority of the attorney general, takes the lead in preventing terrorist attacks and is supported by all federal, state, and local law enforcement in meeting this mission objective. The covert action policy is not legal within our borders, so the CIA and the State Department play a purely supportive role.

The federal government, led by DHS, coordinates and integrates the development and delivery of *protection* capabilities. Federal departments and agencies implement statutory and regulatory responsibilities for a wide array of protective programs and provide needed assistance in funding, acquisition, research, coordination, oversight, implementation, and enforcement. The federal government supports the private sector in protecting its critical infrastructure facilities, personnel, and cybernetworks with data and intelligence.

National *response* is needed when an incident occurs that exceeds or is anticipated to exceed local or state resources—or in cases where the federal government has unique capabilities or responsibilities such as responding to an attack that involves a weapon of mass destruction. The federal government response involves all necessary departments and agency capabilities and provides coordination with all response partners, especially state and local governments. The recent coronavirus pandemic is one example of an incident or situation that exceeded local and/or state resources, almost immediately.

The federal government assists state, local, and private leaders in the development of urban and rural *recovery* plans, and leverages resources to build and rehabilitate communities so that they are more disaster resistant and resilient.

Risk Management Approach to Resource Allocation

The homeland security effort is highly complex, both in terms of the number of players involved and the number and diversity of potential programs to be funded. As a nation, the United States simply cannot afford to fund every possible homeland security program. Therefore, the government adopted a risk management approach to prioritize programs for funding, defined as the "process of identifying, analyzing, assessing, and communicating risk and accepting, avoiding, transferring or controlling it to an acceptable level considering associated costs and benefits of any actions taken."[4] As such, risk management is the fundamental paradigm for making resource allocation decisions for the homeland security effort—for deciding how much to spend on the programs that prevent, protect from, mitigate, respond to, and recover from the various threats to homeland security.

Let's assume for a minute that the United States will be hit with multiple disasters in the future, regardless of how much it is willing to spend, or where money is directed. Regardless of where people live or what they do for a living, everybody faces threats from natural disasters, man-made but accidental disasters, pandemics, and terrorist attacks. There is no way to completely eliminate floods, earthquakes, hurricanes, blizzards, and other natural disasters. Accidents such as power grid outages and chemical spills will occur. And even after the global response following 9/11, the threat of terrorist attacks still remains, as proven by events at Ft. Hood, Boston, and Benghazi.

When this premise is accepted, then the real question becomes how to create a cost-benefit analysis to reduce most efficiently and effectively the likelihood of those threats that can be somewhat controlled (accidents and terrorist attacks) and to mitigate the impact of any disaster that does occur. This question—where should the money go to get the biggest bang for the buck—affects every governmental, private-sector, and public entity, as well as individuals and families.

When it comes to natural disasters and accidents, risk is defined as the product of likelihood and consequence. For terrorism disasters, analysts can postulate likelihood as a function of threat and vulnerability. If plotted on a graph, the likelihood of an event versus the consequence of that event, with the likelihood being the vertical y-axis, and the horizontal x-axis being the consequence of that event, then a visual picture of the risk involved becomes apparent. If the risk is low (lower left-hand quadrant), then the event is unlikely to happen, and even if it does, the consequence is limited. For instance, a snowstorm in Hawaii is both unlikely and of low impact. Therefore, the risk is low and the most appropriate course to follow is to simply accept the risk, not purchase any snow removal equipment, and live with the consequences. However, if the risk and possible consequences are both high (upper right-hand quadrant), then the best course of action is to act immediately to mitigate that risk to the extent possible. For example, the state of Florida is hit by hurricanes on a regular basis, so it makes sense to use wind-resistant buildings for new construction.

Homeland Security and Disaster Prevention and Mitigation

Recent hurricanes that have hit the US mainland and the response to these hurricanes allow us to examine the concepts of disaster prevention and mitigation. Clearly, the National Oceanic and Atmospheric Administration (NOAA) and the National Weather Service (NWS) do an excellent job in telling us what is coming, when it is coming, and where it is likely to strike. They can even estimate such severe conditions as storm surge, the impact of waves and winds on the coastline, the wind speed and direction, and types of damage that result from each level of increasing winds. NOAA can tell us about winter snowstorms and their potential impact on even small parts of large cities. Anybody can get weather alerts about severe thunderstorms from the NWS and even receive warnings of tornados up to fifteen minutes before they strike a location. This is all the result of specific satellite data collection systems, the use of weather balloons released around the world twice daily, the sharing of information with other countries, and multicountry access to space-, ocean-, air-, and ground-based assets. FEMA can prestage equipment and supplies in advance of significant weather events. The National Guard can be mobilized. The US military can relocate significant assets and aircraft out of the way of an oncoming storm and bring them back when conditions stabilize. Local and state agencies can predetermine evacuation areas and routes, arrange contraflow on major roadways, block low-lying roads that might flood, open shelters for evacuees, and coordinate the volunteer services that come flooding in when there is a significant event.

The weather doesn't care if you live in the United States or Canada or England. It is weather and it impacts everybody everywhere. So, the sharing of data, or intelligence related to weather, is essential if people don't want to experience the possibility of a large loss of life when significant events occur.

This is not what happens with terrorism-related events.

Terrorism and Homeland Security

Nearly every agency that has a part within the concept of homeland security has a concurrent part of the process associated with identifying, preventing, mitigating, prosecuting, and deterring terrorist activities. However, they don't prestage assets except for biological warfare response pharmaceuticals. They don't share intelligence very often or efficiently; they certainly avoid sharing intelligence with foreign countries except when absolutely necessary (or if the foreign country is a member of the Five Eyes organization); and they are the last to arrive when a terrorist disaster occurs, and the first to depart after conditions are stabilized.

Nearly every government agency, at the federal, state, and local level, is concerned with enforcing the rule of law, and gathering evidence for subsequent prosecution, when it comes to terrorism. Thus, when a guest at a hotel in Las Vegas makes multiple trips to his room carrying firearms and ammunition in cases, the first calls to 911 come after shots are fired. The response is based on stopping the ongoing shooting, then addressing the wounded and dead, and finally on collecting the evidence to try and determine motive and accomplices for potential prosecution.

This hasn't changed since the days of John Brown.

Yet the intelligence, video evidence, human observations by witnesses are all there before the event occurs. Why are such incidents not interdicted?

The FBI's Role in Homeland Security

Most law enforcement (and by extension, homeland security) is focused at the federal level in the Department of Justice (DOJ). And the dominant agency within government and the Justice Department as far as countering terrorism and, therefore, ensuring homeland security is the Federal Bureau of Investigation. Prior to the 9/11 attacks, the agency worked under specific statutory authorization, and the supervisory agent in each of the fifty-six local field offices was free to set his or her office's priorities and assign agency personnel accordingly. Priorities at local field offices prior to 9/11 were driven by traditional crimes, such as bank robberies, drugs, gangs, and white-collar crimes, and performance evaluations were measured by classical law enforcement statistics such as number of arrests, indictments, prosecutions, and convictions.

Therefore, much like local police agencies, individuals at local field offices made career choices based on local priorities, not national ones.

In addition to the above, the FBI operates under an "office of origin" system as far as investigation of suspect individuals and/or crimes. The agency designates an individual field office to be in charge of an investigation, in order to avoid duplication of effort and reduce any possible redundancy. As one example, the New York field office indicted Osama bin Laden prior to the East Africa bombings; therefore, that office was the office of origin for all subsequent cases related to him. Most of the information the FBI had on him resided there. Other FBI field offices were thus understandably reluctant to allocate much time or resources to subjects over which they had no control and for which they received no credit.

The FBI originated during the presidency of Theodore Roosevelt, in 1908, by the actions of Attorney General Charles Bonaparte. The two men actually met in 1892, when they both spoke at a meeting of the Baltimore Civil Service Reform Association. Roosevelt, at the time civil service commissioner, boasted of his reforms in federal law enforcement and mentioned that Border Patrol applicants were required to pass marksmanship tests, with the most accurate getting jobs. Bonaparte, who followed Roosevelt on the program, countered with the tongue-in-cheek statement that shooting at paper targets was not the most effective way to get the best men. Bonaparte suggested that Roosevelt should have had the men shoot at each other, and given the jobs to the survivors.

Theodore Roosevelt became president in 1901. He and Bonaparte were both Progressives, believing that efficiency and expertise, not political connections, should be the ultimate determination of who gets the job. Four years after he became president, Roosevelt appointed Bonaparte as attorney general. On July 26, 1908, Bonaparte created a corps of Special Agents of the Department of Justice. The newly created unit was ordered by the attorney general to report to Chief Examiner Stanley W. Finch. These former Secret Service men and detectives were the forerunners of the Federal Bureau of Investigation. Both the attorney general and the president recommended in 1909 that the force of thirty-four agents become a permanent part of the Justice Department. Bonaparte's replacement as attorney general, George Wickersham, named the unit the Bureau of Investigation on March 16, 1909. The title of chief examiner was also changed to the chief of the bureau of investigation.

There were very few federal crimes when the Bureau of Investigation was established. The unit primarily investigated violations involving naturalization, bankruptcy, national bank laws, peonage, and land fraud. The first major expansion of the Bureau of Investigation came in 1910 when the Mann (White-Slave Traffic) Act was passed, making it illegal to transport women over state lines for immoral purposes. In addition to giving the new bureau a primary focus for its investigations, the act also provided a selective means for the federal government (through the Justice Department) to investigate suspects who successfully evaded state laws but had violated no other federal laws. The former chief examiner, Stanley Finch, became commissioner of White-Slave Traffic Act violations in 1912. Notable prosecutions under the Mann Act have included Eliot Spitzer (the former New York governor), Charlie Chaplin, Chuck Berry, Frank Lloyd Wright, and Jack Johnson, the first African American heavyweight boxing champion. Johnson was among the first people actually charged under the White-Slave Traffic Act. In 1913, he was accused of transporting a prostitute from Pittsburgh to Chicago. Critics of the action, and of the act, argued that the case against Johnson was racially motivated, since the "prostitute" he was charged with transporting across state lines was actually his white girlfriend.

Field offices existed from the start of the FBI, each controlled by a special agent in charge who was directly responsible to Washington headquarters. Most were located in large cities, with a few near the Mexican border. Those offices concentrated on intelligence collection, neutrality violations, and smuggling. With the onset of World War I, the FBI's work increased again. The bureau was given responsibility for selective service, espionage, and sabotage acts, and was assigned to assist the Labor Department by investigating suspected enemy aliens. With the passage of the National Motor Vehicle Theft Act in October 1919, the bureau had another tool by which to prosecute criminals who attempted to evade the law by crossing state lines. After the end of World War I and the restoration of "normalcy" under President Harding in 1921, the FBI returned to its prewar role of fighting federal crimes, and enforcing the Mann Act.

The period in the United States from 1921 to 1933 was notorious primarily because of the public's almost complete disregard for Prohibition, which made it illegal to sell or import intoxicating beverages. Prohibition not only created a new federal medium for fighting crime, but it also created a tremendous gangster empire for the importation and transportation of illegal alcohol. This major increase in the criminal element in the United States did not directly impact the Federal Bureau of Investigation, however. The Treasury Department, not Justice, had direct jurisdiction over the illegal importation of alcoholic beverages.

So, FBI investigation of the gangsters of the Prohibition era required some creative effort. The agency investigated Al Capone not because of his alleged involvement in importation of alcohol or prostitution, but because he was a "fugitive federal witness." (Capone and three of his gang members were arrested once, traveling by automobile, for "associating with known criminals," each other.) The agency's prosecution of the head of the KKK, dormant since the late 1800s, also required some creativity. For example, the White-Slave Traffic Act was used by the FBI to bring the head of the KKK in Louisiana to justice.

The J. Edgar Hoover era at the agency began on May 10, 1924, when President Coolidge's pick for attorney general, Harlan Fiske Stone, selected Hoover to lead the Bureau of Investigation. Hoover had graduated from George Washington University Law School and worked for the Department of Justice where he had headed the enemy alien operations during World War I and assisted in the General Intelligence Division, investigating alleged anarchists and communists.

At the time Hoover took over, the FBI had 650 employees, which included 441 special agents. Hoover immediately fired those agents he considered unqualified and attempted to professionalize the agency by abolishing the usual seniority rule for promotion and instituting uniform performance evaluations. He also began regular inspections of both headquarters and field offices, established a rule that newly hired agents had to be between the ages of twenty-five and thirty-five, and created a formal training course for new agents. He also returned to the prior preference for special agents to have law or accounting degrees. Hoover also came up with the idea for the country's Ten Most Wanted Fugitives List, which, as the agency captured or killed each one, added publicity to the aura of the "G-Man." As Pretty Boy Floyd, Bonnie and Clyde, or Machine Gun Kelly added to the daily headlines, the public kept track of where their names were on the list.

During the early 1930s several critical decisions helped to solidify the FBI's position as the country's premier law enforcement agency. A federal kidnapping crime act was passed in 1932, and in June 1934 Congress passed the National Firearms Act, which imposed an excise tax on the manufacture and transport of certain firearms and significantly increased the agency's jurisdiction. The Bureau of Investigation was renamed the United States Bureau of Investigation in 1932 and renamed again in 1935 as the Federal Bureau of Investigation, which it has kept since.

Coincident with the increasing communist threat to the country during the Great Depression, authority to investigate communist organizations came in 1936, with President Roosevelt's approval, through Secretary of State Cordell Hull. The 1939 presidential directive also strengthened the bureau's authority to investigate alleged subversive aliens in the United States, and Congress also passed the Smith Act in 1940, which made illegal any attempt at a violent overthrow of the US government.

The outbreak of war in 1939 began the agency's first foray into intelligence and counterintelligence. The responsibilities of the FBI escalated with concerns about sabotage, subversion, and espionage against the United States. At least one agent with special training in defense plant protection was stationed in each of the FBI's forty-two field offices. The organization was the primary defense against subversion by German agents. After France fell to the Germans in 1940, England was the only defense against the increasing Axis threat. Congress reinstated the draft in late 1940, and the FBI became responsible for locating and catching deserters and draft evaders.

During this period the FBI caught both saboteurs and spies. Before US entry into World War II, the FBI uncovered the Frederick Duquesne spy ring, which was the largest catch up to that point in time, leading to the arrest and conviction of thirty-three spies. In June 1942 a German submarine dropped off eight trained operatives with expertise in language, explosives, secret writing, and chemistry at Amagansett, Long Island, and Ponte Vedra Beach in Florida. Fortunately for the country, one of the saboteurs, afraid of capture, went to the FBI multiple times, finally convincing the agency of the danger. All were tried and found guilty. Those who did not cooperate with the authorities were put to death, and the others were given life sentences but were returned to Germany after the war ended. In an early example of what would happen fifty-one years later after the 1993 attempt on the World Trade Center, the almost immediate capture of the saboteurs led the public to believe that fears of Axis subversion were unfounded. The public perception that the Federal Bureau of Investigation could protect the American citizens from any external or internal danger that threatened them effectively prevented any discourse on the actual possibility that that might happen.

Does the Department of Homeland Security Offer a "Feeling" of Safety?

When you get on a commercial aircraft today you have to pass through multiple security screenings of your personal identifying information, your body, your baggage, and anything you are carrying with you on the flight. You cannot carry liquid or gel products greater than 3.4 ounces in carry-on baggage. While there are always exceptions, particularly in the case of law enforcement agents, the average citizen can't carry a knife, mace, pepper spray, police batons, pistols, rifles, crossbows, arrows, and the like through security. The illusion is that everyone must go through the security checks, and the effect of all this, particularly with armed agents in visible presence, is the belief that there is safety inside the airport and when you are on the airplane. This also helps to deter potential attackers from striking out at airports and aircraft.

However, any competent individual can purchase everything needed to manufacture a hand grenade inside the security area of every major airport worldwide. So, who is the intended target of all the security checks and the police presence?

An observant person walks through a building and sees fire axes and fire extinguishers behind glass. They feel safe from the potential of a fire breaking out. They may have never actually used the emergency exits, but they know what that lit sign with the word "Exit" means and are pretty sure they could go down several flights to get out of a building if needed. You might not know where the assembly point is for every building you might be in, but what the heck, you can get out if needed and that's what matters.

Many Americans know what a tornado shelter is, and many who live in tornado-prone regions even know where the closest shelter might be so they can get to it in the event of a tornado warning. They haven't actually entered that particular shelter. They don't know that the university has been using the areas under stairwells (that would be tornado-safe areas for students and faculty in the event of an emergency) as storage for desks and chairs stacked to fill every square foot of space. But that's okay because you see the "Shelter" signs and know that if the alert sounds, you can get there for safety (even if it is unusable).

Much of what is seen around us every day, what people are willing to undergo, and the privacies they are willing to sacrifice are related to the issue of perceptions and have no basis in reality. It is perception that matters when it comes to "feeling" safe. Arguably, the TSA was created to provide the opportunity for Americans to feel safer. The increased waiting times in security lines and multiple identity checks were meant to assure citizens that no terrorist could possibly either pass through the security checks successfully or smuggle anything remotely resembling an explosive or weapon. At least, that was the idea. Reality doesn't come close.

In multiple covert tests by the DHS, including those done in 2017, TSA employees have periodically failed to detect and confiscate explosives, weapons, and/or drugs almost 80 percent of the time. Although the exact failure rate is classified (primarily to protect the somewhat unstable reputations of both the TSA and those in Congress who voted in favor of the Homeland Security Act), sources indicate the failure rate is greater than 70 percent.[5]

The Department of Homeland Security routinely schedules covert "Red Team" tests to check the competency of TSA employees to identify false weapons, a very good idea assuming agency employees could approach or maintain at least an average level of competence. In 2015, the failure rate of TSA was an unbelievable 95 percent.[6] This level of incompetency would not be allowed at any private organization in any country in the world.

Why does Congress continually allow TSA to erode the faith of the American public? One alternative, which could not possibly be any worse in terms of failure rate, would be to switch to private TSA screeners. You can see these security personnel at several major airports in California and other states. They even wear uniforms substantially similar to those worn by TSA employees and use the same screening protocols. This is part of the Screeners Partnership Program, already in place, which allows airports to utilize private screeners instead of the TSA screeners. TSA would retain the responsibility for creating and modifying security standards, and private screeners would provide increased productivity and security and be more cost-effective.

But once again, it is important to ask the question: For what purpose do the TSA and its partners exist? It certainly doesn't make flying any safer.

There is another component of the TSA that actually functions well and with purpose: the TSA agents who work to secure US rail traffic and cargo. Since nearly the entire rail industry across the country is privately owned and operated, the cargo is loaded and unloaded in limited security areas, and switching yards are often open to public access, the presence of TSA cargo and rail inspectors serves to offer a level of security for shipments all across the country. The only federal agency with a more important security function is the National Nuclear Security Agency (NNSA), which provides security forces for the escort of nuclear fuel, enriched uranium, and nuclear weapons across the country. The difference between the TSA and the NNSA is that the TSA has few actual sworn law enforcement officers within its ranks, and none that would use deadly force without first coming under attack themselves.

The NNSA can use deadly force for any reason to protect their shipments. That is risk mitigation at its most effective level.

Conclusion

Before looking at the actual intelligence functions conducted within the DHS as well as other agencies, it is important to review some of the key points already covered.

First, securing the homeland is nothing new. The effort to do so has been around since before the days of John Brown and continues today, with much the same focus.

Second, there are many agencies involved in the homeland security enterprise. Often these agencies work against each other for internal (selfish) interests and goals. Among the problems within this conflict between agencies is that enforcement of the law through prosecution and punishment takes priority over the prevention of actual criminal events.

Third, there is a need to remember that like theater, homeland security has an audience. The actors show the audience what they want to see, and not necessarily what is actually happening. As with a stage play or magician show on the Vegas strip, much sleight of hand and manipulation happen within politically driven agencies. This is particularly true when it is time to submit and defend budgets before Congress.

Finally, the last item to remember in our examination of intelligence for homeland security is that actual intelligence is rarely shared or disseminated in an actionable manner to those actually on the ground securing the homeland.

Notes

1. *The Papers of George Washington*, Revolutionary War Series, vol. 10, *11 June 1777–18 August 1777*, ed. Frank E. Grizzard, Jr. (Charlottesville: University Press of Virginia, 2000), pp. 425–426.

2. Carl von Clausewitz, *On War,* trans. Col. J. J. Graham (London: Kegan Paul, Trench, Trubner & Co., 1918), Vol. 1.

3. US Intelligence Careers, "How Intelligence Works," https://www.intelligence careers.gov/icintelligence.html.

4. *DHS Risk Lexicon: 2010 Edition* (Washington, DC: DHS 2010), p. 30.

5. David Inserra and Ceara Casterline, "Here's How Bad the TSA Is Failing Airport Security. It's Time for Privatization," Heritage Foundation, November 20, 2017.

6. Ibid.

5

The Role of Homeland Security Agencies

With nine separate operational agencies, and an Office of Intelligence and Analysis, the Department of Homeland Security has a massive intelligence-gathering and prosecuting function in defense of the United States. Constraints on size and content necessarily force a focus here on limited functions, but we do so in a manner that demonstrates what information is shared and the reasons (legal justifications) for that intelligence transfer. We also examine the reasons different agencies collect intelligence. For example, the US Secret Service collects intelligence to identify and interdict counterfeiting and money laundering, as well as to protect high-value political persons. The functions of each of these concepts are different. One might be to establish evidence to be used at trial, another to prevent or interdict potential threats to executive office holders and their families; there might also be a need to identify and send money movement records to the Office of the Director of National Intelligence for incorporation into larger-scale investigations into organized crime or terrorist groups. Another example is the concern with chemical, biological, radioactive, and nuclear materials and how US Customs and Border Protection (CBP) follows a long intelligence-gathering process beginning at overseas ports and shippers and finishes with the scanning of containers at US ports of entry. This incorporates the TSA inspections of transportation networks. While weapons of mass destruction (WMD) are an obvious concern to the country, there is also the issue of the CBP agricultural inspectors' approach to protecting against invasive species, which could cause infinitely more damage than a single portable WMD.

The topic of fusion centers is addressed in a later chapter due to its extensive nature.

The Department of Homeland Security

Shortly after the planes struck the Twin Towers in New York City on September 11, 2001, Pennsylvania governor Tom Ridge was appointed as the first director of the White House Homeland Security Office. The Homeland Security Office created a comprehensive national security strategy to safeguard the country and its citizens against any and all future terrorist acts.

In President Bush's initial proposal to create the Department of Homeland Security, he stated,

> The changing nature of the threats facing America requires a new government structure to protect against invisible enemies that can strike with a wide variety of weapons. Today no one single government agency has homeland security as its primary mission. *In fact, responsibilities for homeland security are dispersed among more than 100 different government organizations.* America needs a single, unified homeland security structure that will improve protection against today's threats and be flexible enough to help meet the unknown threats of the future.[1]

The president in his homeland security proposal argued that, as opposed to having multiple government agencies headquartered in Washington, DC, which managed duplicative and redundant activities, there should be one new department whose primary mission was to protect the American homeland. The new department would accomplish this by securing our borders, ports, and other critical infrastructure; synthesizing and analyzing intelligence related to homeland security from various sources; coordinating all important communication between state and local governments, private industry, and the American people concerning threats and preparedness; coordinating any and all efforts against the threat of bioterrorism and other weapons of mass destruction; helping to train and equip first responders; and managing federal emergency response activities.

DHS Organizational Components and Their Intelligence Functions

The Homeland Security Act of 2002 (P.L. 107-296) created the DHS and transferred the funding and personnel from twenty-two affected agencies to the newly created department. The actual divisions created were Emergency Preparedness and Response, Border and Transportation, Science and Technology, and Information Analysis and Infrastructure.

Emergency Preparedness and Response

The Emergency Preparedness and Response division manages and oversees federal aid and assistance in the training of domestic disaster preparedness of first responders and also takes the lead in coordinating all disaster response efforts at the federal level. Through this component, DHS manages and administers all grants for first responders, including police, firefighters, and emergency personnel, managed previously by FEMA officials. FEMA became an intrinsic part of the department when DHS was created.

While FEMA has no intelligence-gathering functions, it is a primary user of intelligence and earth science data collected by NOAA, which is in the Department of Commerce. FEMA also extensively utilizes data and analysis created by the United States Geological Survey, a component of the Department of the Interior.

The US Coast Guard carries out extensive emergency preparedness and response functions in and on the waterways of the United States. As such, it is not only a military service and a branch of the armed forces (US Navy) at all times under Title 14 of the US Code, but it is also a valued member of the US intelligence community under Title 50.

Office of Intelligence and Analysis

The Office of Intelligence and Analysis (I&A) is one of the agencies within the Department of Homeland Security that is directly involved with intelligence. The mission of the agency was originally to furnish the homeland security enterprise with the timely and relevant information it needs to keep the United States safe and resilient. I&A is the only agency within the US intelligence community statutorily charged with delivering information to state, local, tribal, territorial, and private-sector partners, and with collecting and analyzing information from those partners for dissemination within the department and the intelligence community. Although initially the Homeland Security Act of 2002 gave the DHS, through the Information Analysis and Infrastructure Protection Directorate, a mandate for collecting, analyzing, and integrating law enforcement intelligence related to domestic intelligence threats, the creation of the Terrorist Threat Integration Center by the Bush administration effectively downgraded the subsequent role of I&A.[2]

DHS Intelligence and Analysis is charged with looking at persons of interest in the United States who have the potential for radicalization and/or violence, and also with painting a detailed picture of any and all domestic terrorist intelligence threats within the continental United States, relative to current vulnerabilities.[3] In order to accomplish this mission, agents of I&A work with members of the intelligence community as well as local, state, federal, tribal, and private officials. I&A not only gathers information from these sources but also shares intelligence it has compiled in order to warn other sectors of the government about impending threats.

The Secret Service

The US Secret Service is a federal law enforcement agency currently under the Department of Homeland Security charged with creating and conducting criminal investigations and protecting the nation's leaders (and potential leaders) and their families. Until 2003, the Secret Service was a part of the Department of the Treasury. At that point it was transferred to the DHS.

The Secret Service has both a protective mission and an investigative mission. In terms of its protective mission, the agency ensures the safety of the president and vice president of the United States, their immediate families, former presidents and their spouses and children under the age of sixteen, presidential and vice presidential candidates and spouses, and visiting foreign heads of state. Physical security for the White House complex, the Treasury Department building, the vice president's residence, and all foreign diplomatic residences in Washington, DC, is also provided by the Secret Service. Protection of the above also incorporates operations to coordinate manpower and logistics with local and state law enforcement agencies, as well as proactive intelligence necessary to investigate all threats made against all persons considered to be under agency protection. In addition, it is the lead agency for planning, coordination, and implementation of security for events designated as National Special Security Events.

The investigative mission of the Secret Service includes the protection of the payment and financial systems of the United States from all manner of financial and electronic-based crimes. Financial crimes include the counterfeiting of US currency, mail and wire fraud, bank and financial institution fraud, illicit financing operations, and major conspiracies. Cybercrime, identity theft, access device fraud, network intrusions, credit card fraud, and intellectual property theft are all included in electronic crimes. The Secret Service is a member of the High Intensity Drug Trafficking Areas Task Force, which seeks to reduce or eliminate drug trafficking in certain areas of the country, as well as the FBI's Joint Terrorism Task Force, which combats domestic and international terrorism. The agency is also a member of the National Center for Missing and Exploited Children.

The first responsibility of the Secret Service was to combat the counterfeiting of US currency following the Civil War. Following that, the Secret Service evolved into the first US domestic intelligence and counterintelligence agency. Subsequently, many of the agency's original responsibilities were taken over by other agencies such as the CIA; Drug Enforcement Administration; Bureau of Alcohol, Tobacco, Firearms, and Explosives; FBI; and IRS Criminal Investigation Division.

The Secret Service was created on July 5, 1865, in Washington, DC, primarily to reduce or eliminate counterfeit currency. One-third of the currency in the country at that time was counterfeit. Secret Service Chief William P. Wood was sworn in by Secretary of the Treasury Hugh McCulloch. The actual legislation creating the agency was on President Abraham Lincoln's desk the night he was killed at the Ford Theatre. At that time in the United States, the only other federal law enforcement agencies were the US Park Police, the US Post Office Department's Office of Instructions and Mail Depredations (also known as the Postal Inspection Service), the US Marshals Service, and the US Customs Service. At the time, the US Marshals did not have enough manpower to investigate all federal crimes, so the new agency began investigating a range of crimes from bank robbery to murder to illegal gambling.

President William McKinley was assassinated in 1901. After that, Congress asked the Secret Service to provide presidential protection. A year later the agency assumed official and full-time protection for the president and his family.

The first meeting between a sitting US president and a Mexican president occurred in 1909, between President William H. Taft and

Mexican president Porfirio Díaz in El Paso, Texas, and Ciudad Juárez, Mexico. The proposed meeting resulted in serious assassination threats, so the head of the Secret Service asked for some added security. The Texas Rangers, 4,000 Mexican and US military, US Marshals, and an additional 250-man private security detail led by Frederick Russell Burnham were all called in by Chief John Wilkie. Burnham discovered a man holding a concealed pistol standing at the El Paso Chamber of Commerce building, along the procession route, the day of the summit, a few feet from the two presidents. The man was captured and disarmed.

President Harry S. Truman was residing in the Blair House, across the street from the White House, while it was being renovated in 1950. That November 1, two Puerto Rican nationalists, Oscar Collazo and Griselio Torresola, went to Blair House with the intent of killing the president. The two men opened fire on several White House police officers, including Private Leslie Coffelt. Mortally wounded, Coffelt returned fire, killing Torresola with a shot to his head and wounding Collazo. Collazo spent twenty-nine years in prison for the assassination attempt before returning to Puerto Rico in 1979. As of this date, Private Coffelt is the only member of the Secret Service to die while protecting a US president from an assassination attempt.

As a direct result of Robert F. Kennedy's assassination in 1968, Congress authorized the protection of major presidential candidates as well as vice presidential candidates and nominees. Congress also authorized the lifetime protection of the spouses of deceased presidents unless they remarry and also the children of former presidents until they turn sixteen. The Secret Service Presidential Protective Division safeguards the president and his or her immediate family while in the White House and while traveling via plane, helicopter, or limousine.

Congress passed the Comprehensive Crime Control Act in 1984, which increased the Secret Service's jurisdiction over credit card and computer fraud. Six years later, in 1990, the agency launched Operation Sundevil, ostensibly to investigate and arrest hackers, allegedly responsible for disrupting telephone service across the country. The operation affected a large number of people unrelated to hacking, and led to zero convictions. The end result was a number of successful lawsuits against the Secret Service.

The Secret Service created the New York Electronic Crimes Task Force (ECTF) in 1996 in order to combine the resources of the private sector, academia, and state, federal, and local law enforcement agencies to attempt to control and eliminate computer-based threats to US financial payment systems and critical infrastructures. The USA PATRIOT

Act of 2001 required the Secret Service to create a nationwide network of ECTFs in addition to the one already created in New York. Investigations conducted by the forty ECTFs include bank fraud, access device fraud, internet threats, computer system intrusions and cyberattacks, computer-generated counterfeit currency, phishing/spoofing, assistance with internet-related child pornography and exploitation, money laundering, and identity theft. Additionally, the Secret Service has established forty-six Financial Crimes Task Forces that combine the resources of the private sector and other law enforcement agencies in an organized effort to combat threats to US financial payment systems and critical infrastructures.

Money laundering. The United Nations Office on Drugs and Crime estimates that annual illegal profit totaled more than $2 trillion globally, and proceeds within the United States were approximately $300 billion in 2015.[4] For an illegal enterprise to succeed, criminals must be able to move money covertly. That is why people use money laundering, which involves hiding the source of illegally derived profits so that the proceeds appear legitimate, or masking the source of money used to promote illegal conduct. Money laundering requires three steps: placing the money into the financial system; layering, which separates the money from its illegal origins; and integrating the use of legitimate transactions to reintroduce the funds into the economy.

The crimes that generate most of the illegal proceeds in the United States include drug trafficking, human smuggling and trafficking, organized crime, fraud, and corruption. The various types of fraud are believed to create the largest share of illegal profit. These include healthcare fraud, bank fraud, securities fraud, and tax refund fraud. Healthcare fraud by itself generates approximately $100 billion each year, according to the 2018 *National Money Laundering Risk Assessment*.[5] Many healthcare frauds involve complicit healthcare professionals submitting fraudulent bills to insurers. Considering the high cost of both drugs and healthcare, it is easy to understand how fraud like this continues. Insurance payments may continue through the banking system and look indistinguishable from legitimate transfers.

Cybercrime involves a variety of illegal activities, including malware attacks, phishing, and cyber-related crime such as business email compromise, ransomware, credit card fraud, and consumer scams, such as fake lottery and romance schemes, and offers of employment that invariably require the victim to send money. Unfortunately, these internet-based crimes can originate from anywhere in the world, which compromises legal jurisdiction and has contributed to the increase in global money laundering groups. These people utilize complicit merchants, financial service professionals, and individuals to launder money on behalf of multiple criminals and organizations.

Cash transactions are highly vulnerable to money laundering. Cash is anonymous and portable. It has no record of its previous owners, source, or legitimacy. Forms of cash are used globally, and it is very difficult to trace once it is spent. In general, cash in bulk form can be relatively easily concealed and transported in vehicles, aircraft, boats, luggage, or commercial shipments. People regularly use these methods to smuggle bulk cash in shipments across US borders.

Sources of illegal income for money laundering include contraband smuggling, fraud, illegal gambling, extortion, bribery, kidnapping, and prostitution. By far the most profitable, however, is drug smuggling. Cash is used to purchase street-level drugs from dealers, and the dealers use the same cash to purchase their supply from mid-level distributors. The same cash is then used by the mid-level dealers to purchase from wholesalers, and the wholesalers use cash to buy from their suppliers, all the way up the chain. Drug cartels in Mexico who supply most of the drugs to American buyers usually rely on multiple money laundering methods, including bulk smuggling of cash, to move the drug profits across the US border into Mexico.

Mexico remains the primary conduit for the majority of illegal drugs entering the United States. The usual procedure is for the money launderers to acquire possession of the drug profits inside the United States and then facilitate the laundering process, which can involve a combination of structured bank deposits, funnel accounts, and bulk money smuggling. This usually takes place as a collection of smaller accounts into a single account as a result of small cash deposits at bank branches throughout the country, then either wiring the money to Mexico or withdrawing it in cash near the border for direct smuggling into Mexico. However, when it comes to today's opioid epidemic, the primary drug comes from China.

On October 12, 2018, the Department of Justice announced its first ever indictments against Chinese manufacturers of fentanyl and other opiate substances. The attorney general noted in his announcement that "this was an elaborate and sophisticated conspiracy. They used the internet, about 30 different aliases, cryptocurrency, off-shore accounts, encrypted communications, and they allegedly laundered funds internationally through third parties."[6] Earlier that year the Treasury Department issued sanctions against Jain Zhang and his companies under the

Foreign Narcotics Kingpin Designation Act as part of a "whole-of-government approach to combating fentanyl trafficking."[7] The article continues, "The four key financial associates of Zhang designated today—Na Chu, Yeyou Chu, Cuiying Liu, and Keping Zhang—conducted financial transactions through money service businesses to launder illicit narcotics proceeds for Zhang and his organization, which shipped or arranged for the shipment of fentanyl and analogue controlled substances to the United States."[8]

Another common means of laundering is trade-based, where a cycle of money brokers and exporters of goods work together to disguise and move drug money. The sale of intermediate goods effectively launders the drug money and provides drug suppliers with payment in local currency. Honest merchants who receive payment by check or direct wire for their goods may be completely unaware they are indirectly participating in a drug money laundering scheme. After cash is exchanged for legal goods, it is very difficult for law enforcement to trace the source of the illicit funds. In addition, this form of money laundering harms legitimate businesses. According to the US Department of the Treasury's *National Money Laundering Risk Assessment*, transnational criminal organizations routinely put goods purchased with drug money into the legitimate market simply to expedite the money laundering process, which places legal businesses at a huge disadvantage.

Banks are also utilized to facilitate money laundering. Banks in the United States routinely handle trillions of dollars on a daily basis. Most US citizens use some form of depository financial institution to conduct transactions, including credit unions, savings and loan associations, and commercial banks. Some citizens use money services businesses, such as check cashers, currency exchangers, money transmitters, or businesses that market prepaid access devices, money orders, or traveler's checks. Some money services businesses use commercial banks to settle transactions, and some banks may hold accounts in other banks in order to facilitate transactions in the country of the bank where the account is held. The tremendous volume of money transactions that banks handle on a daily basis makes them significantly vulnerable to money laundering risks. In most money laundering cases, criminals and criminal organizations utilize banks at some point to hold or move illicit funds.

Bank Secrecy Act. The Bank Secrecy Act (BSA; 31 USC 5311) established recordkeeping and reporting requirements for federal savings associations, federal banks, and agencies of foreign banks. The Office of the Comptroller of the Currency (OCC) of the US Department of the Treasury prescribes regulations, conducts supervisory actions, and sometimes takes enforcement action to ensure that national banks, federal branches, federal savings associations, and agencies of foreign banks have the controls in place and provide the necessary information to law enforcement agencies to detect money laundering, terrorist financing and other illegal acts, and the misuse of US financial institutions. The OCC examines national banks, federal branches, federal savings associations, and agencies of foreign banks in the United States in order to determine BSA compliance. The OCC uses both informal and formal enforcement actions to ensure that all conform to BSA compliance.

Under the Bank Secrecy Act and related anti–money laundering laws, banks must do the following:

- Establish effective BSA compliance programs.
- Establish effective customer due diligence systems and monitoring programs.
- Screen against Office of Foreign Assets Control and other government lists.
- Establish an effective suspicious activity monitoring and reporting process.
- Develop risk-based anti–money laundering programs.

Effective BSA programs instituted by banks nationwide are often the front line in anti–money laundering efforts. Successful programs help financial institutions detect efforts to launder illegal profits, which can prevent those funds from entering the US financial system. Accurate suspicious activity reports can be a critical source of information relative to money laundering for US law enforcement efforts. Suspicious activity reports are produced by bank security individuals based on lists of suspicious customers with unusually high deposit accounts or suspicious sources of funds, or both. Banks utilize software programs for data-mining purposes to produce lists of suspicious clients, which are then investigated by bank personnel. If suspicious activity reports are produced, then those are sent digitally to law enforcement personnel for further action.

Certain individuals may seek to evade these requirements by structuring cash deposits to avoid threshold reporting requirements, or attempt to locate merchants who will accept illegal funds without reporting the transactions. Individuals may also utilize correspondent banking services to facilitate money laundering, which creates challenges for US bank personnel who may not have a relationship with the originator of a payment when they receive funds from a correspondent bank.

Virtual currencies are also becoming common in money laundering, being the preferred form of payment for purchasing both drugs and other illicit goods online as well as paying off the perpetrators of ransomware attacks (as in a recent case in Baltimore, Maryland). Money laundering syndicates have added the option of moving money through virtual currencies as another way to layer transactions to hide the source of illegal funds.

The greatest money laundering risks in this country include the misuse of cash, lax compliance at US financial institutions, anonymity in transactions, and complicit individuals and financial service employees. Individuals involved with illegal operations such as human smuggling and trafficking, illicit retail transactions, drug trafficking, and other activities associated with organized crime tend to prefer US currency because of its widespread use in the United States as well as overseas. Virtual currencies also provide anonymity due to the lack of regulation and supervision in most jurisdictions. The reach and depth of money laundering in the United States are mitigated by the imposition of anti–money laundering programs, customer recordkeeping requirements in financial institutions, and suspicious and currency transaction reporting.

Counterfeiting. Counterfeit money mimics official or "real" currency without the legal sanction of the state or government in a deliberate attempt to duplicate real currency and deceive the intended recipient. Producing counterfeit money is an attempt to defraud or commit forgery. Prior to the introduction of paper money, the usual method of forging money involved mixing base metals with some pure gold or silver. The value of the coin was based on the intrinsic value of the metal used. Counterfeiters would simply scrape off some of the precious metal from the original coins and utilize it to plate or cover some base metal and then attempt to pass it off as a legitimate coin. Plated copies of early Lydian coins have been found that are believed to be some of the oldest counterfeit coins.

Another form of counterfeiting was the introduction of documents by legitimate printers in response to official orders from governments. For example, during World War II, Nazi printers forged US dollars and British pounds in an attempt to drive down the value of the originals and help their side win the war. There has been significant counterfeiting of euro banknotes since 2002, but much less than for the US dollar. Counterfeiting of US currency is very popular—according to the US

Treasury Department, approximately $70 million in counterfeit bills is in circulation at any point in time.

Even though the Treasury Department handles production and protection of the currency of the country, when it comes to investigating counterfeit currency the Treasury still uses the Secret Service.

Cybersecurity and Infrastructure Security Agency

The Cybersecurity and Infrastructure Security Agency (CISA) protects the nation's critical infrastructure from physical and cyber threats. This mission requires effective coordination and collaboration among a broad spectrum of government and private-sector organizations. CISA's National Cybersecurity and Communications Integration Center provides 24/7 cyber situational awareness, analysis, incident response, and cyber defense capabilities to the federal government; state, local, tribal, and territorial governments; the private sector; and international partners.

CISA supplies cybersecurity tools, incident response services, and assessment capabilities to safeguard the networks that support the essential operations of federal civilian departments and agencies. It also coordinates security and resilience efforts using trusted partnerships across the private and public sectors, and delivers training, technical aid, and assessments to federal stakeholders as well as to infrastructure owners and operators nationwide.

National Risk Management Center

The National Risk Management Center allows CISA to supply consolidated all-hazards risk analysis for US critical infrastructure. In one of its most important functions, and one of the critical lessons learned through the 9/11 Commission Report, CISA enhances public safety interoperable communications at all levels of government, providing training, coordination, tools, and guidance to help partners across the country develop their emergency communications capabilities. The organization works with stakeholders across the country to conduct extensive, nationwide outreach to support and promote the ability of emergency response providers and relevant government officials to continue to communicate in the event of natural disasters, acts of terrorism, and other man-made disasters.

The National Risk Management Center is a planning, analysis, and collaboration center that works to find and address the most significant risks to our nation's critical infrastructure. It works in close coordination with the private sector and other key stakeholders in the critical infrastructure community to identify, analyze, prioritize, and manage the most strategic risks to the US National Critical Functions.

Countering Weapons of Mass Destruction Office

WMD are a concern for all Americans and all branches of the military. The Countering Weapons of Mass Destruction Office (CWMD) has the mission to obstruct attempts by terrorists or other threat actors to carry out an attack against the United States or its interests through the use of a weapon of mass destruction. As such, it works to enhance the nation's ability to prevent terrorists or other threats from using WMD, supports its operational partners such as CBP and the Coast Guard to close capability gaps, and invests in and develops technologies to help its partners to meet requirements and improve operations.

While the CWMD isn't out there actively working to identify and interdict WMD, it is providing the technology for CBP to scan cargo at points of shipment, assisting the TSA in securing the rail systems cargo, and helping to protect ports of entry through development of technologies to sense potential threats through a variety of means.

Science and Technology Directorate

This is the primary research and development arm of DHS. The people of the Science and Technology Directorate work across all branches of DHS to develop better border and immigration screening technology; to develop and deploy chemical and biological weapons sensing devices as well as to study and determine potential threats associated with chemical and biological weapons precursors; to develop explosives detection systems for use in protecting aviation; and to find ways to make unmanned aerial systems more usable for the homeland security enterprise, among other functions. The Science and Technology Directorate is also the behind-the-scenes gadget manufacturer.

Other Intelligence Elements

The Office of Intelligence and Analysis is the only component of the national intelligence community statutorily charged with delivering intelligence products to state, local, tribal, territorial, and private-sector partners. It also is tasked by law with developing intelligence from those partners for use by DHS and the intelligence community. The top priority of I&A is to align its intelligence resources across the intelligence enterprise to identify and enable the effective mitigation of threats. I&A is an operational component of the DHS. The authors feel it is important to single it out from the other operational components of DHS due to its intelligence-specific functions. The DHS Intelligence Enterprise includes the Transportation Security Administration, US Immigration and Customs Enforcement, Customs and Border Protection, Citizenship and Immigration Services, the Federal Emergency and Management Agency, Cybersecurity and Infrastructure Security Agency, I&A, and the Coast Guard intelligence agency, but only I&A and the intelligence arm of the Coast Guard are DHS members of the IC.

Because of the changing nature of Homeland Security Intelligence, while the following information is sourced from the DHS Intelligence and Analysis website, the authors strongly advise the reader to evaluate the most recent information provided at dhs.gov/topic/intelligence-analysis.

I&A manages the department-wide processes for coordinating and executing the intelligence cycle at both the federal and local levels. By integrating its capabilities with those of other DHS components, I&A enhances threat identification, mitigation, and response across the mission areas described above. Additionally, I&A formulates and implements key strategies and initiatives that address critical barriers to information sharing.

I&A regularly applies several methodologies to assess the mission centers' impact on operational priorities. To that end, I&A develops and implements several management metrics that support internal quality control and effectiveness of select training programs, among others. These baseline performance metrics supply the ability to observe operational changes as the mission centers become more established. I&A uses these observations to measure progress and offer insight into how well the mission centers are meeting their mandates and commitments to their partners.

Mission Centers

Five mission centers serve as the department's center of gravity for intelligence-driven integration of analysis, technology, skills, and functions to counter the most critical threats facing the homeland today.

Each mission center is tasked with a topical mission goal focused on mitigating enduring threats to the homeland. Mission centers collect information to address DHS and national intelligence priorities and provide available reporting gathered by DHS components and state, local, tribal, and territorial (SLTT) partners to the intelligence community and other customers. Many of the mission centers utilize the Homeland Security Information Network (HSIN) to share sensitive but unclassified information. This network is used to manage operations, analyze data, send alerts, and share the information that is necessary to ensure the homeland is safe, secure, and resilient. Among these functions there are several outcomes the agency attempts to meet:

- Provide customers timely, relevant, and actionable intelligence for operational and policy-level decisionmaking
- Bring IC capabilities and intelligence to the DHS homeland security enterprise
- Mitigate the dynamic and sophisticated adversaries that threaten our homeland
- Leverage DHS-unique data, fused with IC data for DHS mission use
- Integrate intelligence across DHS and the IC
- Develop collection platforms and requirements needs across DHS
- Provide key intelligence support to state, local, tribal, territorial, and private-sector partners

Counterintelligence Mission Center. The Counterintelligence Mission Center (CIMC) promotes a departmental approach to the current and emerging counterintelligence threats facing the DHS intelligence enterprise and the intelligence community. Employees of CIMC collect and deliver intelligence on threats posed by foreign adversaries and intelligence services. Through integrated and coordinated efforts, they are able to effectively refine the response to such threats. CIMC also works closely with the larger DHS intelligence enterprise and IC partners to identify large-scale threats, implement countermeasures, and enhance resilience across intelligence networks.

Counterterrorism Mission Center. The Counterterrorism Mission Center (CTMC) synthesizes and integrates counterterrorism (CT) intelligence to enable a unified departmental approach to protect the homeland from domestic terrorism. CTMC serves as the focal point for collaboration throughout the DHS intelligence enterprise by coordinating with SLTT, international, private-sector, and IC partners. CTMC produces all-source finished intelligence at the lowest classification possible to provide the CT decision advantage to the secretary, the department, and their partners. CTMC also refines CT intelligence questions from customers, identifies and manages comprehensive collection requirements and gaps, and advocates for CT intelligence issues and equities across the interagency and the IC.

Cyber Mission Center. The Cyber Mission Center (CYMC) is the department's premier provider for cyber threat analysis. CYMC employees deliver finished intelligence to enable the department's mission of ensuring cybersecurity and resilience of the federal government, SLTT partners, and critical infrastructure networks. CYMC works to expand this capability while also evolving the DHS intelligence enterprise cyber program through closer integration across intelligence networks.

Economic Security Mission Center. The Economic Security Mission Center provides intelligence to drive decisions and define the department's intelligence equities in the economic security space. Employees provide intelligence on trade, finance, and transportation activity that is harmful to domestic industry and evasive of US trade laws; their intelligence informs foreign engagement, trade policy, and other economic security decisions. They also regularly interface with the Department of the Treasury, DHS trade policy, DHS components, and their partners in the intelligence community.

Transnational Organized Crime Mission Center. The Transnational Organized Crime Mission Center serves as the preeminent strategic center in DHS for integrated intelligence to counter transnational organized crime networks and facilitators. It focuses primarily on major drug smuggling organizations, transnational gangs, human smuggling, weapons trafficking, child exploitation, illicit trade, and the movement of illicit proceeds on behalf of these criminal enterprises. It also assesses transnational organized crime exploitation outside of the United States and provides opportunity analysis to support engagements with its foreign partners.

Other intelligence elements. In addition to five threat-focused mission centers, I&A is also equipped with three other intelligence elements: the Current and Emerging Threats Center (CETC), Field Operations Division (FOD), and Homeland Identities, Targeting and Exploitation Center

(HITEC). These three components enable the successful completion of I&A's topical mission objectives by enhancing partner collaboration, technological innovation, and information sharing. Through unique directives and capabilities, CETC, FOD, and HITEC collect, analyze, and disseminate actionable intelligence that is crucial for the success of I&A's mission and the security of the homeland.

Current and Emerging Threats Center. The CETC provides 24/7 indications and warnings of threats directed against the homeland. CETC employees specialize in the collection, first-line analysis, and dissemination of current, relevant, and actionable intelligence. This center works closely with SLTT and intelligence community partners.

Field Operations Division. The FOD focuses on integrating, producing, and delivering actionable intelligence by leveraging unique relationships with SLTT partners. FOD is responsible for three primary functions: leading the intelligence cycle execution in its areas of responsibility; supporting threat-related information sharing to and from SLTT partners, the DHS intelligence enterprise, and the intelligence community; and supporting fusion center partners in applying IC resources to execute the intelligence cycle.

Homeland Identities, Targeting and Exploitation Center. HITEC accelerates the discovery and delivery of identity- and network-based intelligence to counter national security threat actors. The intelligence is delivered by adopting and applying advanced exploitation methods, emerging technologies, and sound tradecraft. HITEC conducts advanced technical exploitation and counternetwork targeting analytic services to interpret and integrate leads derived from digital media and identity analysis. It is also responsible for the DHS Watchlisting Enterprise, which requires specialization in standards, certification, program management, and technologies to enable enterprise operations.

Conclusion

The Department of Homeland Security is a huge, wide-ranging, expansive organization with possibly the greatest number of responsibilities of any federal agency spanning the country and the world. Of course, this statement is made with an acknowledgment of the size and scope of the Department of Defense (DOD), which dwarfs DHS. However, within the borders of the United States, the DOD has very limited functions and responsibilities as it is primarily an external protector of the nation and a means of presenting US politics and foreign policy by other means in foreign entanglements. You can see DHS in every city with an international airport, major railyard, port of entry, agricultural component, or cyber and critical infrastructure across the nation and its territories, making it the most visible federal agency to the US population.

With this understanding, it is clear to see the reasons for the wide-reaching intelligence and operational functions of the agency. More so, DHS deploys Customs and Border Protection as well as agricultural inspectors to nearly a hundred overseas ports where cargo originates en route to national ports of entry. You also see many CBP immigration officers in overseas airports where direct flights to the United States originate. When all added together this becomes a massive consumer of advanced intelligence products with a statutory responsibility to disseminate those products to federal, state, local, tribal, and territorial consumers as well as private partners.

Notes

1. George W. Bush, *The Department of Homeland Security* (June 2002), https://www.dhs.gov/xlibrary/assets/book.pdf. Emphasis in the original.

2. Darren Tromblay, *Spying: Assessing US Domestic Intelligence Since 9/11* (Boulder: Lynne Rienner, 2019), p. 117.

3. Ibid.

4. US Department of the Treasury, *National Money Laundering Risk Assessment 2018* (2018), https://home.treasury.gov/system/files/136/2018NMLRA_12 -18.pdf.

5. Ibid.

6. US Department of Justice, "Attorney General Sessions Announces New Indictments in International Fentanyl Case," April 27, 2018, https://www.justice .gov/opa/speech/attorney-general-sessions-announces-new-indictments -international-fentanyl-case.

7. US Department of the Treasury, "Treasury Sanctions Chinese Fentanyl Trafficker Jian Zhang," April 27, 2018, https://home.treasury.gov/news/press-releases /sm0372.

8. Ibid.

6

The Role of Other Security Agencies

There are many state, local, tribal, and federal agencies that are not among the Department of Homeland Security direct reporting agencies that have significant intelligence functions directly affecting the DHS. The first and probably largest agency most readers will immediately identify is the Federal Bureau of Investigation, a component of the Department of Justice. We look into the FBI and related agencies because of their focus on domestic terrorism and counterterrorism as well as their investigative and prosecutorial functions. We examine the FBI through use of official documents and narrative stories of real events.

The FBI uses the criminal case system to identify and interdict potential terrorist attacks, as well as to assist other countries in the same when it supports US interests. However, this routinely leaves potential gaps in the other components of FBI responsibility such as kidnapping, racketeer influenced and corrupt organizations, and espionage. For example, the FBI is officially responsible for cybercrime while DHS is responsible for cybersecurity, and every federal and state agency has its own, separate cybersecurity program—yet the FBI approach is one geared toward development of criminal cases after the fact, not prevention.

It is also important to examine the Food and Drug Administration (FDA) concerns with bioterrorism and the US agricultural infrastructure. Then there is the Department of Transportation (DOT) and its regulation of transportation systems, and the Federal Aviation Administration (FAA) regulation of airline security. Getting to all the various federal agencies and state agencies is difficult as there are so many. This necessarily requires us to focus on just some of the aspects and some of the agencies and how their intelligence efforts either do or do not support homeland security and national security. The FBI is a law enforcement agency tasked with criminal investigations for development of prosecutable cases—not a good choice for counterterrorism or homeland security/national security intel operations, evaluation, and dissemination. Terrorism by actors within the United States is considered a criminal act, frequently involving political or radical groups, whose origins may be domestic or international or a combination of both. Terrorism as an act of violence related to political demands is an act of war. Shouldn't it fall under military judicial processes if it does not originate wholly within the United States? This is a continually debated question at all levels of government as well as among the citizenry. The recent Uzbek terror attack in New York City and the call by President Trump to treat the perpetrator as an enemy combatant and send him to the military prison at Guantanamo Bay, Cuba, is an example. The failure of the FBI to identify and act is also instructive because they see things from a criminal case focus.

The Federal Bureau of Investigation

The FBI is the domestic intelligence and security service of the United States and its principal law enforcement agency. The FBI reports to both the attorney general and the director of national intelligence, since it operates under the jurisdiction of both the Department of Justice and the US intelligence community. The FBI has jurisdiction over violations of more than 200 categories of federal crimes. FBI domestic activities in terms of counterterrorism and counterintelligence are comparable to those of the British MI5 agency. It is primarily a domestic agency, maintaining more than fifty-six field offices in major cities throughout the country. The FBI also maintains an international presence, with sixty Legal Attaché (Legat) offices in US embassies abroad.

As noted in Chapter 4, the agency was created in 1908 as the Bureau of Investigation. The FBI's first official task was to enforce the White-Slave Traffic Act, or Mann Act, passed on June 25, 1910, which regulated interstate and foreign commerce by prohibiting the transportation of women and girls across state lines for immoral and other purposes. The agency's name was changed in 1935 to the Federal Bureau of Investigation. The headquarters is the J. Edgar Hoover Building, located in Washington, DC. The FBI's primary goals are to protect the United States, uphold and enforce the criminal laws of the country, and provide leadership and criminal justice services to federal, state, local, and international agencies and partners.

J. Edgar Hoover initially was the director of the Intelligence Section of the FBI, but within five years he became the director of the FBI, serving from 1924 until 1972, a combined forty-eight years. He was known, primarily, as the creator of the Scientific Crime Detection Laboratory, or the FBI Laboratory, which opened in 1932, as part of his work to professionalize criminal investigations by the agency. Hoover was a genius at marketing, and he wanted to get the FBI's name in the papers, as often as possible, so he created an FBI Most Wanted list of criminals and then tasked his agents to investigate and arrest them, making sure the local reporters were alerted to each event. FBI agents captured or killed a number of well-known criminals during the "war on crime" in the 1930s, including Baby Face Nelson, Ma Barker and her sons, Alvin Karpis, John Dillinger, and Machine Gun Kelly.

Using Wiretaps

Hoover and the FBI began using wiretapping during Prohibition in the 1920s to collect evidence to use in court against bootleggers. In the 1928 case *Olmstead v. United States,* federal agents installed wiretaps in the basement of Olmstead's building, and in the streets near his home, without judicial approval (warrants). He was convicted of bootlegging with evidence directly obtained from the wiretaps, and for conspiracy to violate the National Prohibition Act by importing, possessing, and selling illegal liquors. The Supreme Court held that the FBI wiretaps did not violate Olmstead's Fourth Amendment rights as unlawful search and seizure as long as the government did not physically break into a person's home to complete the taping of the conversation.[1] The legal consensus at the time was that unless a physical intrusion into a dwelling took place, there was no Constitutional violation of the Fourth Amendment. After the repeal of Prohibition, Congress passed the Communications Act of 1934, which outlawed nonconsensual phone tapping, but continued to allow wiretapping.

Based on a tip that Charles Katz was using a pay telephone to communicate gambling information to clients in other states, federal agents attached a wiretap device to the outside of a public phone booth used by

the alleged gambler in 1967. Based on wiretap recordings, Katz was convicted under an eight-count indictment for the illegal transmission of
wagering information from Los Angeles to Boston and Miami. Katz
challenged his convictions on appeal, arguing that the recordings had
been made illegally, infringing his Constitutional Fourth Amendment
rights. Based on prior cases, including the Olmstead case in 1928, the
court of appeals rejected Katz's appeal, noting the absence of a physical
intrusion into the phone booth itself. However, the Supreme Court, in a
landmark decision, held that Katz was entitled to Fourth Amendment protection for his conversations, and that a physical intrusion into the area he
occupied *was not necessary* to bring the amendment into play. For the
first time, a person was entitled to Fourth Amendment protection through
a "reasonable expectation" of privacy, not a physical environment.[2]

Wiretapping came up again during the 1970s as a direct result of the
Watergate scandal, which began on the morning of June 17, 1972, when
several burglars were arrested in the offices of the Democratic National
Committee (DNC), located in the Watergate complex in Washington,
DC. The FBI later discovered the intruders were connected with President Nixon's reelection campaign; they were caught wiretapping phones
and attempting to steal classified documents from the DNC. In a
remarkable example of civilian investigation, *Washington Post* reporters
Bob Woodward and Carl Bernstein broke the story and wrote the book
All the President's Men, which won them a Pulitzer Prize. Much of the
information relayed in the book came from an anonymous source
known at the time as Deep Throat, who in 2005 was revealed to be W.
Mark Felt, a former associate director of the FBI.

Changing Mission Focus

Beginning in the 1940s, the FBI began investigating cases of espionage
against the United States and its allies. Eight Nazi agents were arrested
and convicted of planning sabotage against the United States, and six of
the eight were executed. During the same period, a successful US and
UK effort, called the Venona Project, to break a Soviet code allowed
American and British agents to read Soviet communications.[3] This effort
confirmed the suspicion that Americans were working in the United
States as spies for Soviet intelligence.

Apparently, the director of the FBI at the time had a major concern
about homosexuals working for the federal government, in any capacity.
On April 10, 1950, the FBI launched a "sex deviate" program, when J.
Edgar Hoover forwarded to the US Civil Service Commission, the

White House, and branches of the armed services a list of 393 federal employees who had been arrested in Washington, DC, since 1947, on alleged charges of "sexual irregularities." In June 1951 Hoover expanded the program to include nongovernment jobs. It is important to remember that in that era homosexuality was illegal and often punishable by imprisonment. This created a situation where a practicing homosexual could be blackmailed by foreign powers or corrupt/criminal enterprises; it was, therefore, considered to be a national security issue.

The agency created the Top Hoodlum Program in 1953 in response to increased media attention to organized crime. The FBI directed its field offices to collect information on persons affiliated with mob operations in their territories and to send any and all to Washington to create a centralized database on mobsters in the United States. After the Racketeer Influenced and Corrupt Organizations (RICO) Act was passed in 1970 to combat organized crime, the FBI used it to prosecute Prohibition-era criminal groups and apply civil penalties for racketeering activity performed as part of an ongoing criminal enterprise. The FBI's organized crime work was done undercover and from within the organizations. Over time the agency made headway and dismantled several of the groups, including those headed by Sam Giancana and John Gotti. The RICO Act is still used today against certain individuals and groups that fall under the act's provisions.

During the 1950s and 1960s the FBI administration became increasingly worried about the possibility that civil rights leaders had become unduly influenced by communists and persons with leftist leanings, and they were criticizing the FBI because of it. As an example, in 1956 Dr. T. R. M. Howard, a wealthy civil rights leader and surgeon, had been vocal in criticizing the agency's "inaction" involving the investigation of the recent murders of George W. Lee, Emmett Till, and other Blacks in the South. Also, Dr. Martin Luther King Jr. had been critical of the FBI for what he believed was insufficient attention to White supremacist groups for the use of alleged terrorism. In response, the FBI carried out a controversial domestic surveillance program, COINTELPRO (for "COunterINTELligence PROgram"), targeting what it considered to be militant dissident political organizations, including the Southern Christian Leadership Conference, whose clergy included Dr. King.[4]

A group known as the Citizen's Commission to Investigate the FBI was allegedly responsible for a burglary at the residential office of an FBI agent in Media, Pennsylvania, in March 1971. Several files were taken and subsequently distributed to newspapers, including the *Harvard Crimson,* primarily focusing on the controversial COINTELPRO, which had targeted a Black student group at a Pennsylvania military college and the daughter of Congressman Henry Reuss of Wisconsin. The revelations included accusations of alleged assassinations of political activists, as well as phone surveillance of some members of Congress, including House Majority Leader Hale Boggs.

Fighting Terrorism

In 1982 the FBI created an elite antiterrorism unit named the Hostage Rescue Team (HRT) to protect athletes and others attending the 1984 Summer Olympics held in Los Angeles, as a result of the hostage situation in 1972 at the Summer Olympics in Munich, Germany, when terrorists murdered the Israeli athletes. The HRT is a dedicated FBI SWAT team dealing primarily with counterterrorism scenarios. The antiterrorist Hostage Rescue Team does not conduct investigations; it focuses on additional tactical proficiency and capabilities. The Computer Analysis and Response Team was also created in 1984.

The focus of the FBI changed from foreign counterintelligence to violent crime during the late 1980s to the early 1990s, and more than 300 agents were reassigned to the latter from the former. Because terrorism was no longer considered a major threat after the collapse of the USSR and the end of the Cold War, the FBI assisted local and state police in tracking wanted fugitives who had crossed state lines attempting to evade justice.

On February 26, 1993, a small group of terrorists detonated a truck bomb filled with approximately 1,200 pounds of explosives in a rental van in the underground parking garage at the World Trade Center, in an attempt to bring both towers down.[5] The terrorists, who had links to a local radical mosque and broader terrorist networks, fled the area after setting a timer. The subsequent explosion killed six people and created a five-story crater in the lower levels of the towers as well as undermining the floor of an adjoining hotel. The attack killed John DiGiovanni, Stephen Knapp, Robert Kirkpatrick, Wilfredo Mercado, William Macko, and Monica Rodriguez Smith, and injured more than a thousand people.[6] Approximately 50,000 people were evacuated from the World Trade Center complex. Electrical power was knocked out for significant sections of both towers, which affected the operation of emergency communication, elevators, ventilation systems, and lighting. The explosion also damaged emergency power generators, which shut down after twenty minutes.

Based primarily on the February 1993 World Trade Center attack, the FBI increased its counterterrorism role. This was further intensified after the 1995 Oklahoma City bombing when a truck filled with explosives was detonated just outside the Alfred P. Murrah Federal Building, killing 168 people and injuring hundreds.[7] The explosion was carried out by antigovernment militants Timothy McVeigh, who was executed in 2001, and Terry Nichols, his co-conspirator, who was sentenced to life in prison.[8] The explosion occurred shortly after 9:00 a.m. on April 19, 1995, and blew off the building's entire north wall. The deceased included nineteen children who were in the building's daycare center when the blast occurred. More than 650 people were also injured by the explosion, which damaged or destroyed over 300 other buildings in the surrounding area.

McVeigh, Nichols, and others in their group were radicalized by events such as the August 1992 confrontation at Ruby Ridge, Idaho, between federal agents and survivalists led by Randy Weaver at his rural cabin, as well as the Waco siege of April 1993, where seventy-five members of the Branch Davidian cult were killed. As a response to the events of both Ruby Ridge and Waco, McVeigh planned his attack on the Murrah Building, which contained multiple federal agencies, including the Secret Service, the ATF, and the Drug Enforcement Agency. The ATF was the agency that had launched the initial raid on David Koresh and the Branch Davidian compound in Texas. On the two-year anniversary of the end of the Waco siege, McVeigh parked a rental truck loaded with a diesel fuel–fertilizer mixture bomb outside the Murrah Building and then fled before it exploded. He was convicted on all eleven counts against him on June 2, 1997, and in 2000 McVeigh asked a federal judge to cease all appeals of his convictions and set a date for his execution. He died by lethal injection on June 11, 2001, at the age of thirty-three. He was the first federal prisoner to be executed since 1963.

The Unabomber

The case of the Unabomber is interesting and a primary subject of this chapter for several reasons. One of the most important is that it is representative of how the FBI approaches a typical case: obtain clues, investigate how they may point to a particular suspect, and then perform a link analysis on any and all victims of related crimes to see if any person or persons surface as a viable connection to the crimes. In other words, are the victims related in any way? Does that relationship point to a specific person who may have known all of them? Is there a particular victim type that may indicate a particular person or group?

Theodore John Kaczynski, also known as the Unabomber, is an American domestic terrorist. He was also a former mathematics professor and anarchist author. In the years between 1978 and 1995, he sent multiple mail bombs in an attempt to start a revolution by targeting people involved with modern technology, which he hated.

Kaczynski was born on May 22, 1942, in Chicago, Illinois, to a working-class family, Wanda Theresa and Theodore Richard Kaczynski, a sausage maker. In 1952, three years after his younger brother David was born, the family moved to southwest suburban Evergreen Park, Illinois, and Ted transferred to Evergreen Park Central Junior High School, where his IQ was scored at 167. He skipped the sixth grade, which he later described as a pivotal event in his life: previously he had socialized with his peers, but after skipping ahead he felt that he no longer fit in with the older children and was bullied.

Kaczynski later attended Evergreen Park High School, where he excelled academically. Although he was a member of several clubs, including mathematics, German, coin, and biology, he was considered an outsider by his classmates. He became intensely interested in mathematics at this point, spending hours studying and solving advanced problems. Placed in an advanced mathematics class, he soon mastered the material and skipped the eleventh grade, graduating at the age of fifteen. He entered Harvard a year later, at sixteen, and was assigned to the Eliot House on Prescott Street, designed to house the youngest and most precocious freshmen in a small, intimate living space. He was described by fellow students as reserved but not unfriendly. He graduated with his bachelor of arts degree in mathematics four years later, in 1962, with a GPA of 3.12.

Kaczynski participated in a psychological experiment for three years, between his sophomore and senior years, that was later described as "purposely brutalizing" and was led by Harvard psychologist Henry Murray. Students who volunteered for the experiment were told to write essays describing their personal beliefs and aspirations, and that these would be used in a debate on personal philosophy. The personal essays were later turned over to an anonymous attorney who would, in videotaped sessions, confront and belittle the subject, making sweeping and personally abusive attacks on the individuals, using their essays as ammunition, while electrodes attached to the subjects monitored their psychological and physiological reactions. The subjects' taped reactions of anger and rage were later played back to them repeatedly. Each week for three years someone verbally abused and humiliated Kaczynski. He spent 200 hours as part of the study. Kaczynski's lawyers later linked his hostility toward mind control techniques to his participation in Murray's experiment.

Some have suggested that Murray's study was part of the CIA's Project MK-Ultra, a study in mind control approved by then CIA director Allen Dulles in the early 1950s, which generally centered around behavior modification via a variety of extremes, including hypnosis, radiation, electroshock therapy, and drugs, toxins, and chemicals, including LSD.[9] The test subjects came from a wide variety of populations: some freely volunteered, some participated under coercion, and some had absolutely no idea they were involved in a sweeping grandiose defense research experiment, including some CIA employees. The Central Intelligence Agency particularly liked using prisoners, as they were willing to give consent in exchange for extra recreation time or a (possible) shortened sentence. For example, Whitey Bulger, a former organized crime boss, convicted murderer, and FBI informant, wrote of his experience as an inmate test subject in the MK-Ultra project: "Eight convicts in a panic and paranoid state . . . total loss of appetite. . . . Hours of paranoia and feeling violent . . . horrible periods of living nightmares. . . . I felt like I was going insane."[10] Bulger claimed that he had been given LSD, lysergic acid diethylamide, one of the CIA's key interests for its mind control program.[11] Considering the extremely wide sweep of the MK-Ultra program, including an operation called Midnight Climax, which involved hiring prostitutes to lure unsuspecting johns into safe houses in San Francisco where they would be given LSD and then taped by the CIA and the Federal Narcotics Bureau to test the effects of the drug, the notion that Kaczynski's Harvard experiment was tied to MK-Ultra does not seem irrational or illogical.

Kaczynski enrolled at the University of Michigan in 1962 to obtain his master's and doctoral degrees in mathematics in 1964 and 1967. Michigan was not his first or second choice, but it was the only school that offered him an annual grant and a teaching post. In graduate school, Kaczynski's field of study was geometric function theory, a subset of complex mathematical analysis. His academic ability impressed several of his professors. His graduate studies at Michigan produced twelve As and five Bs, an above-average performance. Kaczynski's doctoral dissertation, "Boundary Functions," won the Sumner B. Myers Prize for Michigan's best mathematics dissertation of the year. His dissertation adviser called it "the best I have ever seen." After graduation from the

University of Michigan in 1967, Kaczynski accepted an offer to teach and became the youngest assistant professor of mathematics in the history of the University of California at Berkeley, where he taught courses in geometry and calculus. His teaching evaluations indicate some level of discomfort in the classroom; he taught straight from the textbook and refused to answer questions from the students. He resigned unexpectedly and without an explanation two years later, in June 1969.

In 1969 Kaczynski moved from Berkeley to his parents' home in Lombard, Illinois, and then, two years later, to a small remote cabin he had built outside Lincoln, Nebraska, where he could live a simple life without running water or electricity. He did odd jobs and received some economic support from his family. His goal was to learn survival skills and live without the benefits of civilization. He learned how to farm, track game, and identify edible plants, as well as other survival techniques. He used an old bicycle for transportation into town and visited the local library to read classics in their original languages.

In what may have been the final push into madness for Kaczynski, the destruction of wildlands near his cabin led him to believe it was impossible for him to live peacefully in nature. He began acting on his hatred and distrust of modern technology by performing sabotage against nearby developments in 1975, and he started reading about sociology and political philosophy. At some point in the succeeding three years he decided to add violence to his survival skills.

Kaczynski mailed or hand-delivered sixteen bombs between 1978 and 1995, increasingly sophisticated explosives that killed or maimed twenty-six people.[12] All but the first few bombs contained the initials "FC," which Kaczynski later stated stood for Freedom Club, inscribed on different parts of the bombs. He left misleading clues in the explosives in order to fool investigators and took great care in not leaving any fingerprints for the FBI to find. The first bomb that Kaczynski sent was indirectly targeted at Buckley Crist, a professor of materials engineering at Northwestern University. On May 25, 1978, a package was found in a parking lot at the University of Illinois at Chicago, bearing Crist's return address. When the package was "returned" to Crist, he became suspicious because he had not sent it, so he contacted campus police. Officer Terry Marker opened the bomb, which exploded and injured his hand.

After the 1978 bombing incident, other explosive devices were sent to airline officials. In 1979 a bomb was placed into the cargo hold of an American Airlines flight from Chicago to Washington, DC. The bomb actually did not explode, due to a faulty timing mechanism, but it succeeded in producing a lot of smoke, which forced an emergency landing. Because placing a bomb in a plane is a federal offense, the FBI became involved—and it designated the situation as UNABOM for university and airline bomber.[13] The media, taking a direct cue, then designated the person responsible as the Unabomber.

In this case, what limited the FBI investigation was an almost complete lack of physical evidence that was probative. Virtually everything used in the bombings was either easily obtainable from literally thousands of stores nationwide, or it was evidence placed by the bomber simply to mislead the investigators (which it did). Additionally, the FBI never saw the perpetrator as somebody to be stopped from committing future terrorist attacks, but as a criminal to be investigated and brought to trial for their crimes. Since its creation in 1908, the FBI has been an agency with at least some confusion as to its primary focus: Is it an intelligence agency, a law enforcement agency, a source for local law enforcement, a counterintelligence agency? Or should its main focus be counterterrorism?[14]

FBI Involvement

The first explosive device that caused serious injury was sent in 1985 when John Hauser, a graduate student and captain in the US Air Force, opened a box and lost four fingers and one eye. A computer store owner in Sacramento, California, Hugh Scrutton, was killed the same year when a bomb placed in the parking lot of his store exploded. Another bomb attack occurred two years later at a computer store in Salt Lake City, Utah. The bomb, disguised as a piece of wood, injured Gary Wright when he attempted to pick it up and move it from the store's parking lot. Kaczynski mailed a bomb to David Gelernter, a computer science instructor at Yale University, in 1993. Shortly thereafter he also mailed a bomb to Charles Epstein from the University of California at San Francisco. Epstein lost several fingers after opening the device. In 1994, Thomas J. Mosser, a Burson-Marsteller executive, was killed after opening a mail bomb Kaczynski sent to his home in North Caldwell, New Jersey. The last death occurred in 1995 when Gilbert Brent Murray, the president of the timber industry lobbying group California Forestry Association opened a mail bomb addressed to the previous president, William Dennison, who had retired.

The same year, Kaczynski mailed multiple letters to media outlets demanding that his 35,000-word essay "Industrial Society and Its Future" (labeled the UNABOMBER Manifesto by the FBI) be printed by a "major" newspaper.[15] In his letters, he stated that he would "desist from terrorism" if his demand was met, and the manifesto was printed. Attorney General Janet Reno and FBI director Louis Freeh both recommended its publication in the hope that a reader could possibly identify the person responsible. The *Washington Post* and the *New York Times* printed the essay on September 19, 1995.[16] This was likely the first time there was a massive politically motivated tome published that related directly to terrorist activities and demands.

In his essay, Kaczynski wrote that technology has had a destabilizing effect on the human race, caused widespread suffering, and made life as a whole unfulfilling. He stated that because of technology, most people spend a majority of their lives in useless pursuits (he termed them "surrogate" activities) for artificial goals, such as entertainment, scientific work, or following sports teams. He argued that future technological advances would result in extensive genetic modifications to allow human beings to become adjusted to meet the needs of the social systems, not vice versa. He believed that technological advances could be stopped, unlike people who believe that it is inevitable, and that the erosion of human freedom was a natural product of an industrial society. Fortunately, according to the author, the industrial system had not yet gained complete control over human behavior and was in a desperate struggle to overcome certain problems that threatened its survival, and that the way forward was to promote "social stress and instability" in order to create an ideology that opposed technology.

The suspect was initially labeled the "Junkyard Bomber" by the US postal inspectors who had original jurisdiction over the case. Terry Turchie was appointed to head the FBI-led investigation and task force, which included 125 agents from the ATF, US Postal Inspection, and the FBI. Later the task force would grow to more than 150 full-time agents, but detailed analysis of the bomb fragments recovered from the blast sites proved to be of little use in identifying the perpetrator. John Douglas, a member of the FBI's Behavioral Sciences Unit, created a psychological profile of the bomber in 1980. He indicated that the suspect would likely be a man of above-average intelligence with connections to the academic world. Later Douglas refined the profile to add that the suspect was most likely a neo-Luddite (a person who distrusted and hated technology) and also held an academic degree in the hard sciences. Although completely correct, this psychologically based profile was discarded in 1983, replaced by another profile based on evidence collected from the bombings, which described the perpetrator as a blue-collar airplane mechanic. To add some leads to the investigation, the

FBI authorized a $1 million reward for information leading to the arrest of the suspect.

David Kaczynski, Ted's brother, was encouraged by his wife to contact the FBI prior to the publication of "Industrial Society and Its Future" because she believed that Ted could be the Unabomber. David was hesitant at first, but after reading the published essay he began to take the possibility more seriously. Searching through family papers dating back to the 1970s, he found letters to newspaper editors protesting the use of technology and using phrases similar to ones found in the manifesto.

The FBI had been sure, prior to the publication of the manifesto, that he worked in or had some real connection to the Salt Lake City area, and that he was originally from Chicago, since the bombings began there (many criminals commit their first crimes in areas they are familiar with, their "comfort zone"), and also by the 1990s that he had some association with the San Francisco Bay area. In response to the million-dollar offer for information leading to the possible arrest and conviction of the Unabomber, as would be expected the FBI received over a thousand phone calls and tips a day for months. Many letters that people thought might have been written by the perpetrator were also sent in, and the agency had to follow through on any and all leads. While the agency was working through thousands of new leads, Kaczynski's brother was hiring a private investigator in Chicago, Susan Swanson, to discreetly investigate Ted's activities. He later hired a Washington, DC, attorney, Tony Bisceglie, to coordinate and organize the private investigator's findings in preparation for contacting the FBI. He was trying to protect his brother from the danger of an FBI raid like the Ruby Ridge and Waco sieges.

An investigator working with Bisceglie contacted former FBI hostage negotiator and profiler Clinton Van Zandt in early 1996 to ask him to compare the manifesto sent by the Unabomber to copies of typewritten letters David had received from his brother Ted. The initial analysis by Van Zandt estimated a better than 60 percent chance that the same person had written both the letters and the essay. A follow-up analysis by another Van Zandt team indicated an even higher correlation percentage. Based on the above, Van Zandt recommended that Bisceglie's client contact the FBI.

Also in early 1996 Bisceglie gave a copy of a 1971 essay by Ted Kaczynski to the FBI's Molly Flinn, who forwarded it to the task force in San Francisco. FBI profiler James Fitzgerald used linguistic analysis to determine that the same author likely wrote both the essay and the manifesto. Based on this determination as well as a timeline analysis of the bombings and Kaczynski's life, the head of the task force decided to apply for a search warrant.

David Kaczynski had received assurances from the FBI that his brother would not learn who turned him in, but his identity was somehow leaked to CBS News in April 1996. Dan Rather called the FBI director Louis Freeh, who asked for twenty-four hours before CBS broke the story. The FBI scrambled to finish the search warrant before the story hit the evening news. Later, the FBI launched an internal investigation to learn the source of the leak, but it was no more successful than the seventeen-year search for the bomber prior to the release of the manifesto. The source was never identified.

The FBI arrested Ted Kaczynski at his cabin on April 3, 1996. The search incident to the arrest revealed 40,000 handwritten journal pages, bomb components, one live bomb, and descriptions of Unabomber crimes. Also found was what appeared to be the original typed manuscript of "Industrial Society and Its Future." Kaczynski was indicted by a federal grand jury the same month on ten counts of illegally transporting, mailing, and using bombs, as well as three counts of murder. Kaczynski's attorneys attempted to enter a plea of insanity to avoid the death penalty, but he was against that. He requested to dismiss his lawyers and hire an attorney who had previously agreed not to use the insanity defense, Tony Serra, and instead use the suspect's anti-technology views in his defense. This request was turned down and Kaczynski attempted to commit suicide by hanging on January 9, 1998. Several (but not all) forensic psychiatrists who examined him gave a clinical diagnosis of paranoid schizophrenia. In his book *Technological Slavery*, Kaczynski said that two prison psychologists who saw him regularly for four years told him they saw no indication of paranoid schizophrenia.

Kaczynski was declared competent to stand trial on January 21, 1998, and prosecutors sought the death penalty. Kaczynski avoided that by pleading guilty on all counts on January 22 and accepting life imprisonment without any possibility of parole. Later, Kaczynski attempted to withdraw his plea, claiming it was involuntary, but Judge Garland Ellis Burrell Jr. denied the request, and the Ninth Circuit Court of Appeals upheld the decision. Kaczynski is currently at the maximum-security prison ADX in Florence, Colorado, serving eight life sentences with no chance of parole.

At the time of Theodore Kaczynski's arrest, it should be noted, the FBI had not solved the case, had changed its profile of the suspect several times, and was essentially looking in the wrong part of the country. The agency was attempting to gather evidence and build a criminal case to deliver to prosecutors, not prevent an ongoing terrorist operation from killing and maiming individuals across the country. In the end, it was Ted's brother who solved the case, at the urging of his wife, using his own time and money and then delivering a complete investigative package to the FBI for action. Even then, the FBI nearly lost the chance to arrest the suspect when the story and identity of the terrorist were leaked to a news agency.

Ruby Ridge

Although the general public perception of the FBI was good following the 1993 World Trade Center bombing in New York City, the Oklahoma City bombing in 1995, and the 1996 arrest of the Unabomber, the agency did not fare nearly as well during both the 1992 Ruby Ridge and the 1993 Waco sieges. During the Ruby Ridge situation, self-proclaimed white separatist Randy Weaver, his family, and a friend named Kevin Harris engaged in an eleven-day standoff with FBI agents and US Marshals in an isolated cabin in Boundary County, Idaho. During the siege, Weaver's wife Vicki, his fourteen-year-old son Sammy, the family dogs, and US Marshal William Degan were all killed.[17]

A former US Army engineer, Weaver moved his family to a cabin he had built in 1983 on Ruby Ridge, about forty miles south of the Canadian border. His problems with the US government began when he attended meetings of the Aryan Nations, a white supremacist group in Hayden Lake, Idaho, in the 1980s, and met a member of the group who was also an informant of the ATF, and who allegedly bought two illegal sawed-off shotguns from Weaver in October 1989.[18]

Federal agents first asked Weaver to become an informant, which he refused; they then pursued a weapons charge against him. He was originally arrested and released, and a trial date was set for February 19, 1991. When the trial was moved to February 20, Weaver was sent a letter incorrectly stating the trial had been moved to March 20. After Weaver failed to show up for trial on February 20, the court issued a bench warrant for his arrest. On August 21, the US Marshals initiated a stealth operation to arrest Weaver, and the situation became violent after the Weavers' dog began barking at six heavily armed US Marshals inside the property. One of the marshals shot and killed the dog, and in an exchange of fire Sammy Weaver (age fourteen) was shot in the back and killed. Kevin Harris, a family friend who was visiting the Weavers and who was with Sammy trying to find out what had the dogs aggravated, then shot and killed US Marshal Degan.[19]

The FBI dispatched the Hostage Rescue Team to Ruby Ridge on August 21. The next day, FBI sniper Lon Horiuchi opened fire from approximately 200 yards, when he believed that Weaver and Harris were about to open fire on an FBI helicopter circling overhead. Horiuchi's first shot hit Weaver in the arm. He fired his second shot, meant for Harris, as they were running back into the cabin. The bullet hit Weaver's wife in the face as she was standing in front of the door holding her infant daughter, and it injured Harris. Vicki soon died on the living room floor of the cabin in front of her daughters while Harris nearly bled to death while awaiting some form of medical assistance. Vicki's body remained in the cabin for the eleven days of the standoff.[20]

Harris and Weaver surrendered to the FBI on August 30, when the federal agents finally allowed the local sheriff to approach the cabin in an armored vehicle to check on the condition of the family.[21] The men were charged with murder, conspiracy, and assault. Harris was acquitted by an Idaho jury of all charges, and Weaver was convicted only of failing to appear for the original firearms charge. He served a year in federal prison and was then released.[22]

The FBI was criticized by the Justice Department for failing to gather the necessary intelligence prior to the stealth operation to attempt to arrest Weaver and for not ordering the occupants of the cabin to surrender before engaging them in a firefight. The inquiry also concluded that the sniper's second shot was unconstitutional because both men were running for cover and, therefore, were not imminent threats.[23]

The examples of the Unabomber and Ruby Ridge are demonstrative of how the federal law enforcement system is not conducive to addressing domestic terrorism; it results in law enforcement overreach and coercion; and often they only find their suspects when civilians are participants in the process. There are a number of other examples, such as that of Major Nidal Hasan, the Boston Marathon bombings and subsequent hunt for the Tsarnaev brothers, and the inability of federal agents from any agency to address the rise of MS-13, its spread across the country, and the continuing presence of these criminal cartel-type terrorists in the United States. The same can be said for the original Los Zetas Mexican drug cartel, which has penetrated deep into the United States. There are also concerns about African refugees who are being resettled in Minnesota or Colorado without any concern for their strong Salafist Islamic terrorist leanings. This leads us to a recent case of a legal immigrant who was radicalized after coming to the United States and convinced by an online Islamic extremist journal to commit murder.

The Strange Radicalization of an Uzbek Immigrant

On October 31, 2017, a rented pickup truck driven by Sayfullo Saipov rammed into pedestrians and cyclists on a walking path near the World Trade Center location in New York City, killing eight. Saipov, a twenty-nine-year-old Uzbek national had come to the United States in 2010.[24] He was taken into custody after crashing, exiting the truck holding two handguns (later determined by police to be nonlethal), and being wounded by the police. The alleged perpetrator was not from countries normally associated with terrorist attacks against the United States, such as Saudi Arabia, Afghanistan, or Syria; he was from Uzbekistan, a Central Asian country with a history of domestic religious violence, and one whose citizens are increasingly susceptible to terrorist propaganda.

Saipov came to the United States from Tashkent, the Uzbek capital, using the Diversity Immigration Visa (also known as the Green Card Lottery) program, run by the State Department, which allows a percentage of applicants living in areas overseas to receive a US Permanent Resident card. The Immigration Act of 1990 established the current and permanent Diversity Visa program, through which the State Department issues 55,000 permanent visas annually.

Apparently not radicalized prior to coming to the United States, Saipov worked periodically as an Uber driver. Acquaintances from Uzbekistan described his family as not particularly religious. He was a college graduate and worked as an accountant before immigrating to the United States. After being interrogated by investigators, he told them that he had started planning the attack the previous year and was inspired by viewing Islamic State propaganda videos on the internet. ISIS (Islamic State of Iraq and Syria), also known as ISIL (Islamic State of Iraq and the Levant), claims religious authority over all Muslims and has been increasingly using instructional videos to teach would-be supporters how to do everything from choosing the best vehicle to picking the ideal target. The November edition of its online journal included a three-page feature explaining the right way to carry out a vehicle attack, including a picture of a typical U-Haul truck and a list of suggested targets.

The alleged perpetrator's trial has been delayed, subsequent to defense counsel accusations that the government had their client under surveillance, possibly illegally, for years prior to the October 31, 2017, attack. They are suggesting that Saipov's international communications could have been "vacuumed up by the government's dragnet collection" of metadata. In a court filing in March 2019, they requested more information on US collection of overseas communications between Saipov and his acquaintances.

If it is true that federal agency dragnet sweeps of data and international communications are ongoing, as claimed by Saipov's defense attorneys and demonstrated by the releases made by Edward Snowden, then somebody, somewhere, should have flagged this individual for subsequent investigation. Unfortunately, nothing has been presented, nor any indication made by the FBI or US Attorney that he was ever under surveillance or suspicion. In all likelihood the result will have to wait for court evidence to be made public.

Fusion Centers

According to the DHS website,

> Fusion Centers are state-owned and operated centers that serve as focal points in states and major urban areas for the receipt, analysis, gathering and sharing of threat-related information between State, Local, Tribal and Territorial (SLTT), federal and private sector partners.
>
> The National Network of Fusion Centers (National Network) brings critical context and value to Homeland Security and Law Enforcement that no other federal or local organization can replicate. Fusion Centers accomplish this through sharing information, providing partners with a unique perspective on threats to their state or locality and being the primary conduit between frontline personnel, state and local leadership and the rest of the Homeland Security Enterprise.
>
> The National Network of Fusion Centers is the hub of much of the two-way intelligence and information flow between the federal government and our State, Local, Tribal and Territorial (SLTT) and private sector partners. The fusion centers represent a shared commitment between the federal government and the state and local governments who own and operate them. Individually, each is a vital resource for integrating information from national and local sources to prevent and respond to all threats and hazards. The enhanced collaboration between the federal government, SLTT and private sector partners represents the new standard through which to view homeland security.[25]

As of September 25, 2019, there were eighty fusion centers spread across all states, Puerto Rico, Guam, and the District of Columbia. These fusion centers are of two types:

- Primary Fusion Centers: A primary fusion center typically provides information sharing and analysis for an entire state. These centers are the highest priority for the allocation of available federal resources, including the deployment of personnel and connectivity with federal data systems.
- Recognized Fusion Centers: A recognized fusion center typically provides information sharing and analysis for a major urban area. As the Federal Government respects the authority of state governments to designate fusion centers, any designated fusion center not designated as a primary fusion center is referred to as a recognized fusion center.[26]

Fusion centers are relatively new, only coming into being starting in 2004. "The development and exchange of intelligence is not an easy task. Sharing this data requires not only strong leadership, it also requires the commitment, dedication, and trust of a diverse group of men and women who believe in the power of collaboration."[27] These centers are built on the National Criminal Intelligence Sharing Plan, which "contains over 25 recommendations that were vetted by law enforcement officials and experts from local, state, tribal, and federal agencies. It embraces intelligence-led policing, community policing, and collaboration and serves as the foundation for the Fusion Center Guidelines."[28] These guidelines define what a fusion center is:

a "collaborative effort of two or more agencies that provide resources, expertise, and information to the center with the goal of maximizing their ability to detect, prevent, investigate, and respond to criminal and terrorist activity." Among the primary focuses of fusion centers are the intelligence and fusion processes, through which information is collected, integrated, evaluated, analyzed, and disseminated. Nontraditional collectors of intelligence, such as public safety entities and private sector organizations, possess important information (e.g., risk assessments and suspicious activity reports) that can be "fused" with law enforcement data to provide meaningful information and intelligence about threats and criminal activity. It is recommended that the fusion of public safety and private sector information with law enforcement data be virtual through networking and utilizing a search function. Examples of the types of information incorporated into these processes are threat assessments and information related to public safety, law enforcement, public health, social services, and public works. Federal data that contains personally identifiable information should not be combined with this data until a threat, criminal predicate, or public safety need has been identified. These processes support efforts to anticipate, identify, prevent, monitor, and respond to criminal activity. Federal law enforcement agencies that are participating in fusion centers should ensure that they comply with all applicable privacy laws when contemplating the wholesale sharing of information with nontraditional law enforcement entities.[29]

Thus fusion centers focus on terrorism, criminal, and public safety matters in support of securing communities and enhancing the national threat picture. They receive, analyze, gather, produce, and disseminate a broad array of threat-related information and actionable intelligence to appropriate law enforcement and homeland security agencies. Owned and operated by state and local authorities, they are supposed to include a multidisciplinary group of representatives with the ability to individually contribute, share, and act upon disparate information from law enforcement, public safety, fire services, emergency response, public health, and critical infrastructure organizations, businesses, and agencies.

It is important to note that in fusion centers without an FBI presence there tends to be good exchange of information and intelligence between the agencies staffing the center. Unfortunately, it has been uniformly reported by fusion center employees that as soon as the FBI becomes involved in any particular case the information is immediately locked down, not shared, and people are prosecuted or fired for attempting to share the information under statutes that prohibit interference in any federal law enforcement criminal investigation. It has also been noted that there is nearly no private-sector participation in fusion centers. This stems from a duality of fear on the part of participants. Law enforcement in general doesn't ever want sensitive information to get into the hands of "civilians" as it might corrupt or interfere with developing a prosecution in the future, and of course they can't trust the private sector and certainly not academia. Alternatively, the private sector is afraid to share information with fusion centers because they might inadvertently become the focus of law enforcement investigators. This will continue to be a major issue in the effectiveness and functionality of the fusion center concept.

What's Working and What Isn't

The primary benefit of fusion centers is the sharing of intelligence and crime data between federal, state, local, tribal, and territorial law enforcement agencies. There are also a number of fusion centers with emergency management and fire services representatives that participate in the information sharing. Some fusion centers are strictly strategic in their approach while others act as real-time crime centers for local law enforcement and federal agencies such as the Drug Enforcement Agency (DEA).

The largest complaint about fusion center functionality is that the information flowing upward from local agencies lacks any contribution to counterterrorism efforts. The same can be said for direct counterintelligence efforts. However, the success of fusion centers in sharing information between diverse agencies that previously didn't communicate has been beneficial and is improving (except with the FBI). Additionally, there have been notable successes in communications to address forest fires in Colorado and narcotics trafficking in Arizona.

Joint Terrorism Task Forces

Joint Terrorism Task Forces (JTTFs) differ from fusion centers in being SLTT groups led and managed by the FBI. The JTTFs focus primarily on terrorism and other criminal matters related to various aspects of the counterterrorism mission. They also conduct counterterrorism investigations and provide information for assessments and intelligence products that are shared, when appropriate, with law enforcement and homeland security agencies. JTTFs are multijurisdictional task forces and include other federal and SLTT law enforcement partners, which together act as an integrated force to combat terrorism on a national and international scale.

Field Intelligence Groups

The FBI's Directorate of Intelligence oversees field intelligence operations through fifty-six Field Intelligence Groups (FIGs). The directorate was established in February 2005, and the FBI's intelligence program was established in August 2014. The FIGs perform intelligence functions through integrated teams of intelligence analysts, language analysts, physical surveillance specialists, and a dedicated number of special agents. The FIGs coordinate, manage, and execute all of the functions of the intelligence cycle in the field.

- Requirements: They help determine what it is the agency doesn't know about the threats the country is facing—and what the FBI needs to know to combat them.

- Planning, direction, and collection: They help ensure that agents in the field collect—through interviews, searches, and electronic and physical surveillances—the kind of information the agency's partners in the law enforcement and intelligence communities are looking for.
- Processing and exploitation: They extract the information from cases being worked in their field offices and put it into a form usable by analysts. They do this using a variety of methods, including decryption, language translation, and data reduction.
- Analysis and production: They put the information into context by answering questions such as, What does it mean? And why is it important?
- Dissemination: They compile the information into reports and disseminate them to FBI headquarters, other law enforcement and intelligence agencies, and key decisionmakers, including the president and the attorney general. Often, the dissemination process leads to generating new requirements, and the process starts over again.

FIGs collect, analyze, produce, and disseminate actionable intelligence to lead and support FBI investigative intelligence programs, and to inform the intelligence community and other federal and SLTT law enforcement partners. The FIGs focus on broad counterterrorism, national security, and criminal intelligence collection operations and serve as the FBI's primary intelligence link with fusion centers, the intelligence community, and JTTFs. FIGs are operated by the FBI and staffed with FBI intelligence analysts, language analysts, and special agents.

Fusion centers, JTTFs, and FIGs are supposed to operate collaboratively to leverage their analytic and investigative capabilities to safeguard the homeland and prevent criminal and terrorist activities.

Food and Drug Administration

The Food and Drug Administration is a federal agency within the Department of Health and Human Services. As for its relationship to homeland security intelligence, the FDA

is responsible for protecting the public health by ensuring the safety, efficacy, and security of human and veterinary drugs, biological products, and medical devices; and by ensuring the safety of the nation's food supply, cosmetics, and products that emit radiation. . . .

FDA is responsible for advancing the public health by helping to speed innovations that make medical products more effective, safer, and more affordable and by helping the public get the accurate, science-based information they need to use medical products and foods to maintain and improve their health.

FDA also plays a significant role in the Nation's counterterrorism capability. FDA fulfills this responsibility by ensuring the security of the food supply and by fostering development of medical products to respond to deliberate and naturally emerging public health threats.[30]

When it comes to homeland security and related intelligence activities, one of the most worrisome issues the nation faces is the potential that a terrorist will acquire the means to deliver a "dirty bomb" (radiological dispersion device) to a city or military base. Often people think that ports of entry are the place where such detection and deterrence efforts are focused. However, everything a terrorist needs to create a dirty bomb can be found in nearly every community in the United States. All a terrorist needs are basic explosives components, found in every hardware store, and a radioactive source. Where do you find radioactive materials? Dentist offices. Hospitals. Medical clinics and urgent care facilities. Most veterinary clinics. Any industrial welding facility. Oncology treatment centers have huge amounts of radioactive materials, some quite deadly, that are disposed of daily in waste containers. These radioactive materials are regularly transported in and through virtually every city in the United States on a daily basis. It is the FDA that is responsible for knowing where all this radioactive material is located, who is handling it, how it is being handled and moved, and to where and when.

The other major issue handled by the FDA in relation to homeland security intelligence is food defense. The FDA works with the private sector and other government agencies on activities related to food defense, including conducting research and analysis, developing and delivering training and outreach, and conducting exercises. In addition, the FDA has developed a number of tools and resources to help food facilities prevent, prepare for, respond to, and recover from acts of intentional adulteration of the food supply. Consider the last time you heard about a recall of lettuce or beef. It was the FDA that initiated that recall and notified the media in all areas of the United States that might have been affected. What would happen if somebody intentionally adulterated the food supply? It wouldn't be the DHS or FBI that informed the community—it would be the FDA. What if there was an outbreak of bovine spongiform encephalopathy (mad cow disease) at a cattle feed lot that provided the beef that is distributed through your grocery stores? The Department of Agriculture would take action to isolate the feed lot and identify each and every potentially affected animal and where it might have gone—but it would be the FDA that would alert the public, recall potentially affected beef and other products, and protect the community.

Department of Transportation

The Department of Transportation (DOT) has nine operational components that address issues related to homeland security, primarily through critical transportation infrastructure. These are aviation, roadways and bridges, trucking and motor coaches, railways, public transit, maritime, automobiles, pipelines and hazardous materials, and the St. Lawrence Seaway. The DOT has been around since 1966 and works to ensure the United States has "the safest, most efficient and modern transportation system in the world, which improves the quality of life for all American people and communities, from rural to urban, and increases the productivity and competitiveness of American workers and businesses."[31]

Imagine that a major hurricane strikes the East Coast of the United States. Before FEMA can deploy recovery and support assets to the potentially devastated region it has to know which roadways have been damaged, which bridges can still carry their rated weight capacity, which railroads are no longer functional, which airports are open and with what restrictions, and so forth. Before the US Coast Guard or US Navy can provide recovery and rescue assets they have to know the status of ports, piers, and logistic centers. They also have to know which local and regional airports can accept rescue aircraft and deal with the delivery of injured and displaced people.

All of these same issues would apply in the event of an earthquake, with the added problems related to potential pipeline integrity. There are extensive pipelines across the United States that move hazardous materials such as crude oil and natural gas. Other pipelines are the primary fresh water supplies to communities while still others move sewage to treatment plants. Knowing the status of these is essential before any agency can enter into recovery operations.

Thus, communication between the experts of the DOT and the relative components of the DHS is essential for a multitude of reasons. Let's take a quick look at all the agencies within the DOT that have a direct impact on the functionality of homeland security and how the intelligence these agencies provide leads to a better understanding of the interconnected nature of how homeland security intelligence functions.

The Federal Highway Administration

The Federal Highway Administration (FHWA) coordinates highway transportation programs in cooperation with states and other partners to enhance the country's safety, economic vitality, quality of life, and the environment. Major program areas include the Federal-Aid Highway Program, which provides federal financial assistance to the States to construct and improve the National Highway System, urban and rural roads, and bridges. This program provides funds for general improvements and development of safe highways and roads.

The Federal Lands Highway Program provides access to and within national forests, national parks, Indian reservations and other public lands by preparing plans and contracts, supervising construction facilities, and conducting bridge inspections and surveys. The FHWA also manages a comprehensive research, development, and technology program.[32]

The Federal Railroad Administration

The Federal Railroad Administration (FRA) promotes safe and environmentally sound rail transportation. With the responsibility of ensuring railroad safety throughout the nation, the FRA employs safety inspectors to monitor railroad compliance with federally mandated safety standards including track maintenance, inspection standards and operating practices.

The FRA conducts research and development tests to evaluate projects in support of its safety mission and to enhance the railroad system as a national transportation resource. Public education campaigns on highway-rail grade crossing safety and the danger of trespassing on rail property are also administered by FRA.[33]

The Federal Transit Administration

The Federal Transit Administration (FTA) assists in developing improved mass transportation systems for cities and communities nationwide. Through its grant programs, FTA helps plan, build, and operate transit systems with convenience, cost and accessibility in mind. While buses and rail vehicles are the most common type of public transportation, other kinds include commuter ferryboats, trolleys, inclined railways, subways, and people movers. In providing financial, technical and planning assistance, the agency provides leadership and resources for safe and technologically advanced local transit systems while assisting in the development of local and regional traffic reduction.

The FTA maintains the National Transit library (NTL), a repository of reports, documents, and data generated by professionals and others from around the country. The NTL is designed to facilitate document sharing among people interested in transit and transit related topics.[34]

The Maritime Administration

The Maritime Administration (MARAD) promotes development and maintenance of an adequate, well-balanced, United States merchant marine, sufficient to carry the Nation's domestic waterborne commerce and a substantial portion of its waterborne foreign commerce, and capable of serving as a naval and military auxiliary in time of war or national emergency. MARAD also seeks to ensure that the United States enjoys adequate shipbuilding and repair service, efficient ports, effective intermodal water and land transportation systems, and reserve shipping capacity in time of national emergency.[35]

It is important to note that prior to the establishment of the Department of Homeland Security, the US Coast Guard was a DOT agency and carried out many of these functions. It still does but as a separate agency, leading to a sense of dysfunction between the DOT, MARAD, and the Coast Guard.

The National Highway Traffic Safety Administration

The National Highway Traffic Safety Administration (NHTSA) is responsible for reducing deaths, injuries and economic losses resulting from motor vehicle crashes. NHTSA sets and enforces safety performance standards for motor vehicles and equipment, and through grants to state and local governments enables them to conduct effective local highway safety programs. NHTSA investigates safety defects in motor vehicles, sets and enforces fuel economy standards, helps states and local communities reduce the threat of drunk drivers, promotes the use of safety belts, child safety seats and air bags, investigates odometer fraud, establishes and enforces vehicle anti-theft regulations and provides consumer information on motor vehicle safety topics.

Research on driver behavior and traffic safety is conducted by NHTSA to develop the most efficient and effective means of bringing about safety improvements. A toll-free Auto Safety Hotline, 1-888-DASH-2-DOT, furnishes consumers with a wide range of auto safety information. Callers also can help identify safety problems in motor vehicles, tires and automotive equipment such as child safety seats.[36]

The Pipeline and Hazardous Materials
Safety Administration

The Pipeline and Hazardous Materials Safety Administration (PHMSA) oversees the safety of more than 800,000 daily shipments of hazardous materials in the United States and 64 percent of the nation's energy that is transported by pipelines. PHMSA is dedicated solely to safety by working toward the elimination of transportation-related deaths and injuries in hazardous materials and pipeline transportation, and by promoting transportation solutions that enhance communities and protect the natural environment.[37]

The Saint Lawrence Seaway Development Corporation

The Saint Lawrence Seaway Development Corporation (SLSDC) operates and maintains a safe, reliable and efficient waterway for commercial and noncommercial vessels between the Great Lakes and the Atlantic Ocean. The SLSDC, in tandem with the Saint Lawrence Seaway Authority of Canada, oversees operations safety, vessel inspections, traffic control, and navigation aids on the Great Lakes and the Saint Lawrence Seaway.

Important to the economic development of the Great Lakes region, SLSDC works to develop trade opportunities to benefit port communities, shippers and receivers and related industries in the area.[38]

Federal Aviation Administration

The Federal Aviation Administration (FAA) oversees the safety of civil aviation. The safety mission of the FAA is first and foremost and includes the issuance and enforcement of regulations and standards related to the manufacture, operation, certification and maintenance of aircraft. The agency is responsible for the rating and certification of airmen and for certification of airports serving air carriers. It also regulates a program to protect the security of civil aviation, and enforces regulations under the Hazardous Materials Transportation Act for shipments by air.[39]

As a part of the Department of Transportation, the FAA stands separate when it relates to homeland security. The sheer number of aircraft in the skies over the United States, entering and departing US airspace daily, and the tonnage of air cargo as well as the number of passengers make the agency special. Using fiscal year 2019 data (most recent available) it is possible to understand the size of this undertaking (see Table 6.1).

Table 6.1 Air Traffic Management System Overview (for fiscal year 2019)

Flights Handled Yearly	
Scheduled	10,390,000
Unscheduled	6,015,000
Total	16,405,000
Airspace (millions of sq. miles)	
Oceanic	24.1
Domestic	5.3
Total	29.4
Airports (total number in the United States)	
Public	5,082
Private	14,551
Total	19,633
Air Traffic Control Towers	
Federal	264
Contract	256
Total	520
General Aviation Aircraft (2018)	
Fixed wing	167,600
Rotorcraft	10,000
Experimental, lightcraft, or other	34,200
Total	211,800
General Aviation Flight Hours (FY2018)	25,506,000

Sources: Compiled from FAA data.

One of the key issues that makes the FAA important to homeland security intelligence is that the system failures on 9/11 allowed for three of the hijacked aircraft to make it to their targets. This was a noted component of the 9/11 Commission Report, and in the nearly two decades since those terrorist attacks a significant effort has been put in place to track aircraft, improve the monitoring and notification systems to report aberrations in flight paths by commercial and private aircraft, and to establish protocols to communicate between the FAA and the DOD and DHS.

Conclusion

There are hundreds of agencies throughout the US federal, state, and local governments that are directly responsible for the safety of everything a person is exposed to on a daily basis. From the quality of your drinking water, to the food provided through your grocery stores, to the purity of the alcohol in your evening beer or other beverage, somebody, somewhere, is testing, certifying, and demonstrating that products are okay to be sold, purchased, and consumed. Elsewhere, people are sitting at radar screens directing aircraft from their place of origin to their destination and ensuring that somebody hasn't decided to fly that aircraft into a building where you might live or work. Other people are checking the bridges you drive over to ensure they aren't going to collapse while you happen to be on them. Still others are looking at how the metro system in your community is operating, investigating accidents, and looking for ways to improve your transportation to avoid making you a victim of an accident or simply a faulty signal or computer.

All of these agencies and people are part of the overall homeland security intelligence process. From the water quality technician who is sampling the local water supply down the road from your home to the veterinarian testing for salmonella at the local chicken processing plant—when they find something, or when they see something, they say something. So too should you.

Notes

1. Olmstead v. United States (277 U.S. 438), 1928.
2. Katz v. U.S., 389 U.S. 347, 1967.
3. Peter Kross, "The Venona Project," HistoryNet, https://www.historynet.com/the-venona-project.htm.
4. FBI, "COINTELPRO," https://vault.fbi.gov/cointel-pro.
5. FBI, "First Strike: Global Terror in America," February 26, 2008, https://archives.fbi.gov/archives/news/stories/2008/february/tradebom_022608.
6. Ibid.
7. "Oklahoma City Bombing," History.com, https://www.history.com/this-day-in-history/truck-bomb-explodes-in-oklahoma-city.
8. Ibid.
9. "MK-ULTRA," History.com, June 16, 2017, https://www.history.com/topics/us-government/history-of-mk-ultra.
10. Ibid.
11. Ibid.
12. "Why It Took 17 Years to Catch the Unabomber," History.com, October 25, 2018, https://www.history.com/news/unabomber-letter-bombs-investigation-arrest.
13. FBI, "Unabomber," FBI Famous Cases and Criminals, https://www.fbi.gov/history/famous-cases/unabomber.
14. Darren Tromblay, *Spying: Assessing US Domestic Intelligence Since 9/11* (Boulder: Lynne Rienner, 2019).
15. FBI, "Unabomber."
16. Ibid.

17. "Ruby Ridge," *Encyclopedia Britannica,* https://www.britannica.com/event /Ruby-Ridge.

18. James Phelps has met and worked with Kevin Harris, and the information he provides, which is the same as evidence later presented in a wrongful death lawsuit against the government, is significantly different from that provided by federal agents to prosecutors. It is important to note that Randy Weaver never sold any shotguns, modified or not, to the ATF informant. In the end, to get a prosecutorial case through the US Attorney, the ATF provided their informant with a shotgun, who then gave it to Weaver, who sawed off the barrel and cleaned it up so that the firearm would function without injuring the user. Weaver then returned the modified firearm to the informant. The ATF then acquired an arrest warrant for Randy Weaver and executed that warrant. Weaver was released from jail on bail. ATF and the US Attorney changed the court dates, and Weaver was never informed of the changes. When he failed to show for a changed court date, the ATF raid on his cabin commenced.

19. "Ruby Ridge," *Encyclopedia Britannica.*

20. A major failing of the federal investigation is that friends and neighbors were allowed into the cabin and shed to clean up the horrible mess caused by the death and decay of Vicki's and Sammy's bodies lying in the open air for over eleven days. This resulted in the destruction of a crime scene and evidence. Later, while Weaver was incarcerated, the FBI directed the entire property along with the cabin, shed, and all locations used by the federal agents to be bulldozed and hauled away from the scene. This left no physical evidence for the subsequent court cases brought against the government.

21. "Ruby Ridge," *Encyclopedia Britannica.*

22. Ibid.

23. The sniper received an award for his performance of duty even though there is reason to believe he shot a fourteen-year-old boy and the boy's mother, who was unarmed and holding a baby in her arms, with intent to kill them.

24. Corey Kilgannon and Joseph Goldstein, "Sayfullo Saipov, the Suspect in the New York Terror Attack," *New York Times,* October 31, 2017, https://www .nytimes.com/2017/10/31/nyregion/sayfullo-saipov-manhattan-truck-attack.html.

25. DHS, "Fusion Centers," https://www.dhs.gov/fusion-centers.

26. DHS, "Fusion Center Locations and Contact Information," https://www.dhs .gov/fusion-center-locations-and-contact-information.

27. US Department of Justice, *Fusion Center Guidelines: Developing and Sharing Information and Intelligence in a New Era* (Washington, DC: DOJ Office of Justice Programs, 2006), p. 1.

28. Ibid., p. 2.

29. Ibid., pp. 2–3.

30. FDA, "What We Do," https://www.fda.gov/about-fda/what-we-do.

31. US Department of Transportation, "Mission," https://www7.transportation .gov/about.

32. US Department of Transportation, "U.S. Department of Transportation Administrations," https://www.transportation.gov/administrations.

33. Ibid.

34. Ibid.

35. Ibid.

36. Ibid.

37. Ibid.

38. Ibid.

39. Ibid.

7

Counterintelligence Missions

At this point you know what intelligence is and how agencies apply it to carry out their missions. This chapter looks at counterintelligence and how it is employed by homeland security agencies. To accomplish that, it is important that we start by creating an operational definition of counterintelligence (CI).

The CIA tells us that the concept of strategic counterintelligence remains relatively undeveloped in theory or implementation. Within the DOD, counterintelligence is a component of the agencies that carry out military intelligence, and they define counterintelligence as activities to detect, identify, assess, counter, exploit, and/or neutralize adversarial foreign intelligence services, international terrorist organizations, and insider threats to the US military. Executive Order 12333, as amended, defines counterintelligence as information gathered and activities conducted to identify, deceive, exploit, disrupt, or protect against espionage, other intelligence activities, sabotage, or assassinations conducted for or on behalf of foreign powers, organizations, or persons, or their agents, or international terrorist organizations or activities, but not including personnel, physical, document, or communications security programs.[1]

The *Cambridge Dictionary* defines counterintelligence as "secret action taken by a country to prevent another country from discovering its military, industrial, or political secrets."[2]

Merriam-Webster defines counterintelligence as "organized activity of an intelligence service designed to block an enemy's sources of information, to deceive the enemy, to prevent sabotage, and to gather political and military information."[3]

The Association of Former Intelligence Officers defines counterintelligence in an article published in 2013 in their *Journal of U.S. Intelligence Studies* as "both an intelligence discipline and a national security mission and involves catching spies and putting them in jail; a set of tactical activities to protect and enable successful intelligence operations; the national security function that supplies insights into foreign intelligence threats to the United States, including options to defeat them as national policy may direct; and 'an intellectual exercise of almost mathematical complexity.'"[4]

The DOD Center for Development of Security Excellence further defines counterintelligence as "information gathered and activities conducted to identify, deceive, exploit, disrupt, or protect against espionage or other intelligence activities, sabotage, or assassinations conducted for or on behalf of foreign powers, organizations, or persons or their agents, or international terrorist organizations or activities."[5]

This set of definitions clearly puts counterintelligence within the realm of the FBI, the DOD, and the CIA. There is no homeland security–related CI function except as a feeder of data into the other organizations for analysis and action.

The United States does have a National Counterintelligence Strategy published by the National Counterintelligence and Security Center (NCSC). The 2020–2022 strategy was published on January 7, 2020, under the auspices of and with the signature of President Trump. The strategic objectives of the strategy are as follows:

Protect the Nation's Critical Infrastructure
- Protect the nation's civil and commercial, defense mission assurance, and continuity of government infrastructure from foreign intelligence entities seeking to exploit or disrupt national critical functions. . . .

Reduce Threats to Key U.S. Supply Chains
- Reduce threats to key U.S. supply chains to prevent foreign attempts to compromise the integrity, trustworthiness, and authenticity of products and services purchased and integrated into the operations of the U.S. Government, the Defense Industrial Base, and the private sector. . . .

Counter the Exploitation of the U.S. Economy

- Counter the exploitation of the U.S. economy to protect America's competitive advantage in world markets and technological leadership, and to ensure our economic prosperity and security. . . .

Defend American Democracy Against Foreign Influence

- Defend the United States against foreign influence to protect America's democratic institutions and processes, and preserve our culture of openness. . . .

Counter Foreign Intelligence Cyber and Technical Operations

- Counter foreign intelligence cyber and technical operations that are harmful to U.S. interests.[6]

Within the strategy, the term *homeland security* occurs once, buried in a footnote that references the US election infrastructure as a component of critical infrastructure within the Government Facilities Sector. Otherwise, the whole concept of homeland security is missing from the National Counterintelligence Strategy.

Counterintelligence Within the FBI

The FBI operates a CI program to identify and neutralize ongoing national security threats and is the lead agency responsible for CI. Within the FBI, CI is housed in the National Security Branch. The FBI is the lead agency for exposing, preventing, and investigating intelligence activities on US soil. One way this is clearly demonstrated is that the Department of Energy (DOE) also has an Office of Counterintelligence, established under 42 US Code §7144b to "reduce the threat of disclosure or loss of classified and other sensitive information" at DOE facilities.[7] The DOE CI program must submit annual reports on the effectiveness of its operations to the FBI, the CIA, and Congress.

The goals of the FBI CI organization are as follows:

- Protect the secrets of the U.S. Intelligence Community, using intelligence to focus investigative efforts, and collaborating with our government partners to reduce the risk of espionage and insider threats.
- Protect the nation's critical assets, like our advanced technologies and sensitive information in the defense, intelligence, economic, financial, public health, and science and technology sectors.

- Counter the activities of foreign spies. Through proactive investigations, the Bureau identifies who they are and stops what they're doing.
- Keep weapons of mass destruction from falling into the wrong hands, and use intelligence to drive the FBI's investigative efforts to keep threats from becoming reality.[8]

DHS Program

The DHS Office of Inspector General conducted a review of DHS counterintelligence activities and reported,

> The DHS Counterintelligence Program conducts the department's counterintelligence mission activities at the direction of, and under the authority of the Secretary. The primary mission of DHS' Counterintelligence Program is to prevent adversaries from penetrating the department to exploit sensitive information, operations, programs, personnel, and resources. In addition, the United States Coast Guard provides Coast Guard specific counterintelligence support to the department. Their primary mission is to preserve operational integrity by shielding operations, personnel, systems, facilities, and information from intelligence threats.[9]

Within the DHS Office of Intelligence and Analysis is a Counterintelligence Mission Center, or CIMC. The CIMC promotes a departmental approach to the current and emerging counterintelligence threats facing the country. They collect and deliver intelligence on threats posed by foreign adversaries and intelligence services, and through integrated and coordinated efforts they are able to effectively refine their response to such threats. They also work closely with the larger DHS intelligence enterprise (IE) and national IC partners to identify large-scale threats, implement countermeasures, and enhance resilience across intelligence networks. Through fusion centers DHS shares intelligence between the IC and state, local, tribal, and territorial law enforcement agencies while gathering intelligence from those agencies to share with the IC overall.

Strategic Plan 2020–2024

In the DHS Office of Intelligence and Analysis strategic plan for the five-year period 2020–2024, the term *counterintelligence* only appears thirteen times. All except two of these appearances occur on a single page. The first time *counterintelligence* appears is at the very end of the summary of the homeland strategic environment where the summary concludes,

> During this era of dynamic threats that cross borders in both the physical and digital arenas, I&A (Intelligence and Analysis) will continue to ensure it is positioned to provide intelligence and information on transnational organized crime, terrorism, cyber-threat actors, counterintelligence vulnerabilities, economic security, and other developing threats that pose a critical danger to the Nation's security and our democratic way of life.[10]

Here the idea is to address counterintelligence vulnerabilities. The second time it appears is on page 10 where it is the first of five topical mission goals: "Counterintelligence addresses threats from foreign intelligence entities [FIE] and implements appropriate countermeasures."[11] Note that the application of CI is toward foreign intelligence entities. This raises the question about domestic terrorist organizations' efforts to gather intelligence. Does DHS simply defer that function to the FBI?

Counterintelligence: The Topical Mission Goal

Rather than attempt to recreate and summarize an already very concise topical mission goal of DHS counterintelligence, the authors choose to reprint here the entire page from the plan.

> The current and emerging counterintelligence challenges facing DHS and the HSE [Homeland Security enterprise] require an integrated, whole-of-Department response. Rapid technological advances allow a broad range of Foreign Intelligence Entities (FIE) to field increasingly sophisticated capabilities, and aggressively target the government, private-sector partners, and academia. FIEs are proactive and use creative approaches—including the use of cyber tools, malicious insiders, espionage, and supply chain exploitation—to advance their interests and gain advantage over the U.S. These activities intensify traditional FIE threats, place U.S. critical infrastructure at risk, erode U.S. competitive advantage, and weaken our global influence. In order to effectively identify and assess current and future FIE efforts targeting DHS and the HSE, I&A will drive innovative counterintelligence solutions, further integrate counterintelligence responses into Department business practices, advance Component integration, effectively resource programmatic efficiencies, and continuously assess and refine counterintelligence programs to ensure the HSE remains relevant, responsive, and effective.
>
> Goal 2.1: Expand counterintelligence coordination across DHS, SLTTP [state, local, tribal, territorial, and private], and federal partners to rapidly recognize the contemporary threat environment, identify vulnerabilities, and implement appropriate countermeasures.

- Objective 2.1.1: Advance integrated IE [intelligence enterprise] intelligence activities and collection, including operationalizing DHS-wide datasets, to develop insights and improve understanding of evolving FIE threats against the U.S. Homeland and interests.
- Objective 2.1.2: Increase the production of all-source counterintelligence analytic products on FIE threats, at the lowest classification possible, and joint analytic efforts on FIEs to support counterintelligence activities.
- Objective 2.1.3: Operationalize DHS datasets using data as a service, developing and implementing new intelligence capabilities, to strategically target foreign intelligence operations against the HSE.
- Objective 2.1.4: Increase DHS counterintelligence education and awareness training to identify and report FIE threats against the HSE and the IC.
- Objective 2.1.5: Practice and promote comprehensive, integrated, and unified DHS counterintelligence activities to create a robust DHS-wide counterintelligence program.
- Objective 2.1.6: Increase interaction with SLTTP on FIE threats to critical infrastructure, enabling SLTTP partners to implement appropriate countermeasures.

A FIE is any known or suspected foreign state or non-state organization or persons that conduct intelligence activities to acquire information about the U.S., block or impair intelligence collection by the U.S. Government, influence U.S. policy, or disrupt systems and programs owned or operated by or within the U.S. The term includes foreign intelligence and security services, international terrorists, transnational criminal organizations, and drug trafficking organizations conducting intelligence-related activities.[12]

Note that the focus is on cyber tools, malicious insiders, espionage, terrorists, criminal organizations, supply chain exploitation, and critical infrastructure. Yet, the FBI maintains the primary responsibility for investigating and preventing all cyber crime, international and domestic terrorism and associated organizations, organized crime including transnational criminal organizations, along with the DEA when narcotics are involved. Threats to critical infrastructure are addressed primarily by the various agencies and private corporations that own or operate the infrastructure, such as the National Park Service, Department of the Interior, US Army Corps of Engineers, and the extensive number of private civilian corporations. DHS has no function related to intelligence gathering or actions in any of these areas except where it involves interdicting cross-border efforts where people or contraband are actually attempting to enter or exit the country illegally.

DHS and Counterintelligence

As with much of the DHS enterprise, in the case of counterintelligence, the agency is reaching for some form of validity within its assigned duties and responsibilities while other federal agencies have been clearly designated as the lead for all such activities. Again, you can see in the world of counterintelligence another poorly defined and planned effort to accommodate congressional and presidential directives that are already addressed in federal law and policy as well as in budgets.

When President George W. Bush signed the legislation into place establishing the DHS, he declared somewhat idealistically that

> With my signature, this act of Congress will create a new Department of Homeland Security, ensuring that our efforts to defend this country are comprehensive and united. The new department will analyze threats, will guard our borders and airports, protect our critical infrastructure, and coordinate the response of our nation for future emergencies. The Department of Homeland Security will focus the full resources of the American government on the safety of the American people. This essential reform was carefully considered by Congress and enacted with strong bipartisan majorities.[13]

The DHS was at that point responsible for doing something that had never been done before: coordinating information sharing and collaboration across all levels of federal, state, and local governments as well as traditional and nontraditional intelligence partners. It would do this, theoretically, by incorporating and analyzing information from the FBI, the CIA, the NSA, and others, cross-referencing that information in terms of possible threats to US critical infrastructure; forging lasting relationships with other federal agencies, state and local governments, as well as the private sector, so that needed information flows quickly and effectively; addressing the increasing cyberterrorism threat, in addition to nuclear, biological, and chemical terrorism; and creating effective security efforts focused on protecting the nation's coastline, border, and transportation environments. This effort essentially transformed the intelligence community from one in which there existed the always pragmatic mantra of the "need to know" to the infinitely more expansive "responsibility to share," thus exponentially increasing the number of people with security clearances, along with the associated increased danger of important information getting into the hands of the wrong people.

The Department of Homeland Security was the first federal agency charged with information sharing and collaboration on a relatively huge scale. Specifically given the responsibility was the Intelligence and Analysis section within DHS, although originally named the Office of Information Analysis and Infrastructure Protection. The new department was supposedly going to create a new era of collaboration, integration, and coordination in order to prevent any and all attacks of any kind on the United States, as well as respond to and recover from all said attacks. Of course, no agency had ever done this, effectively, and probably no agency, including DHS, ever will. Some critics of the plan pointed out that the expanded mission of the new department conflicted directly with the mission of the Federal Bureau of Investigation, and wondered whether that would cause confusion, or worse. Areas of ambiguity include those where threats are neither clearly national security nor obvious law enforcement threats, which usually results in an expansion of duplicative intelligence-related activities and an environment in which no agency clearly has primacy.

According to the DHS Office of Inspector General, the primary mission of the DHS Counterintelligence Program is to prevent adversaries from penetrating the department to exploit sensitive information, operations, programs, personnel, and resources. This establishes that DHS CI is fundamentally charged to protect the agency itself from outside attempts at penetration, not to actually carry out national-scale counterintelligence to protect the homeland. The secondary function of DHS CI is to share the information up, down, and across their federal, state, local, tribal, and territorial law enforcement partners. It was initially believed that this would be accomplished primarily through fusion centers.

Fusion Centers and Counterintelligence

According to the DOJ Office of Justice Programs, "The ultimate goal of a fusion center is to provide a mechanism where law enforcement, public safety, and private partners can come together with a common purpose and improve the ability to safeguard our homeland and prevent criminal activity. A police officer, firefighter, or building inspector should not have to search for bits of information. They should know to call one particular place—the jurisdiction's fusion center."[14] In addition to "normal" intelligence, one would think that fusion centers would be interested in gathering and disseminating counterintelligence information. That is an effort that is missing.

The goal of fusion centers to remedy information-sharing shortfalls was one of the primary recommendations of the 9/11 Commission. One of the major failures of the intelligence community prior to 9/11 was an almost complete lack of interagency counterintelligence efforts, for various reasons. Since 9/11, the federal government has strengthened the connection between collection and analysis on transnational organizations and other threats. Terrorism-related information sharing across the intelligence community has seemingly greatly improved, but counterintelligence efforts are still restricted to individual agencies and the FBI.[15]

Moreover, DHS has strengthened the ability to convey intelligence on threats to the homeland in a context that is useful and relevant to law enforcement and homeland security officials at the state and local level. In addition, DHS continues to improve and expand the information-sharing mechanisms by which officers are made aware of the threat picture, vulnerabilities, and what it means for their local communities. Fundamental to this process is the Nationwide SAR (Suspicious Activity Reporting) Initiative (NSI).

Unfortunately, fusion centers do not have any counterintelligence functions or capabilities. One would think that an NSI would work to share counterintelligence as the attacks on one agency are going to be similar to those on another agency and likely conducted by the same entities in the cyber age.

Nationwide SAR Initiative

The NSI is a joint collaborative effort by the US Department of Homeland Security, the Federal Bureau of Investigation, and state, local, tribal, and territorial law enforcement partners. This initiative provides law enforcement with another tool to help prevent terrorism and other related criminal activity by establishing a national capacity for gathering, documenting, processing, analyzing, and sharing SAR information. These are the agencies that participate in the NSI:

- US Department of Justice's Global Justice Information Sharing Initiative
- Crime Stoppers USA
- Criminal Intelligence Coordinating Council
- International Association of Chiefs of Police
- Association of State Criminal Investigative Agencies
- Major Cities Chiefs Association

- Major County Sheriffs of America
- National Fusion Center Association
- National Sheriffs' Association
- Federal Bureau of Investigation
- US Department of Homeland Security
- Office of the Program Manager, Information Sharing Environment
- Bureau of Justice Assistance, Office of Justice Programs, DOJ[16]

The NSI is a standardized process—including stakeholder outreach, privacy protections, training, and technology assistance—for identifying and reporting suspicious activity in jurisdictions across the country and also serves as the unified focal point for sharing SAR information. Much of this is accomplished through fusion centers.

The NSI initiated operations in March 2010 with the challenge of ensuring that regardless of where in the country suspicious activity is reported, these potential indicators of terrorist activity can be shared, analyzed, and compared with other information nationwide. The NSI works to incorporate the informal processes that traditionally exist within law enforcement agencies into the standards, policies, and processes developed by the NSI that allow fusion centers and law enforcement agencies to easily share information with the critical partners that need it to help identify and prevent terrorist threats.

The NSI continues to work with key partners at the SLTT and federal levels of government, as well as with advocacy groups through development of a comprehensive program that includes community and law enforcement outreach, standardized processes, training, privacy protections, and enabling technology. The goals are not only to develop and update the policies and processes of the NSI but also to ensure that Americans' privacy, civil rights, and civil liberties are protected throughout implementation and institutionalization of these processes. The NSI has worked with various advocacy groups, such as the American Civil Liberties Union, to develop protections that make up a comprehensive NSI Privacy Protection Framework. The NSI requires each fusion center to consider privacy throughout the SAR process by fully adopting this framework prior to NSI participation. Working with different advocacy groups and stakeholders in states across the country has served an important role in successfully shaping and implementing NSI policies and processes.

Technology plays a vital role in the NSI process. For the information to be shared across the country, each agency must have a process and a system in place to share SAR. To support the operational mission, the NSI leverages the National Information Exchange Model, which allows the interoperability and seamless exchange of SARs. Through the NSI technology platform, NSI participants can make their SARs available to fusion centers and other NSI participants in an effort to instantaneously share critical information. The NSI was developed to ensure that information received and vetted by a fusion center, regardless of what mechanism is used to receive the information, can be quickly reviewed by the FBI's JTTFs for possible investigation and shared with fusion centers and FBI FIGs for additional analysis.

The Building Community Partnerships initiative was established to assist fusion centers and law enforcement agencies in engaging with and developing productive relationships with the critical sector and community stakeholders they serve to enable partnerships in the protection of critical infrastructure and the prevention of crime and terrorism. The DHS's "If You See Something, Say Something" campaign is a simple and effective program to raise public awareness of indicators of terrorism and terrorism-related crime and to emphasize the importance of reporting suspicious activity to the proper local law enforcement authorities. Both the "If You See Something, Say Something" campaign and the NSI underscore the concept that a secure homeland begins with hometown security, where an alert community plays a critical role in keeping the nation safe.

Suspicious Activity Reporting

Suspicious activity reporting is a concept in which law enforcement and citizens report suspicious activities so that proper evaluation can be conducted and the subsequent information shared with appropriate law enforcement agencies through fusion centers or the FBI Joint Terrorism Task Forces. The easiest way to explain how SAR works is through a personal example. Some years ago, while visiting Houston, Texas, the authors were driving through an area with large petroleum storage tanks and refineries, occasionally stopping to take photos in support of upcoming terrorism training for the Houston Police Department (HPD). At one point, when finishing at the refineries, a security vehicle pulled us over to ask what we were doing. After explaining ourselves, and after the driver of the vehicle showed his HPD badge, we continued on our way to where our training was going to take place. During the training, some of the photos of vulnerabilities in the refinery area were shown, and one of the HPD sergeants in the group shouted out that we were the ones they had received an SAR about. Clearly, the system of recognizing suspicious activity, reporting it even though it wasn't criminal activity, and having the Houston Real Time Crime Center take that report and distribute it through the FBI JTTF, created a situation where multiple agencies were knowledgeable of what could have been terrorist intelligence-collecting activities. Every person should take the initiative to practice the "See Something, Say Something" counterintelligence function, and all law enforcement agencies, even those not part of fusion centers or JTTFs, should be trained in documenting and reporting such activities.

The NSI establishes standardized processes and policies that provide the capability for law enforcement and homeland security partners to share timely, relevant suspicious activity reports while working to ensure that privacy, civil rights, and civil liberties are protected. The NSI SAR Data Repository (SDR) serves as the technology solution for the NSI. State, local, tribal, territorial, and federal law enforcement agencies and state and major urban area fusion centers have multiple options for entry of suspicious activity reports, including the eGuardian User Interface, the SAR Vetting Tool, and various records management systems connected to the SDR.[17]

Before a suspicious activity report can move from an agency system to be shared in the NSI SDR, two levels of vetting must occur: (1) supervisors at source agencies, which initially receive suspicious activity reports or other tips or leads from law enforcement officers, public safety agencies, private-sector partners, or citizens, must initially review each report to determine whether it is eligible for consideration as a terrorism-related suspicious activity report, and (2) trained analysts or investigators at a participating federal agency or fusion center must then analyze the report and make a determination, based on the relevant context, facts, and circumstances, whether the suspicious activity report has a potential nexus to terrorism. If so, the resulting report can be submitted to the SDR for sharing with NSI participants. Throughout the submission, vetting, and sharing process, privacy, civil rights, and civil liberties are vigilantly and actively protected.

Note that the entire basis of the SDR and sharing with NSI is terrorism based!

Suspicious Activity Reporting Indicators and Behaviors

Table 7.1, created by the NSI, shows indicators and behaviors related to SAR.

Table 7.1 Suspicious Activity Reporting: Indicators and Behaviors

Behaviors	Descriptions

Defined Criminal Activity and Potential Terrorism Nexus Activity

Behaviors	Descriptions
Breach/attempted intrusion	Unauthorized personnel attempting to enter or actually entering a restricted area, secured protected site, or nonpublic area. Impersonation of authorized personnel (e.g., police/security officers, janitor, or other personnel).
Misrepresentation	Presenting false information or misusing insignia, documents, and/or identification to misrepresent one's affiliation as a means of concealing possible illegal activity.
Theft/loss/ diversion	Stealing or diverting something associated with a facility/infrastructure or secured protected site (e.g., badges, uniforms, identification, emergency vehicles, technology, or documents [classified or unclassified]), which are proprietary to the facility/infrastructure or secured protected site.
Sabotage/ tampering/ vandalism	Damaging, manipulating, defacing, or destroying part of a facility/infrastructure or secured protected site.
Cyberattack	Compromising or attempting to compromise or disrupt an organization's information technology infrastructure.
Expressed or implied threat	Communicating a spoken or written threat to commit a crime that will result in death or bodily injury to another person or persons or to damage or compromise a facility/infrastructure or secured protected site.
Aviation activity	Learning to operate or operating an aircraft, or interfering with the operation of an aircraft in a manner that poses a threat of harm to people or property and that would arouse suspicion of terrorism or other criminality in a reasonable person. Such activity may or may not be a violation of Federal Aviation Regulations.

Potential Criminal or Non-Criminal Activities Requiring Additional Information During Vetting[a]

Behaviors	Descriptions
Eliciting information	Questioning individuals or otherwise soliciting information at a level beyond mere curiosity about a public or private event or particular facets of a facility's or building's purpose, operations, security procedures, etc., in a manner that would arouse suspicion of terrorism or other criminality in a reasonable person.
Testing or probing of security	Deliberate interactions with, or challenges to, installations, personnel, or systems that reveal physical, personnel, or cybersecurity capabilities in a manner that would arouse suspicion of terrorism or other criminality in a reasonable person.

(continues)

Table 7.1 continued

Behaviors	Descriptions
Recruiting/ financing	Providing direct financial support to operations teams and contacts or building operations teams and contacts; compiling personnel data, banking data, or travel data in a manner that would arouse suspicion of terrorism or other criminality in a reasonable person.
Photography	Taking pictures or video of persons, facilities, buildings, or infrastructure in an unusual or surreptitious manner that would arouse suspicion of terrorism or other criminality in a reasonable person. Examples include taking pictures or video of infrequently used access points, the superstructure of a bridge, personnel performing security functions (e.g., patrols, badge/vehicle checking), security-related equipment (e.g., perimeter fencing, security cameras), etc.
Observation/ surveillance	Demonstrating unusual or prolonged interest in facilities, buildings, or infrastructure beyond mere casual (e.g., tourists) or professional (e.g., engineers) interest and in a manner that would arouse suspicion of terrorism or other criminality in a reasonable person. Examples include observation through binoculars, taking notes, attempting to mark off or measure distances, etc.
Materials acquisition/ storage	Acquisition and/or storage of unusual quantities of materials such as cell phones, radio control toy servos or controllers; fuel, chemicals, or toxic materials; and timers or other triggering devices, in a manner that would arouse suspicion of terrorism or other criminality in a reasonable person.
Acquisition of expertise	Attempts to obtain or conduct training or otherwise obtain knowledge or skills in security concepts, military weapons or tactics, or other unusual capabilities in a manner that would arouse suspicion of terrorism or other criminality in a reasonable person.
Weapons collection/ discovery	Collection or discovery of unusual amounts or types of weapons, including explosives, chemicals, and other destructive materials, or evidence, detonations or other residue, wounds, or chemical burns, that would arouse suspicion of terrorism or other criminality in a reasonable person.
Sector-specific incident	Actions associated with a characteristic of unique concern to specific sectors (e.g., the public health sector), with regard to their personnel, facilities, systems, or functions in a manner that would arouse suspicion of terrorism or other criminality in a reasonable person.

Source: DHS, Nationwide SAR Initiative, "Suspicious Activity Reporting: Indicators and Behaviors," https://www.dhs.gov/sites/default/files/publications/16_0208_NSI_SAR-Indicators-Behaviors-Tools-Analysts-Investigators.pdf.

Note: a. When the behavior describes activities that are not inherently criminal and may be constitutionally protected, the vetting agency should carefully assess the information and gather as much additional information as necessary to document facts and circumstances that clearly support documenting the information as an ISE-SAR (Information Sharing Environment–Suspicious Activity Report).

Suspicious activity reporting has also been designed for and implemented in relation to maritime operations, campus safety, and safety for faith-based events and houses of worship. There are also specialization programs for public health and health care institutions, places where precursor chemicals are sold, fire and emergency medical services, the private security sector, probation/parole/corrections agencies, and public safety telecommunications.

Conclusion

The Department of Homeland Security was created in a time immediately after the United States was attacked, to provide a federal-level agency whose sole purpose was protecting this country from each and every external threat that could conceivably occur, at any point in the future, and also to prove to the American people that their leaders have/had their interests at stake. The first part has more or less come true (with a few notable exceptions), more due to luck than a focused effort applied to the "correct" target. There has been effort, particularly on the part of multiple DHS secretaries, each of whom attempted to recreate the type of department the people expected and the country actually needs, and each failing for different reasons.

When it comes to counterintelligence, DHS has no formal function or capabilities and is dependent upon other federal, state, local, tribal, and territorial agencies. The only indirect counterintelligence function DHS maintains is the interagency sharing of intelligence within fusion centers. It is also responsible for protecting the agency itself from potential penetration by intelligence operatives from other countries, transnational criminal organizations, and the like. As noted in other areas of the text, this has sometimes been successful, yet there are still US Border Patrol (USBP) agents and CBP officers who are working along the US-Mexico border who are former/current drug cartel members or closely related to people within those organizations.

DHS is still unfocused, more due to the initial cacophony of agencies thrown together than anything else. There is no directly enhanced effort toward domestic counterterrorism analysis, which is precisely what America needs, among other things. Somehow, the United States should place into the Department of Homeland Security functions that directly impact domestic security and remove those functions that do not, and that could be better applied in other federal agencies.

Notes

1. Executive Order 12333, 46 Fed. Reg. 59941, 3 CFR (December 4, 1981), https://www.archives.gov/federal-register/codification/executive-order/12333.html.

2. *Cambridge Dictionary*, "Counterintelligence," https://dictionary.cambridge.org/dictionary/english/counterintelligence.

3. *Merriam-Webster's Dictionary*, "Counterintelligence," https://www.merriam-webster.com/dictionary/counterintelligence.

4. M. K. Van Cleave, "What Is Counterintelligence? A Guide to Thinking and Teaching About CI," *Journal of U.S. Intelligence Studies* 20, no. 2 (Fall/Winter 2013): 58.

5. Center for Development of Security Excellence, "Counterintelligence Glossary," https://www.cdse.edu/documents/glossary/CI-glossary.pdf.

6. Office of the Director of National Security, *National Counterintelligence Strategy of the United States of America, 2020–2022* (Washington, DC: ODNI, 2020), https://www.hsdl.org/?abstract&did=833930&utm_source=hsdl_cr&utm_medium =email&utm_campaign=hsdl_cr_2020-02-12.

7. 42 US Code §7144b Office of Counterintelligence.

8. FBI, "What We Investigate: Counterintelligence," https://www.fbi.gov/investigate/counterintelligence.

9. DHS Office of Inspector General, "DHS' Counterintelligence Activities (Summary)," July 29, 2010, p. 1, https://www.oig.dhs.gov/assets/Mgmt/OIG_10-97_Jul10.pdf.

10. DHS, *Office of Intelligence and Analysis Strategic Plan FY 2020–2024* (Washington, DC: DHS, 2020), p. 5.

11. Ibid., p. 10.

12. Ibid., pp. 11–12.

13. George W. Bush, *The Department of Homeland Security*, June 2002.

14. *Fusion Center Guidelines: Developing and Sharing Information and Intelligence in a New Era* (Washington, DC: US Department of Justice, 2006), pp. 1–4.

15. Darren E. Tromblay, *Spying: Assessing US Domestic Intelligence Since 9/11* (Boulder: Lynne Rienner, 2019).

16. DHS, "NSI Partners," https://www.dhs.gov/nationwide-sar-initiative-nsi/nsi-partners#.

17. Nationwide SAR Initiative, http://nsi.ncirc.gov.

8

Domestic Threats and National Security

Many of the threats to homeland security are also threats to national security. These include the issues of narcotics trafficking, terrorism (both domestic and international), critical infrastructure protection and vulnerabilities, and cyberthreats. Some are wholly within the borders of the United States while others span the globe. Yet both homeland and national security functions of the government have a responsibility to address all of these threats, among others.

Narcotics Trafficking

The greatest narcotics trafficking threat to US security is posed by the Mexican drug trafficking organizations (DTOs), primarily because of their geographical proximity and history of smuggling and violence within Mexico.[1] These organizations are considered to be the greatest criminal threat due to their ability to operate relatively freely in Mexico and to the existence of smuggling networks throughout the United States.[2] They have been identified for their strong links to drug trafficking, money laundering, and other criminal enterprises, and have trafficked heroin, cocaine, methamphetamine, marijuana, and, increasingly, the synthetic opioid fentanyl. In fact, overdoses of opioids sharply increased in 2016 due to expanded control of the heroin and synthetic opioid markets by Mexican criminal organizations.[3] Further, the primary drug trafficking organizations have increased their expansion into illegal criminal activity such as extortion, kidnapping, and oil theft.

The number and breadth of Mexico's DTOs has changed in recent years. Former Mexican president Felipe Calderón (2006–2012) began an aggressive campaign against the drug trafficking organizations after he took office. By 2006 there were four dominant DTOs: the Tijuana/Arellano Félix (AFO) organization, the Juárez/Vicente Carrillo Fuentes (CFO) group, the Gulf Cartel, and the Sinaloa Cartel. Operations to remove leadership of the cartels resulted in much instability within the groups and continued violence between the groups and the government.

After leaders were removed, either by arrest or death, larger and relatively stable organizations fractured, leading the US Drug Enforcement Administration (DEA) and other analysts to list seven major DTOs: Los Zetas, Tijuana/AFO, Juárez/CFO, Sinaloa, Gulf, Beltrán Leyva, and La Familia Michoacana. These include what are considered to be the "traditional" drug trafficking organizations, although several have fractured further, leaving as many as nine (or possibly as many as twenty) major organizations currently in operation. A new transnational criminal organization, which split from Sinaloa in 2010, the Jalisco New Generation Cartel, has used brutal violence in an attempt to become dominant.

Mexico has seen a spike in homicides, passing 29,000 in 2017.[4] The DTOs exercise significant geographical influence in parts of the country, especially near drug production hubs and along drug trafficking routes. Total homicides in the country rose 7 percent during 2015, 22 percent in 2016, and 23 percent in 2017.[5] Simply killing individuals does not seem to be the ultimate goal, since beheadings, public hanging of corpses, and murders of dozens of media personnel as well as government officials seem to be almost daily occurrences. The drug cartels want to see their work on the front pages of every newspaper in the larger cities in Mexico.

The violence has spread geographically, from the border with the United States to the interior of Mexico, from the Pacific states of Guerrero and Michoacán, in the border state of Tamaulipas, and in Chihuahua and Baja California, where the largest border-region cities of Tijuana and Juárez are located. Criminal organizations have both splintered and turned to diverse activities, including kidnapping, auto theft, human smuggling, oil smuggling, extortion, retail drug sales, and other illicit operations.

Concerns have also been raised regarding possible human rights violations attributed to Mexican military and police forces, which, at times, allegedly have been assisting Mexico's drug trafficking organizations within both Mexico and the United States.[6] The Mexican armed forces injured or killed some 3,900 people in domestic operations between 2007 and 2014, with official reports labeling the deaths as related to "civilian aggressors." The actual death rate was very high (about 500 were injuries and the rest were killings by Mexican officials), which indicates the extreme lethality of any and all encounters with Mexican military and police.

Official reports did not note how many of the civilians were armed or were merely innocent bystanders. Significantly, official statistics were no longer made available by the Mexican government after 2014.[7]

Violence is an intrinsic part of the illicit drug trade. Violence is used to instill fear in subordinates in order to maintain discipline and discourage possible theft of drugs and/or money as well as to settle disputes and maintain order with creditors, suppliers, and buyers. However, the violence associated with Mexican drug cartels in that country currently is not only related to settling disputes or maintaining discipline but also has been directed toward political candidates, the media, and government officials. This inter-cartel rivalry and associated narcotics-related violence has crossed into major US cities since the early 1980s.

Capturing the leaders of the cartels and extraditing them to the United States has been an agenda for Mexican presidents since the 1980s and the era of Pablo Escobar, the head of the Medellín Cartel in Colombia. Historically, cartel leaders have been afraid of the possibility of extradition to the United States for good reasons, among them the increased difficulty of breaking out of US maximum-security prisons as opposed to Mexican institutions of incarceration. The Mexican government increased the number of extraditions between 2007 and 2012, as part of much closer US-Mexican security cooperation. The majority of the persons undergoing extradition were wanted by the US government on drug trafficking and related charges. A possibly unintended consequence of the increase in the number of extraditions was a corresponding increase in the number of accusations of human rights violations against the Mexican military, largely untrained in domestic policing operations.

When Peña Nieto took office as the new president of Mexico in 2012, he began a "militarized" strategy toward the drug cartels, theoretically more focused on reducing the violence toward civilians and businesses by the cartels, and less on removing the cartel leadership. The Mexican attorney general in 2012, Jesús Murillo Karam, said that the Mexican government faced between sixty and eighty criminal groups operating in the country, including drug cartels, whose proliferation he attributed directly to the prior president's "kingpin strategy" of arresting or killing the most notorious leaders of the organizations.[8] Analysts note that, in spite of the public statements of both the president and attorney general in 2012, the strategy of taking down by arrest or execution the leaders of the cartels has apparently continued unabated.

The Mérida Initiative, an anticrime package between the United States, Mexico, and Central American countries, began in 2008 and focused at that time on the United States providing Mexico with antinarcotics trafficking money and police/military hardware, including aircraft, scanners, and other equipment. The initiative, which began under President Calderón, cost the United States $2.9 billion (through 2017) and has recently shifted focus to US training and technical assistance for Mexico's local and state police, southern border security enhancements, and crime prevention. After some reorganization of initiative efforts, the Nieto administration continued the Mérida programs.

The potential violence attributed to Mexico's transnational criminal organizations, including the drug cartels, is due at least in part to their efforts to transport their drugs and to expand aggressively into the heroin (plant-based) and synthetic opioid markets. Mexico is the major supplier of heroin to the United States, according to the DEA, and opium poppy cultivation has increased in recent years, reaching an estimated 32,000 hectares in 2016. The increase in Mexican poppy production led to tripling the amount of heroin produced between 2013 and 2016, estimated by the DEA to have risen from twenty-six to eighty-one metric tons.[9]

According to the Wilson Center's Mexico Institute, "Since surging into the market in 2013, fentanyl has become the most lethal category of opioid in the United States." The Centers for Disease Control and Prevention (CDC) estimated that more than 47,000 people died from an opioid overdose in 2017 in the United States—28,000 of those deaths were due to synthetic opioids, which the CDC says is largely the result of the uptick in abuse of fentanyl.[10] According to the DEA's National Forensic Laboratory Information System, in 2012 there were fewer than 700 identification requests that showed fentanyl-family results in the United States. In 2016 the number of fentanyl-family results had risen to over 32,000 cases, which jumped to 56,530 cases in 2017.[11] Additionally, the market share of fentanyl-family opioids jumped from second place in 2016 to first place in 2017, exceeding all other opioids including pharmaceutical drugs.[12]

Fentanyl and its precursors are primarily sourced from China and routed to the United States through Mexico. The US State Department reports there are an estimated 160,000 chemical companies operating legally or illegally in China where the poor regulation of the industry allows fentanyl precursor chemicals such as ANPP (4-anilino-N-phenethyl-4-piperidine) and NPP (N-phenethyl-4-piperidinone) to be diverted by criminal groups. IBISWorld reported in 2018 that China has become the world's second largest producer of pharmaceuticals and precursor chemicals, bringing in annual revenue of $122 billion legally and illegally. According to Dudley et al., Mexico has become the primary transit point for shipments of synthetic opioids, such as fentanyl, primarily through the ports of Manzanillo in the state of Colima and Lázaro Cárdenas in Michoacán, where the port managers, customs officials, and others have been corrupted by drug cartels, particularly the Familia Michoacana. Dudley et al. report that the precursors are shipped to storage and production points in and around Mexico City, Guadalajara, and Culiacán before being processed into pill form and shipped to the United States concealed within otherwise legitimate shipments.[13]

Fentanyl has fueled the ongoing drug wars in Mexico along with the fracturing of the larger DTOs into smaller groups and gangs. It is a ready and easy form of revenue for up and coming criminal groups without the large-scale production and logistical needs of the crystal methamphetamine and heroin producers. The creation of smaller criminal groups, both transnational criminal organizations and local small mafias with trafficking or other crime specialties, has made the overall intelligence situation more diffuse and much more difficult in terms of addressing the criminal behavior from a homeland security perspective.

The Changing Nature of Transnational Crime Organizations

The larger hierarchical drug trafficking organizations have in some cases morphed into flatter, more responsive organizations that tend to be more loosely networked. The smaller criminal groups tend to use more outsourcing of some aspects of trafficking and resist any restrictions on violence. The increase in the number of groups has produced continued violence, and in some cases has created the extremes of brutality seen in newspaper headlines in an attempt to intimidate competitors, the public, or the government. Or, the cartels seek to mask their crimes by somehow insinuating that other cartel agents are responsible. Sometimes shootouts are not reported due to media or government self-censorship or because the bodies simply disappear.[14]

A major issue with the decapitation of Mexican cartel leadership is that with the ongoing combat between and within organizations the level and manner of violence have escalated significantly. Continued efforts to accurately tabulate the number of persons who simply disappear have been stymied, a problem exacerbated by underreporting, as well as the problem that twenty of Mexico's thirty-one states have no biological databases needed to identify unclaimed bodies. Government estimates of the exact number of people who have simply disappeared have varied, particularly those who have gone missing as a result of possible force or homicide. Sometimes bodies simply turn up in mass graves, as in the case of the missing forty-three students in Iguala, Guerrero, where the Mexican police and victims' families located scores of unmarked graves.[15] In March 2017 a mass grave was unearthed near Veracruz that contained approximately 250 skulls and other remains, some of which were years old. A general estimate of the total number of disappeared persons during the term of former governor Javier Duarte, in office from 2010 to 2016, is greater than 5,000 people.[16]

Drug trafficking organizations have operated with relative impunity in Mexico for a very long time. DTOs can be described practically as global criminal organizations with linkages for managing real-time supply and distribution in various countries. Much like modern corporations, they operate their business to maximize efficiency to increase profits. Mexican drug cartels are the primary wholesalers of illegal narcotics in the United States and are attempting to gain control of retail-level distribution using alliances with US gangs. Currently, the violence directly associated with their operations is distinctly less than in Mexico even though they reportedly have a presence in multiple US jurisdictions.[17] Drug cartels use bribery and corruption, and if that doesn't work, they resort to the threat of violence or actual violence to achieve their ends. Cash from drug sales or money laundering is used to corrupt US and Mexican border officials.[18] In addition, Mexican police and military are paid by the DTOs to either ignore or actively support and protect DTO drug shipments.[19] In the early 1900s Mexico was a source of heroin and marijuana to the United States, and by the 1940s the situation was much worse. The government in Mexico during that time was under one-party rule by the Institutional Revolutionary Party, which governed for a total of seventy-one years. It tolerated and protected some drug operations in certain parts of the country, which facilitated the growth of the industry. For many years, particularly during the

1970s and 1980s, the Mexican government pursued an overall policy of accommodation with the drug cartels. Some arrests and crop eradications took place, primarily for some newspaper space, but overall there existed a "working relationship" between the government and cartel leaders in Mexico and surrounding countries, including Colombia, such as Pablo Escobar, the leader of the Medellín Cartel in the 1980s and 1990s.[20] In order to understand the current threat from drug cartels, it is necessary to take a look at the history of drug smuggling in North and South America.

Police officers in the United States are well aware of a phenomenon that occurs when law enforcement attempts to shut down a particular type of crime in a specific location. US law enforcement has learned by experience that by focusing resources (officers, plainclothes detectives, etc.) in the area and concentrating on stopping the criminal activity, whatever it is, it is possible to do so, at least temporarily. However, what usually happens is that once the criminals have left that area, they simply move to another area or jurisdiction and continue their operations. This is known as displacement, and it happens every year in every major city in the United States. Something similar happened in Colombia in the 1980s and 1990s in the drug trade.

Pablo Escobar and the Medellín Cartel

The biggest and most feared drug dealer in the twentieth century was born on December 1, 1949, in Rionegro, Colombia, a collection of relatively prosperous cattle farms outside Medellín. His full name was Pablo Emilio Escobar Gaviria. He died violently on December 2, 1993, in Medellín, as the head of the Medellín Cartel and was at the time arguably the world's most powerful drug trafficker. *Forbes* magazine listed Escobar as the seventh-richest man in the world in 1989, and his violent reputation made him the most feared terrorist in the world.[21]

The story of Pablo Escobar and the Medellín Cartel is the precursor to today's chaotic world of drug cartels and criminal organizations that are growing and smuggling billions of dollars' worth of narcotics into this country and others—after a declared war on drugs by the United States in the early 1980s. In spite of a major national effort, drug trafficking cannot be stopped. Apparently, neither can it be slowed down, and neither can Mexico or Colombia stop it. The heads of current drug cartel organizations learned from Pablo Escobar. He grew up on the streets and obtained the equivalent of an advanced degree in "street psychology" that taught him how to control production, harvest, marketing, transportation, and retail of the world's most dangerous narcotic. Others are doing the same thing now, following in Escobar's footsteps and using his methods. The threat to this country is real, and growing.

Escobar understood the power of the outlaw mystique and built on his and nurtured it. He was a vicious sociopathic thug, with a social conscience. He built homes, hospitals, and playgrounds for the poor. When he died, he was mourned by thousands. Escobar was a complex contradiction, with a genius for manipulating public opinion, but the crowd-pleasing quality he possessed was also his downfall. He simply was not content to just be very rich and extremely powerful. He wanted to be respected and loved.

In the mid-1970s something happened that transformed Escobar and his friends from fairly successful lower-level criminals into international drug smugglers: the American pot generation discovered cocaine, which became the fashionable drug of choice for young professionals. By the end of the decade, Escobar, Jorge Ochoa and his brothers, José Rodríguez Gacha, and Carlos Lehder earned phenomenal wealth by forming what became the Medellín Cartel. By 1980 they controlled more than half the cocaine shipped to the United States, resulting in a profit measured in billions of dollars. This became the largest export industry in Colombia, and by the mid-1980s Escobar owned nineteen residences in Medellín alone, each with a heliport. He owned fleets of boats and planes, properties in Colombia, apartment buildings, housing developments, and banks. In spite of his wealth, and how he had earned it, Escobar sàw himself as a man of the people, correctly or incorrectly, and, as such, felt that he should go into politics, to truly represent his people. In 1978 he ran and was elected as a substitute city councilman in Medellín; that year, he helped underwrite the presidential campaign of Belisario Betancur, who lost. In 1982, however, he ran for Congress as a substitute for Envigado representative Jairo Ortega, and they won the election. But when Escobar tried to take his alternate seat in Congress, he was denounced by the new minister of justice, Rodrigo Lara, as a known criminal and drug dealer. The Medellín newspaper reporters investigated and discovered Escobar's 1976 arrest for cocaine possession. Escobar was dismissed from the New Liberal Party, and a warrant was issued for his arrest. At the same time, the justice minister signed an arrest and extradition order for Carlos Lehder, the first time the new extradition agreement signed in 1979 with the United States was implemented. Three months later the minister of justice was murdered, hit by seven bullets from a fully automatic machine pistol. His family was in Texas, living under assumed names for protection.

The Start of the War on (Medellín) Drugs

In 1982 President Ronald Reagan created a cabinet-level drug task force led by Vice President George H. W. Bush to coordinate the nation's efforts against drug smuggling. At that point, drug cartel leaders became both military and law enforcement targets. A CIA intelligence estimate in June 1983 reported that "these [Colombian] guerrilla groups initially avoided all connections with narcotics growers and traffickers. . . . Now, however, several have developed active links with the drug trade . . . and some apparently use profits from drugs to buy arms."[22] The new Colombian justice minister was completely on board with the US policy and gave permission for the US State Department to test new herbicides on coca fields in Colombia.

In March 1984 government forces struck two heavy blows against the Medellín Cartel. Under orders from Minister Lara, the PNC (La Policia Nacional de Colombia) raided a large cocaine-processing facility on the Yari River, consisting of fourteen labs and camps that housed forty workers. Fourteen metric tons of cocaine were seized, the largest amount seized in history up to that date. In the months preceding the Yari River raid, Colombian troops had destroyed seven airstrips and planes used by the Medellín Cartel, along with 12,000 chemical drums containing over $1 billion worth of cocaine. It had been the worst month ever for the cartel. Less than a month later, Minister Lara was dead, murdered in his chauffeur-driven Mercedes in northern Bogotá by an ex-convict on a motorcycle with a machine pistol.

Lara's murder created a backlash against Escobar and the Medellín Cartel. Cocaine would never again be considered by the public or Colombian politicians as "just another" industry. Killing the minister of justice was considered to be an act of war against the state. President Betancur authorized the National Police to begin confiscating Escobar's estates and other assets, and he vowed at Lara's grave to enforce the extradition treaty with the United States, the only thing that Escobar ever truly feared.

Shortly after the murder of Justice Minister Lara, Pablo Escobar boarded a plane bound for Panama. When he arrived, he found the other leaders of the cartel, José Rodríguez Gacha, Carlos Lehder, and the

Ochoa brothers, already there seeking exile. Several years earlier, a representative of the commander of the army of Panama, Manuel Noriega, had approached the cartel leaders with an offer of safe haven in that country for $4 million, which they had accepted. However, when all of them showed up at the same time, Noriega, now plotting to become dictator of Panama, did not welcome them. His side deals with Oliver North and a burgeoning marijuana smuggling business were already occupying most of his time. One thing he did not want or need was to have Panama become the new world capital of cocaine smuggling.

However, Escobar had no intention of spending the rest of his life in that country. In May, shortly after fleeing Colombia, he and Jorge Ochoa met with a former president of Colombia, Alfonso Lopez, to make an offer: He and the other leaders of the Medellín Cartel would "dismantle everything" and return billions made from cocaine smuggling to the banks in Bogotá. In return, the cartel leaders asked to be officially forgiven for all past crimes, and for a change in the extradition treaty with the United States. All Pablo wanted was to go home and live with his fortune in Medellín without fear of arrest or extradition.

It was a generous offer, at least on paper, but the anger in the country and in the United States over Lara's murder was still so great that the deal was politically untenable. Pablo left Panama after the Panamanian army double-crossed him, raiding one of his lab complexes on the border. Some of Ochoa's men were falsely accused of attempting to murder Noriega. Escobar flew to Managua, where he met with one of his drug-smuggling pilots, Barry Seal.

Seal had been busted by the DEA in Florida and had made a deal with the government to avoid a lengthy prison term: he would become an informant. He flew a C-137 transport plane to Managua in 1984 to pick up a 750-kilogram cocaine shipment. A camera hidden in the cockpit of the plane by Seal prior to the trip to Managua clearly picked up both Pablo Escobar and Rodríguez Gacha as they supervised loading the C-137. When the DEA viewed the film later they wanted to set up a sting to lure Escobar, Gacha, and possibly Lehder and the Ochoa brothers to Mexico where they all could be arrested and flown to the United States for trial. Escobar's orders to Barry Seal were simple: the cartel leader wanted the pilot to bring him ten-speed bicycles, video recorders, Scotch, cigarettes, and $1.5 million in cash.

The DEA film caused a sensation in Washington. Oliver North in particular saw the film as a major public relations coup. It showed Colombian narcotic kingpins shipping cocaine from Nicaragua and was extremely helpful to the Reagan administration in arguing for continued funding for the Contras, the prodemocracy rebels fighting the Sandinista regime. Since it was political dynamite, of course, the film soon leaked, first to the head of the US Army's Southern Command, General Paul Gorman, who told a meeting in San Salvador that the world would "soon see proof" that the Sandinista regime was in league with the cocaine cartels, and then to the *Washington Post*. Articles about the film appeared in the *Post* soon after Seal delivered the goods to Escobar. Seal was murdered two years later in Baton Rouge, Louisiana, by one of Escobar's gunmen, after surprisingly refusing to enter the US Witness Protection Program.

After the mess in Panama and then Nicaragua, Escobar simply returned to Colombia and decided that no matter what, he would never leave home again. Extradition to the United States was the one thing that Escobar feared, along with a cell in a US prison. In the fall of 1985 Escobar once again offered to turn himself in if he was given a promise of no extradition to the United States. Again he was refused.

In November 1985 the guerrilla group M-19 stormed the Palace of Justice in Bogotá and demanded that the government renounce the 1979 extradition agreement with the United States. They also destroyed over 6,000 criminal records, which just happened to include those of Pablo Escobar. It was discovered later that Escobar had paid the group $1 million for the raid.

In April 1986, President Reagan signed the classified National Security Directive 221, declaring the flow of drugs into the United States to be a national security threat. The murder of the Colombian justice minister pushed both the Colombian and US governments to consider the cocaine cartels and their leaders not simply law enforcement targets but also military ones.

In 1986, a highly publicized University of Maryland basketball star became the trigger of a dramatic shift in public support for the president's declared war on drugs. Len Bias, the number one draft pick of the National Basketball Association, had been chosen by the Boston Celtics, one of the premier teams in the United States. In June of that year, after the draft, Bias attended a campus party and, perhaps celebrating his multimillion-dollar draft status, snorted cocaine and collapsed and died. The flirtation of White affluent youth with the infamous drug had more or less run its course by that point, but the death of the college basketball star sealed its fate. Suddenly the glamour drug of movie stars and star athletes became the death drug. Cocaine had been on the streets for at least a decade in the cheaper more obtainable form preferred by Black youths, known as crack, but until the sons and daughters of White congressmen became addicted to the white powder form, it was relatively ignored. However, not so after the widely publicized death of Len Bias. The drug cartel leaders became the authors of a modern-day plague and enemies of the state.

Escobar played all the hands he had. He had his lawyers approach the US attorney general in 1986 with an offer to trade intelligence information about communist guerrilla groups in return for amnesty. He was refused. He also turned in a longtime cartel associate, Carlos Lehder, who was arrested and immediately extradited from Bogotá to Tampa, Florida, by the DEA. Following Escobar's betrayal, Lehder was sentenced to 135 years in prison.

President Reagan was very serious about Escobar and the threat of smuggled cocaine. Declaring drug trafficking a threat to national security opened the door to direct military involvement, which became for the first time a mixture of military power and law enforcement. Beginning that summer, US Army troops joined Bolivian police and DEA agents in raiding cocaine-processing labs in Bolivia.

President George H. W. Bush's administration upped the ante, moving from intercepting boats and planes at the border to attacking the South American poppy plantations. The US government had seized Escobar's Florida homes and property. Bush had campaigned in 1988 saying that he wanted to take direct military action against drug traffickers in other countries, and it was very clear exactly to which countries he was referring. As president, he declared a war on drugs and signed National Security Directive 18, which called for $230 million worth of military, intelligence, and law enforcement assistance to fight the South American drug cartels over the succeeding five years. Another $65 million was authorized by the president for emergency military aid to Colombia alone, and he authorized sending US Special Forces troops to that country to train its police and military in tactics. The president had always said that sending US troops to a country to counter the cartel threats would depend entirely on the approval of the host country, but that was eroding in the face of the perceived increasing danger to the United States. US spending on the war on drugs increased over the next five years from $300 million in 1989 to over $700 million by 1991.

The Use of Operational Intelligence

The hunt for Escobar escalated. Colombia created a special police force to hunt Escobar along with other cartel leaders, such as José Gacha and the Ochoa brothers. In addition, part of the military "package" supplied by the United States was a group of intelligence specialists trained by the army to assist with operational intelligence. The specialists provided timely, specific information (such as the location of the target).

The name of this intelligence operations group had been changed many times, but at that moment it was called Centra Spike. Its primary effectiveness was in locating people via radio or cell phone signals using aerial triangulation. Used in World War II, triangulation could at best locate a signal to a relatively large area. In Vietnam, direction-finding using triangulation could isolate a signal to within half a mile. Twenty years later, in Colombia, Centra Spike could pinpoint a signal to within two hundred yards, and the group could do this from a single small aircraft, by taking readings from multiple points along the plane's semicircular path around a source. The CIA conveniently set up a bogus cover story using a fake corporation name, Falcon Aviation, allegedly hired to conduct a survey of Colombia's VOR (VHF omnidirectional radio range) beacons. VOR beacons are primarily used to establish pathways to airports for planes. Centra Spike used twin-engine Beech-craft 300 and 350 planes with state-of-the-art electronic eavesdropping and direction-finding equipment.

When Centra Spike was first operationalized in Colombia, the first target was someone considered to be one of the top men in the Medellín Cartel, José Rodríguez "El Mexicano" Gacha, who often wore a Panama hat with a snakehead on the headband. With an estimated worth of $5 billion, US intelligence believed him to be the real power in the Medellín Cartel. It did not take the group long to locate the alleged cartel leader. Gacha had been hiding at his estate north of Bogotá and communicating with a woman in Bogotá periodically. When this information was passed to the US embassy and then to the DEA, Centra Spike began listening for his cell phone calls. With direction-finding ability to within two hundred yards, they immediately located him on a *finca* southwest of Bogotá, the only conspicuously elegant place within miles. The location was passed along to the CIA station chief and then to Colombian president Barco, who immediately ordered the Colombian Air Force to launch T-33 fighter-bombers to attack the *finca*. US embassy officials were surprised that the Colombians would immediately make plans to kill everyone there. This did not happen, however, simply because the lead air force officer called off the attack when he saw a small village just beyond the hilltop location where Gacha was staying. If one bomb overshot the target, it would obliterate the village and kill scores of innocent civilians. The planes did fly over the drug kingpin at about fifty feet, which startled him (as well as everybody else at the location). He immediately left the *finca*, which was raided the next day by a police unit using helicopters. The unit confiscated $5.4 million in cash at the villa and arrested several of Gacha's lieutenants who had stayed behind at the compound.

Gacha moved around the country frequently after that, never staying for long at any one place. He finally settled in a cabin near the border of Panama, in a remote, heavily forested area. The Colombian police were able to locate him with the help of an informer, a cocaine smuggler from Cartagena, who had been working as a spy for the Medellín Cartel's rivals in Cali. The Cali Cartel leaders had a vested interest in getting rid of the Medellín Cartel's leaders so they had begun quietly assisting the police. A coordinated police assault was planned for December 15, 1989. Just in case, a group of US Delta Force and Navy SEALs were standing by on the USS *America*, just off the coast. As the police assault helicopters descended on Gacha and his bodyguards, they fled the house and ran toward a nearby banana grove. According to the police report, they fired automatic weapons toward the helicopters and the on-board police used their own Israeli machine guns to cut them down.

Helped by intelligence from Centra Spike, the Colombian police unit assigned to track down Escobar and his associates tightened the ring around Pablo. In June 1990 John Arias was killed, one of Escobar's most trusted *sicario* leaders. The following month the cartel's treasurer, Hernan Henao, was captured. Henao was Pablo's brother-in-law and a trusted associate. On August 9 his closest friend from his days of skipping school and stealing cars, Gustavo Gaviria, was killed "in a shootout with police," as the official report put it. This official phrase was widely regarded as a euphemism for summary execution.

Pablo believed that his cousin and friend was simply captured, tortured, and then executed by the police. In October another of Pablo's cousins, Gustavo's brother Luis, was also "killed in a shootout with the police." The new Colombian president, César Gaviria, also extradited three suspected drug dealers in the first two months of his administration. What happened in the ensuing months was more like a chess match than a life or death struggle within a nation. Escobar continued a series of kidnappings and bombings to increase pressure on the politicians to make him and the other drug kingpins an offer that included no extradition and no prison time. For his part, the new Colombian president was put under increasing pressure to do just that. He did offer better and better deals, including, weeks before Christmas, that those who confessed to a single minor charge would serve only a reduced prison term, with no extradition. Fabio Ochoa gave up and turned himself in on December 18, the day after the president made the public offer. Over the next two months his two brothers in the cartel, Jorge and Juan David, also turned themselves in.

But Pablo wanted a better deal, one with *no* prison or possibility of extradition to any other country, particularly the United States. So, the killings continued. In January and February of 1991 there was an average of twenty killings a day in Colombia. In Medellín, 457 police officers had been murdered since the Colombian police had begun hunting Escobar and the other cartel leaders. Young cartel members were being paid five million pesos for killing a cop.[23] To garner public support for his position, Escobar began to release the hostages he had been holding for months. It somehow all worked. On June 19, 1991, over the protests of US ambassador Thomas McNamara and DEA (Bogotá) chief Robert Bonner, the Colombian Constitutional Assembly voted to formally outlaw extradition. Pablo had won the game.

He was sent to a prison that he had personally overseen construction on, La Catedral, located at the top of Mont Catedral, which overlooked the city of Medellín. Just in case, Pablo and his brother had buried an arsenal of rifles and machine guns on a slope close to where their "cells" would be located. As part of his plea deal, the drug kingpin confessed, more or less, but the lone admission of guilt was for his part in a French drug deal as a middleman, arranged by his dead cousin Gustavo. Pablo emphasized his innocence and noted that he was surrendering only in order to clear his name by appealing his conviction in France of the drug deal.

The prison was gradually turned into a resort. Anything Pablo wanted could be brought in. Escobar had entrusted the cartel operations to two primary families, the Galeanos and the Moncadas, but over time Pablo became distrustful of both, believing they were conspiring to steal from him, and eventually he had both Galeano, Moncada, and their brothers killed. The families of both men went to the police, complaining that both had vanished after visiting Escobar at La Catedral. The Colombian president was finally forced to act.

The president sent for Vice Minister of Justice Mendoza to let him know that he was ordering the army to attack La Catedral and bring Escobar back to Bogotá. Mendoza ended up as a hostage taken by Escobar's men. President Gaviria was furious and ordered Colombian Special Forces to attack the prison. They did, and somehow Escobar escaped through an entire brigade of Colombia's army.

Centra Spike was once again called back to Colombia, along with other agents of the US government. In the latter part of 1989, Defense Secretary Dick Cheney (future vice president Cheney) had sent a memo to military commanders ordering them to define counterdrug efforts as "high-priority national missions" and asking for plans for increased military commitment. Cheney had realized what military commanders had figured out: with the decreased threat of communism, the US military and high-priced espionage agencies had become a highly skilled workforce in search of a role. It did not take a genius to figure out that big budget cuts were on the way, *unless* a new enemy was found, and Escobar and narcoterrorists like him could be that enemy. The CIA and the NSA both wanted to be in the new fight and prove themselves flexible and smart enough to be effective against the new target. Centra Spike was brought back to Colombia, and the CIA moved in a U2 spy plane as well.

Using triangulation, Centra Spike sourced Escobar to a middle-class neighborhood in Medellín called Los Olivas near the city's football stadium. Members of the Colombian Police Search Bloc used CIA direction-finding equipment to isolate the cell source signal to a particular building, based on signal strength and frequency. On December 2, 1993, they found him. Escobar usually tried to confuse his pursuers by speaking from the backseat of a moving taxi, but on that day, he was on a balcony of a second-story apartment building in Los Olivas. Hugo Martínez, a member of the police unit, saw him talking on a cell phone. Police raided the apartment, which had a heavy metal door. The Search Bloc members used a sledgehammer on it. Once inside, they found the first floor empty, but they saw a taxi parked near the rear of the building. Escobar's driver and bodyguard, Limon, jumped out a back window of the second floor of the apartment and was immediately shot by Search Bloc police using automatic weapons. Escobar followed and was also cut down by automatic gunfire. Autopsy reports indicated he was hit three times: one round in the leg above the knee, one in the back just below his right shoulder, and one round directly in his right ear.

Centra Spike and the army intelligence and CIA specialists at the time of Escobar's capture and killing were state of the art, and the best at what they did. When the USSR disbanded in the early 1990s, and the US military realized that they needed a new threat in order to substantiate the billions of dollars allocated each year for military expenditures, they seized on drug cartels and the president's war on drugs as an alternative. Military units and resources were switched from pursuing Cold War/Russian threats to drug interdiction. Upwards of $10 billion per year was allocated to the drug war until the September attacks in 2001. Since that point, resources both military and civilian are still fighting the war (including DHS and homeland security intelligence) and struggling against the ongoing smuggling, with arguable success.

The Sinaloa Cartel

Among the various groups that are currently active, the Sinaloa Cartel is the most dangerous, according to the DEA, due to its historical domination of the Mexican drug trade, its advantageous geographic location, and its organizational adaptability. The Sinaloa Cartel is one of the more dominant Mexican DTOs in recent history. The organization has a diverse history of trafficking many types of drugs, including marijuana, cocaine, methamphetamine, and heroin via distribution centers in large cities such as Phoenix, Los Angeles, and Chicago.[24] It is believed that in 2012 the organization had control of approximately 60 percent of Mexico's drug trade and annual proceeds as high as $3 billion.[25] According to June Beittel, "Sinaloa operatives control certain territories, making up a decentralized network of bosses who conduct business and violence through alliances with each other and local gangs."[26] Sinaloa agents contract local gangs to conduct specific specialized operations for the organization. The leadership structure has been described as horizontal. It is believed that El Chapo served more as a symbolic leader rather than a directly functioning one after being arrested again in 2016. In more recent years there has been splintering within the cartel. Still, the cartel maintains an impressive transnational footprint and key territories in Mexico and the United States that keep the organization profitable.

The geographical advantages of the cartel have truly propelled its business. The cartel started in the Mexican state of Sinaloa but quickly expanded to control vast portions of the US-Mexican border. The cartel controls much of Baja California and Sonora and has fought the Juárez Cartel for control of Chihuahua.[27] These Mexican states form much of the US-Mexican border and stand opposite of California, Arizona, New Mexico, and Western Texas. What is of more concern to US officials are the inroads the Sinaloa Cartel has made deep into the United States. The DEA reports the cartel has trafficking hubs in many cities, including Los Angeles, Phoenix, Denver, and Chicago and operations from Southern California to New England.[28] The DEA reported that a Chicago-based street gang, the Conservative Vice Lords, had a lucrative business relationship with the Sinaloa Cartel. Per the report, the cartel would traffic an average of 1,500–2,000 pounds of cocaine to Chicago monthly, and the gang would return \$4–\$10 million a week to Mexico.[29]

Finally, the last key to the Sinaloa Cartel's success is its organizational adaptability. Like most other Mexican cartels, the Sinaloa Cartel has been affected by the Mexican government's counternarcotics campaign. Following the arrest of El Chapo, cartel operations have continued normally under the Sinaloa banner, with the exception of some infighting for control of the cartel. This is due in large part to the organization's horizontal and decentralized organization.[30] The horizontal distribution of authority allows for greater operational security for the organization as it allows for flexibility in situations when leadership may be captured or killed. Others can quickly step in as temporary or permanent leaders.

The Sinaloa Cartel offers a brief view of the standard Mexican cartel organization. All the large-scale cartels in Mexico follow a flat organizational structure under a central head that directs operations through a group of *plaza* chiefs. When interlopers enter an area under control of a given cartel, the plaza chief is responsible for regaining control and not only chasing away the interlopers but making examples of them so as to discourage other upstarts who might interfere with the cartel's money stream. This has led to significant open and public battles between cartels and plaza chiefs to take lucrative territories away from other cartels. The continuous deadly violence is akin to open warfare, particularly when the decapitation process used by the DEA and Mexican government eliminates cartel leadership. Much like a hydra from mythology, simply removing the head of the organization doesn't kill or eliminate it, but instead offers an opportunity for multiple more vicious heads to rise. This process significantly compounds the difficulty of intelligence gathering and counternarcotics efforts of both US and Mexican government agencies.

Terrorism and Drug Trafficking

Across the globe there are relationships between terror groups and drug trafficking organizations and also terror groups that have incorporated drug trafficking into their own portfolio. This link between terrorism and drug trafficking may be stronger with some groups than others. It is still true, however, that many terror organizations count on drug trafficking as at least a minor income source. This relationship between terrorism and drug trafficking, often referred to as narcoterrorism, is widespread, and governmental efforts to curb its influence have had mixed results.

The United Nations Office on Drugs and Crime (UNODC) offers a brief assessment of terrorism's and drug trafficking's relationship in the *World Drug Report 2017*. The UNODC reports that terror groups in Central Asia, Africa, the Middle East, and South America are involved to some level in the drug trade. Groups in Africa such as Boko Haram and al-Qaeda in the Islamic Maghreb are complicit in assisting the trafficking of cannabis, cocaine, and heroin from Mexico and Colombia.[31] The report also notes that the Taliban is estimated to have made $150 million in 2016 from opium poppy and heroin sales alone.[32] It has been reported that the Islamic State has also embraced the drug trade, and uses amphetamines on its foot soldiers in an effort to bolster their battlefield effectiveness. Additionally, Islamic State members and affiliated groups have been linked to smuggling cocaine through Africa and cannabis through Syria and Turkey.[33] All of these groups have taken advantage of areas where the government does not have the capacity to implement an effective rule of law.

The Sinaloa Cartel is one example of a transnational drug trafficking organization with massive reach in Mexico and the United States. In addition, the cartel is believed to have outposts in Peru and Colombia to facilitate the transport of cocaine.[34] According to the Congressional Research Service, the cartel has a presence in over fifty countries and at its height controlled around 40 to 60 percent of Mexico's drug trade.[35]

In addition to the organization's prolific drug smuggling activities, the Sinaloa Cartel has a long history of using violence to achieve its goals. Mexican drug trafficking organizations have committed atrocious acts of violence including kidnapping, assassination, torture, intimidation, and mass killings.[36] Cartels have used these tactics in many ways. Not only have they targeted and killed rival cartel members, they have used these fear tactics to silence politicians, journalists, and even students.[37]

While drug trafficking organizations may not have a single ideological motivation, their use of violence certainly mirrors that of various terror groups. Commonly, terrorism can be understood as the use of violence to instill fear in a population to coerce the population to submit to the terror group's demands or ideology. The only unifying ideology for drug cartels is that of generating massive financial revenue through illicit activity. Thus, cartels are businesses that use fear in an attempt to intimidate the public into accepting the status quo. Cartels often use the internet to circulate videos of torture and execution, similar to current operations of ISIS and al-Qaeda. They employ their own narco-musicians as popular music bands to sing their praises and generate a public follow-ing. Much like terrorist organizations, cartels often leave bodies and narcomantas in public places where large numbers of people can view the displays as a symbol of the government's and other cartels' and con-ventional criminals' ineffectiveness. While the Sinaloa Cartel and Mex-ican drug trafficking organizations in general may not be conventional terror groups, it is clear that they use similar terror tactics and media outreach to further their criminal ambitions.

The effectiveness of counternarcotic strategy varies depending on the area. One of the worst failures of counternarcotic activities was and is Afghanistan. Despite joint action between the United States, the Afghan government, and the United Nations, the opium poppy contin-ues to thrive in the country. In 2017, twenty-four of Afghanistan's thirty-four provinces cultivated the opium poppy, and potential opium production was estimated at 9,000 tons. This estimated production is 87 percent higher than the previous year.[38] Despite various degrees of US involvement in the country since 2001, the Taliban continues to profit from opium and heroin production, much of which is trafficked to Rus-sia and Europe.

There have been more successful counternarcotic operations in other countries. In South America, particularly in Peru and Colombia, officials have seen drastic reductions in both areas used for drug pro-duction and the number of people killed by nonstate armed groups. Over the period from 1992 until 2015 Peru saw land used to cultivate coca reduced by 70 percent, and Colombia saw a 70 percent reduction from 2000 to 2013.[39] Coinciding with this reduction of coca cultivation, Peru saw killings by nonstate armed groups fall from 818 in 1992 to 6 in 2016.[40] Homicides related to drug smuggling in Colombia fell from 426 in 2000 to 137 in 2013.[41] US participation in South American coun-ternarcotic operations includes multiple departments: the Department of Defense assisting in intelligence sharing; the Bureau of International Narcotics and Law Enforcement Affairs assisting in the destruction of coca plants and cultivation; and the US Agency for International Devel-opment helping to address some of the root causes that motivate rural farmers.[42]

The War on Drugs

The US war on drugs has failed primarily due to the inability to ade-quately quell the demand for drugs. US efforts to curb drug production and trafficking globally have been effective to varying degrees; however, any counternarcotic program progress is undercut if there is still a large population purchasing illegal drugs. The US strategy in large part has hinged on supply interdiction and reducing cultivation, but in order to treat the cause, the United States must implement more policies that address drug consumption domestically and that solve the economic and political problems in foreign nations that lead to drug production.

Largely, the war on drugs has focused (at least in the United States) on shutting down the supply of drugs and arresting drug users and suppliers. Despite the continuing massive cost and effort dedicated to supply interdiction, this has not had the intended result of winning the drug war. The actual result of this strategy is an environment in which the demand for drugs has not been reduced and the legal restrictions levied on the products have created a state of "denied demand." Madsen argues that this state of denied demand is fertile ground from which organized crime can grow and what has led to the development of the powerful drug trafficking organizations of today.[43] Despite these supply interdiction policies, the *World Drug Report 2019* estimates that in 2017 approximately 271 million people aged fifteen to sixty-four had used drugs at least once during the previous year, which corresponds to 5.5 percent of the population; 585,000 people died as a direct result of drug use in 2017, and some 35 million people had drug dependency disorders.[44] During the late 1990s, pharmaceutical companies assured the medical community that patients could not become addicted to prescription opioid pain relievers, and doctors began to prescribe them at greater rates. This led directly to increased usage and misuse of both prescription and nonprescription opioids before it became increasingly clear that these medications could indeed be highly addictive. More than 47,600 people died from an overdose of an opioid in 2017, including prescription opioids, fentanyl, and heroin.[45] Supply reduction efforts are futile if the demand of users is not also reduced concomitantly.

To reduce demand in the United States more emphasis should be given to the public health dimension of reducing drug use. There will always be the need for supply interdiction; however, the most important step is stopping the reason that drugs are flowing to the United States. The success of supply interdiction plans such as the Mérida Initiative and Plan Colombia are often undone by cartels fracturing and reforming or coca production being reduced one year, only to surge the next.[46]

In a recent United Nations special session on drugs, a joint panel hosted by the UNODC and World Health Organization comprised of addiction science experts from UN member nations collaborated to produce a set of recommendations. These recommendations were meant to be used to transform drug abuse reduction policy toward the public health realm. Included in the recommendations are measures to remove stigma from drug abuse, offer more rehabilitation programs to drug users instead of criminal punishment, implement evidence-based prevention and treatment programs, and engage many divergent parties in policymaking.[47] By embracing these concepts, it could be possible to solve the root cause of the drug problem—demand—versus the drug problem's symptoms—crime, abuse, and violence.

The Threat of Terrorism

Terrorism is a topic in its own right, and there are many great resources available to the reader. For the purposes of this text, terrorism is a concern for homeland security intelligence in that interdiction is essential before a terrorist commences an actual attack. As the (now retired) police chief Paul Branham of Greeley, Colorado, once said to students in a terrorism course taught by author Dr. James Phelps, "Once a terrorist leaves his home, somebody is going to die. We have to prevent the terrorist from actually implementing his plan." For homeland security intelligence this is the ultimate goal in addressing terrorism. This problem can be clearly seen in the cases of Major Nidal Hasan, who attacked and killed troops and civilians in a shootout at Fort Hood, Texas, in November 2009,[48] or in the Tsarnaev brothers' attack near the finish line of the Boston Marathon on April 15, 2013.[49] In both instances there were indications ahead of time, other people who knew something but didn't say anything, and the inaction of those people resulted in loss of life.

This problem isn't going to disappear. With the attack on the Murrah Federal Building in Oklahoma City on April 19, 1995, Timothy McVeigh and Terry Nichols implemented a wholly new form of terrorism in the United States.[50] The homegrown terrorist with a penchant for large visual displays of destruction was created. No longer was terrorism restricted to events overseas. No longer was it targeted at small groups of people by highly radicalized political or racial groups with access to small improvised explosive devices and firearms. This was an attack that drew a massive media presence with continuous visuals broadcast around the world. And it was a major failure of intelligence! It was clearly not the last of its kind and was built upon by many others over the decades. Yet such attacks against critical infrastructure, such as a federal building, are rare events. Most attacks against critical infrastructure are lone-wolf attacks but not at the scale of the McVeigh-Nichols bombing. They tend to be single-shooter attacks, with a limited visual impact. Terrorism is primarily about creating a strong visual impact that can be replayed constantly to remind the victims and supporters of the effectiveness of the group and how unsafe individuals might be as a result of their government's actions or inactions.

Domestic terrorism can come from different sources. Violence can originate from right-wing, racially motivated ideologies, or it can come from single-minded individuals with little more than eventual suicide on their minds, such as the recent Las Vegas shooter, Stephen Paddock. On October 1, 2017, Paddock, a former Postal Service worker, accountant, and real estate developer, fired more than 1,100 rounds from his suite on the thirty-second floor of the Mandalay Bay Hotel during the Route 91 Harvest music festival. Paddock, 64, killed 58 and wounded 422 between 10:05 and 10:15 p.m.[51] Approximately an hour later, as police stormed his room, he was found dead from a self-inflicted gunshot wound. According to the FBI, his motive for the shootings remains undetermined. The agency concluded that there was "no single or clear motivating factor" behind the massacre. Lone-wolf shooters like Paddock are extremely difficult to apprehend prior to the act because there is no intelligence or evidence that anyone can find or collect to ascertain possible critical action, beforehand, aside from the acquisition of multiple firearms of different calibers, along with thousands of rounds of ammunition, obtained legally. Right-wing extremism is a form of domestic terrorism.

Right-Wing Extremism

The most well-known forms of right-wing extremism are White nationalist groups that promote White supremacist or White separatist ideologies, but other types exist. Groups such as Aryan Brotherhood, Aryan Brotherhood of Texas, Aryan Nations, Blood and Honour, and Brotherhood of Klans generally all promote White supremacist ideologies and denounce non-Whites as inferior, based solely on race.

Adherents of these groups believe that race should be the primary principle of countries that make up Western civilization. Members advocate for policies that promote White identity and against reverse demographics that do not support an absolute, White majority. A major key is to end non-White immigration, both legal and illegal, for White nationalists who wish to preserve White racial hegemony.

White nationalists want to return to the United States that predated the implementation of the Immigration and Nationality Act of 1965 as well as the 1964 Civil Rights Act. The groups believe that this legislation, in particular, led to White dispossession and the so-called White genocide—the idea that Whites in America are being systematically replaced.

Supporting the above idea are two myths of White nationalists: the narrative of Black-on-White crime, the idea that the White majority is under constant threat of attack by violent people of color; and "human biodiversity," the theory that scientists are working to create a society of humans with non-negligible genetic differences.

Charleston Church Shooting

On June 17, 2015, Dylann Roof, a twenty-one-year-old White supremacist, shot and killed nine African Americans during a prayer service at the Emanuel African Methodist Episcopal Church in Charleston, South Carolina.[52] Three other victims survived the attack. Roof was arrested in Shelby, North Carolina, the morning after the attack. He confessed to the shootings in the hope of starting a race war. The Episcopal Church was founded in 1816 and is one of the oldest American Black churches, and it had long been a site for community organization centered on civil rights. Denmark Vesey, one of the original cofounders of the church, was suspected of plotting a slave rebellion in Charleston in 1822. Charleston residents accepted the claim that a slave rebellion was to begin on June 17, 1822, and thirty-five people, including Vesey, were hanged and the church was burned to the ground. The 2015 shooting occurred on the 193rd anniversary of the alleged uprising.

Shortly after 9 p.m. on Wednesday, June 17, 2015, Charleston police received calls reporting a shooting at the Emanuel African Methodist Episcopal Church. A White man described as around twenty-one years old, approximately five feet nine inches tall, wearing a gray sweatshirt and jeans, opened fire with a Glock 41, a .45 caliber handgun, on a group of people attending a Bible study. In the hour preceding the attack, according to witnesses who survived the shooting, thirteen people including the shooter attended the Bible study. Witnesses claim that Roof walked into the church and asked for the senior pastor, state senator Clementa C. Pinckney, and sat down next to him. He initially listened to others during the study but disagreed when they began discussing Scripture. After waiting for the others in the group to begin praying, he stood up, removed a gun from a fanny pack, and began shooting. Roof reloaded five times, and the shooting lasted for approximately six minutes.

The shooter was found competent to stand trial in federal court, and he was convicted in December 2016 of thirty-three federal murder and hate crime charges stemming from the shooting. Roof was sentenced to death as a result of the federal convictions on January 10, 2017. He was also charged with nine counts of murder in the South Carolina state courts. He pleaded guilty on all counts in order to avoid a second death sentence.

Roof had posted photographs on the internet showing him posing with emblems associated with White supremacy and with the Confederate battle flag. The shooting at the church triggered national debate on the display of the Confederate flag, which resulted in the South Carolina General Assembly voting to remove the flag from State Capitol grounds.

Other state congressional assemblies and city councils also voted to remove Confederate flags and monuments, including the Charlottesville City Council in Charlottesville, Virginia. This led various White supremacist, alt-right, neofascist, and White nationalist groups to plan a rally to protest the decision of the Charlottesville City Council to remove the Confederate monuments and memorials from public places.

Unite the Right Rally

The Unite the Right Rally was a rally organized to promote White nationalism. It occurred in Charlottesville, Virginia, on August 11–12, 2017. Rally protesters were members of alt-right, neo-Confederate, neofascist, neo-Nazi, Klansmen, and White nationalist groups. The stated goals of the organizers of the rally included unifying the American White nationalist movement and protesting the city council decision to remove the statue of Robert E. Lee from Lee Park in Charlottesville.

The rally was initially planned as a result of the controversy surrounding the removal of Confederate monuments throughout the country in response to the Charleston church shooting in 2015. Organizers hoped to counter the negative publicity surrounding both the church shooting and the national outcry to remove any and all monuments to the Confederacy. The rally turned violent after protesters fought with counterprotesters, which left more than thirty people injured. This resulted in the governor of Virginia, Terry McAuliffe, declaring a state of emergency. Shortly after that, the Virginia State Police declared the Unite the Right Rally to be an unlawful assembly. Around 1:45 p.m. local time on August 12, James Alex Fields Jr. rammed his car into a crowd of counterprotesters about a half mile away from the rally, killing Heather Heyer and injuring nineteen other people. Fields initially fled the scene but was arrested shortly afterward. He was later tried and convicted in Virginia state court of premeditated murder. In 2019 Fields pled guilty to twenty-nine federal crimes in a deal to avoid the death penalty.

The rally and associated violence triggered a national backlash against White nationalist and White supremacist groups in the country. Various groups that participated in the rally had subsequent events canceled by universities and social media accounts closed by major companies. President Trump's initial remarks on the rally were criticized because he did not seem to denounce the marchers explicitly when he condemned "hatred, bigotry, and violence on many sides." Later, when he stated that he condemned neo-Nazis and White nationalists, his first statement and his subsequent defenses of it were seen by some as implying moral equivalences between the White nationalist marchers and those who protested against them.

Tree of Life Synagogue Massacre

The right-wing extremist violence continued. On October 27, 2018, Robert D. Bowers walked into the Tree of Life Synagogue in Pittsburgh, Pennsylvania, and began shooting indiscriminately into the crowd of worshipers, killing eleven and wounding four police officers and two other people.[53] After exchanging gunfire with police, he barricaded himself into a third-floor room, eventually surrendering. He was later taken to Allegheny General Hospital and treated for wounds. It was unclear whether his wounds were self-inflicted or he was wounded by the police.

Robert Bowers was forty-six years old at the time of the shooting. He was born on September 4, 1972, and was a resident of Baldwin, Pennsylvania. He attended Baldwin High School from August 1986 until November 1989, when he dropped out and worked as a trucker. Neighbors described him as a loner, rarely interacting with others. Coworkers described him as a staunch conservative, which transformed over time into White nationalism. Online, he promoted anti-Semitic conspiracy theories through social media.

The Tree of Life congregation shooting was the deadliest attack on the Jewish community in the United States. Bowers, according to the *New York Times*, has been charged with twenty-nine federal crimes, including obstructing the free exercise of religious beliefs, a hate crime, and using a firearm to commit murder. In addition to the federal charges, he also faces state criminal charges, including eleven counts of criminal homicide, six counts of aggravated assault, and thirteen counts of ethnic intimidation.[54]

Right-wing extremism continues to be a major threat to the United States. Somehow, Americans must ensure that ethnic hatred does not transpose into indiscriminate violence against individuals.

Threats Against Critical Infrastructure

The real consequential threat of terrorism isn't against individuals or cities, but against critical infrastructure—the networks and assets that are essential for the functioning of a society, its economy, and the public's health and/or safety. This is the place where there can be significant environmental and economic impacts, and with a very large loss of life should a terrorist be successful. Yet, there are few instances of significant attacks against critical infrastructure, the exceptions being the 9/11 attacks against the Pentagon and the World Trade Center, and the Murrah Federal Building in Oklahoma City. However, the attack on the Pentagon had minimal effect and loss of life at the target, in comparison to what happened at the WTC. The World Trade Center was never intended to be brought down. In Bruce Lawrence's *Messages to the World*, Osama bin Laden said the intent was to leave two blackened and smoking fingers pointing to heaven for all to see for years to come, not two holes in the ground filled with rubble.[55] The goal was visual impact. Had the goal been significant economic and cultural impact on the target, the United States, then the planes would have struck the New York Stock Exchange and the Capitol Building during a State of the Union Address.

The only publicized planned terrorist attack against critical infrastructure is that of the Los Zetas drug cartel against Falcon Dam on the lower Rio Grande in 2010.[56] The dam provided an accessible target, and had the attack been carried out, millions of people downstream could have been killed or injured, or at least forced to evacuate. All of the downstream bridges carrying people and commerce across the Rio Grande would have been washed away, significantly impacting US and

Mexican commerce. Wide expanses of farmland would have been removed from production for years. And, from the Zetas perspective, the Golfo Cartel operations to import drugs into the United States would have been ended, thus eliminating a major competitor in the marketplace.

The attack on Falcon Dam was never conducted for any number of reasons, but most likely because the Department of Homeland Security issued a warning based on "serious and reliable sources" to first responders on both sides of the US-Mexico border.[57] The Mexican military stepped up its presence on the approaches to Falcon Dam while the USBP and Texas Department of Public Safety established a strong presence on the US side of the river.

The Cyber Threat

Emil Metropoulos and Jeremy Platt, writing for Marsh & McLennan *Insights,* tell us that in 2017 the dynamic of cyberattacks changed with the introduction of WannaCry and NotPetya.[58] These two attacks alone impacted business and government organizations across over 150 countries, prompted business interruption and financial losses over $300 million, compromised hundreds of thousands of client data, and caused extensive reputational damage to those affected. These two attacks "exposed a systemic risk and affected a broad cross-section of businesses without specific targeting, demonstrating the potential for escalation in the threat of cyber terrorism."[59]

The small-scale or single attacker will continue to be a concern for everybody, and a difficult target for law enforcement to address. However, traditional physical processes carried out by (internet-isolated) industrial control systems—including critical infrastructure industries such as power utilities, water treatment services, and health and emergency systems—are already online. Metropoulos and Platt write that thirty billion connected devices will be in use by 2030, creating more assets susceptible to attack and adding more vulnerabilities to be exploited.[60] The number of highly skilled hackers is increasing, often with support from nation-states such as China and North Korea. This coincides with development of much more sophisticated tools that are constantly seeping into the broader environment through an online black market. As more companies, agencies, governments, and individuals are ever more dependent upon their computer systems and access to data, any interference with those assets can significantly impact market capitalization, endanger individual and corporate financial accounts, and offer the terrorist an opportunity to destabilize entire countries overnight.

Ransomware Strikes: City of Baltimore

Cyberattacks against cities using ransomware is the latest form of cyber threat, at least in the United States. In May 2019 hackers encrypted key files used by the City of Baltimore's service employees. City workers were unable to use their government email accounts or conduct routine city business. This followed an attack a year earlier when a separate cyberattack shut down the city's 911 emergency phone system for about a day. Among other problems, the current ransomware attack had prevented residents within the city from obtaining building permits. As the name suggests, the hackers use malicious software to block access to or take over a computer system or program until the owner pays a ransom to unencrypt or release the system or program. However, there is no guarantee that even if the city pays the money (in this case 13 bitcoin, or approximately $76,280), the system will be released, unharmed, so to speak. Some ransomware attacks end with the data lost and/or unretrievable, even if the ransom is paid. Similar attacks have targeted the United Kingdom's National Health Service, shipping giant Maersk, and various city, county, and state governments in the United States and Canada.

In terms of major threats to the US culture, and survival, however, this is not the most critical of our concerns. The recent coronavirus pandemic is an example of a threat that could (theoretically, at least) result in the contamination of every human on earth.

Future Threats

In 2007 the Idaho National Laboratory initiated the Aurora Generator Test to demonstrate how vulnerable the electrical grid of the United States was to cyberattack.[61] The control system for the electrical generator was air-gapped from the internet, yet a simple change in the operating code through a remote wireless interface caused the generator to physically destroy itself. Today, every electrical grid across the world, and the equipment that generates the electricity transmitted by those grids, is vulnerable to attacks that more than disrupt, they destroy. And this type of attack can originate from anywhere in the world, at any time, and as a result of any provocation, or no provocation at all. How does homeland security intelligence address this threat; contribute to the resiliency of privately owned power generation, transmission, and distribution systems; and still maintain a functional economy? Much like the Japanese attack on the forces in Hawaii on December 7, 1941, this particular danger is not a matter of if, but of when. Can the assets of the homeland security intelligence systems across the country, along with our allies, create a climate and culture of resiliency before the vulnerability is exploited?

Even this may be the least of our intelligence worries. Today, with CRISPR (a ribonucleic acid–guided genome engineering method), it is possible to genetically alter the human genome. Somewhere, in some lab, experiments are being conducted that could possibly kill everybody if released. Not even state and local law enforcement, and certainly not the populace, know where all these bio labs are, or who runs them. Only level 4 bio labs are tracked by the government. A level 3 bio lab could exist in your neighborhood with all the equipment necessary to conduct genetic splicing and modifications and you would never know.

Timothy McVeigh and Terry Nichols simply drove up to a fertilizer sales center and purchased hundreds of pounds of ammonium nitrate, the base of their improvised explosive device. Nobody reported the sale to police. Today, you couldn't do that without somebody asking questions—we hope. However, you can order all the equipment for a full bio lab from Amazon, and it will be delivered to your door, no questions asked. You can order samples of specific viruses from the CDC and they will ship them to you. In March 2018, FedEx shipped five package bombs delivered to their Austin, Texas, facilities to targets in the same city. Even with a massive federal, state, and city law enforcement manhunt for the perpetrator, until a bomb prematurely exploded at the FedEx Ground facility in the Austin suburb of Schertz, Texas, there were no clues as to the perpetrator.[62]

Conclusion

The nature of the terrorism and threats facing society has changed over the past thirty years, and you can expect them to continue to change in the future. In the past, people depended on local law enforcement agencies to conduct counterterrorism investigations and operations after a labor strike, the bombing of a bank or police station by political radicals, or attacks on religious institutions. Then, with the advent of large-scale events, such as the Murrah Building bombing, the shift was to governments and insurers to address mitigation strategies and responses appropriate to wholly new targets. From 9/11 to now Americans have experienced a number of smaller, less sophisticated, yet no less appalling acts of terrorism across the world that involve mass casualties and events intended to instill fear in specific populations. The threat typology will continue to change as new technology and new opportunities become available to terrorist and criminal organizations as well as the disgruntled individual. Homeland security intelligence needs to be constantly evolving as the world changes around us and threats evolve. This is the quandary investigators face: to be reactive or proactive to emerging threats in a rapidly changing world.

Notes

1. DEA, *2017 National Drug Threat Assessment* (Arlington, VA: US Drug Enforcement Administration, 2017).

2. Ibid.

3. June S. Beittel, "Mexico: Organized Crime and Drug Trafficking Organizations" (CRS Report No. R41576, Washington, DC, Congressional Research Service, updated July 28, 2020), https://fas.org/sgp/crs/row/R41576.pdf.

4. Ibid.

5. Laura Calderón, Octavio Rodríguez Ferreira, and David A. Shirk, "Drug Violence in Mexico: Data and Analysis Through 2017" (Justice in Mexico Special Report, University of San Diego, Dept. of Political Science and International Relations, April 2018).

6. James Phelps, Jeff Dailey, and Monica Koenigsberg, *Border Security,* 2nd ed. (Durham: Carolina Academic Press, 2018).

7. S. Fisher and P. J. McDonnell, "Mexico Sent in the Army to Fight the Drug War, Many Question the Toll on Society and the Army Itself," *Los Angeles Times,* June 18, 2018.

8. Patrick Corcoran, "Mexico Has 80 Drug Cartels: Attorney General," InSight Crime, December 20, 2012, https://insightcrime.org/news/analysis/mexico-has-80-drug-cartels-attorney-general/.

9. DEA, *2017 National Drug Threat.*

10. S. Dudley, D. Bonello, J. López-Aranda, M. Moreno, T. Clavel, B. Kjelstad, and J. Restrepo, *Mexico's Role in the Deadly Rise of Fentanyl* (Washington, DC: Wilson Center Mexico Institute, 2019), https://www.wilsoncenter.org/publication/mexicos-role-the-deadly-rise-fentanyl.

11. DEA, "National Forensic Laboratory Information System: NFLIS-Drug 2017 Annual Report" (2018), https://www.nflis.deadiversion.usdoj.gov/Desktop Modules/ReportDownloads/Reports/NFLIS-Drug-AR2017.pdf.

12. DEA, "National Forensic Laboratory Information System: 2016 Annual Report" (2017), https://www.nflis.deadiversion.usdoj.gov/DesktopModules/Report Downloads/Reports/NFLIS2016AR_Rev2018.pdf.

13. IBISWorld, "Pharmaceutical Manufacturing Industry in China: Industry Market Research Report," September 2018, https://www.ibisworld.com/industry-trends/international/chinamarket-research-reports/manufacturing/pharmaceutical/pharmaceutical-manufacturing.html; Dudley et al., *Mexico's Role in the Deadly Rise of Fentanyl*; US Department of State, Bureau of International Narcotics and Law Enforcement Affairs, "2014 International Narcotics Control Strategy Report (INCSR)," March 2014, https:// www.state.gov/j/inl/rls/nrcrpt/2014/vol1/index.htm.

14. Phelps, Dailey, and Koenigsberg, *Border Security*; C. Sherman, "Drug War Death Tolls a Guess Without Bodies," Associated Press, March 26, 2013.

15. J. Bargent, "2014: A Record Year for Disappearances in Mexico," InSight Crime, November 20, 2014.

16. P. J. McDonnell and C. Sanchez, "A Mother Who Dug in a Mexican Mass Grave to Find the 'Disappeared' Finally Learns Her Son's Fate," *Los Angeles Times,* March 20, 2017.

17. DOJ, *National Drug Threat Assessment* (Washington, DC: US Department of Justice, National Drug Intelligence Center, February 2010).

18. L. Riesenfeld, "Mexico Cartels Recruiting US Border Agents: Inspector General," InSight Crime, April 16, 2015.

19. Phelps, Dailey, and Koenigsberg, *Border Security*.

20. F. E. Gonzalez, "Mexico's Drug Wars Get Brutal," *Current History,* February 2009.

21. Mark Bowden, *Killing Pablo: The Hunt for the World's Greatest Outlaw* (New York: Atlantic Monthly Press, 2001).

22. Ibid., p. 43.

23. Ibid.

24. DEA, *2017 National Drug Threat Assessment.*

25. Beittel, "Mexico."

26. Ibid., p. 14.

27. Ibid.

28. DEA, *2017 National Drug Threat Assessment.*

29. DEA, *Cartels and Gangs in Chicago* (Arlington, VA: Drug Enforcement Administration, 2017), https://www.dea.gov/docs/DIR-013-17%20Cartel%20and%20Gangs%20in%20Chicago%20-%20Unclassified.pdf.

30. Beittel, "Mexico."

31. UNODC, *The Drug Problem and Organized Crime, Illicit Financial Flows, Corruption and Terrorism* (Vienna: United Nations Office on Drugs and Crime, 2017).

32. Ibid.

33. C. Clarke, "ISIS Is So Desperate It's Turning to the Drug Trade," *The RAND Blog,* July 25, 2017, https://www.rand.org/blog/2017/07/isis-is-so-desperate-its-turning-to-the-drug-trade.html.

34. P. Chalk, "Profiles of Mexico's Seven Major Trafficking Organizations," *CTC Sentinel,* January 2012, pp. 5–8, https://ctc.usma.edu/profiles-of-mexicos-seven-major-drug-trafficking-organizations/.

35. Beittel, "Mexico."

36. D. Agren, "Mexico Maelstrom: How the Drug Violence Got So Bad," *Guardian,* December 26, 2017, https://www.theguardian.com/world/2017/dec/26/mexico-maelstrom -how-the-drug-violence-got-so-bad; Beittel, "Mexico."

37. Beittel, "Mexico."

38. UNODC, *Afghanistan Opium Survey 2017: Cultivation and Production* (Vienna: United Nations Office on Drugs and Crime, 2017).

39. UNODC, *The Drug Problem and Organized Crime,* p. 40.

40. Ibid., p. 41.

41. Ibid.

42. US Government Accounting Office, *2017 Annual Report: Additional Opportunities to Reduce Fragmentation, Overlap, and Duplication and Achieve Other Financial Benefits,* GAO-17-491SP (Washington, DC: GAO, April 26, 2017).

43. F. G. Madsen, "International Narcotics Law Enforcement: A Study in Irrationality," *Journal of International Affairs* 66 (2012): 123–141, https://blackboard .angelo.edu/bbcswebdav/institution/LFA/CSS/Course%20Material/BOR6306 /Readings/BOR%20CRIJ%206306%20Madsen%202012%20Lesson%207%20DQ .pdf.

44. UNODC, *World Drug Report 2019* (Vienna: United Nations Office on Drugs and Crime, 2019), p. 1, https://wdr.unodc.org/wdr2019/prelaunch/WDR19_Booklet _2_DRUG_DEMAND.pdf.

45. CDC WONDER database, "Mortality," 2018, https://wonder.cdc.gov.

46. V. Duenas, "Recalibrating the U.S. Strategy for the War on Drugs," Carnegie Council for Ethics in International Affairs, 2017, https://www.carnegiecouncil .org/publications/ethics_online/recalibrating-the-u-s-strategy-for-the-war-on -drugs#_ftn23.

47. G. Gerra, V. Poznyak, S. Saxena, N. Volko, and UNODC-WHO Informal International Scientific Network, "Drug Use Disorders: Impact of a Public Health Rather Than a Criminal Justice Approach," *World Psychiatry* 16, no. 2 (2017): 213–214, https://www.ncbi.nlm.nih.gov/pmc/articles/PMC5428163/?report=reader# __ffn_sectitle.

48. S. Stewart, "The Hasan Case: Overt Clues and Tactical Challenges," *Stratfor Security Weekly,* November 11, 2009, https://worldview.stratfor.com/article /hasan-case-overt-clues-and-tactical-challenges.

49. Marcy Kreiter, "What Happened to Dzhokhar Tsarnaev? Update on Boston Marathon Bomber Sentenced to Death," *International Business Times,* April 16, 2017, https://www.ibtimes.com/what-happened-dzhokhar-tsarnaev-update-boston -marathon-bomber-sentenced-death-2526052.

50. FBI, "History: Oklahoma City Bombing," https://www.fbi.gov/history /famous-cases/oklahoma-city-bombing.

51. Vanessa Romo, "FBI Finds No Motive in Las Vegas Shooting, Closes Investigation," NPR, January 29, 2019, https://www.npr.org/2019/01/29/689821599/fbi -finds-no-motive-in-las-vegas-shooting-closes-investigation.

52. History.com, "Charleston Church Shooting," This Day in History, June 17, 2015, https://www.history.com/this-day-in-history/charleston-ame-church-shooting.

53. Campbell Robertson, Christopher Mele, and Sabrina Tavernise, "11 Killed in Synagogue Massacre; Suspect Charged with 29 Counts," *New York Times,* October 27, 2018.

54. Ibid.

55. Bruce Lawrence, *Messages to the World: The Statements of Osama bin Laden* (New York: Verso Books, 2005).

56. D. Schiller and J. Pinkerton, "Agents Feared Mexican Drug Cartel Attack on Border Dam," *Houston Chronicle,* June 2, 2010, https://www.chron.com/news /houston-texas/article/Agents-feared-Mexican-drug-cartel-attack-on-1617694.php.

57. Ibid.

58. E. J. Metropoulos and J. Platt, "Global Cyber Terrorism Incidents on the Rise," MarshMcLennan Insights, 2018, http://www.mmc.com/insights/publications /2018/nov/global-cyber-terrorism-incidents-on-the-rise.html.

59. Ibid.

60. Ibid.

61. J. Meserve, "Sources: Staged Cyberattack Reveals Vulnerability in Power Grid," CNN, September 26, 2007, http://www.cnn.com/2007/US/09/26/power.at .risk/index.html.

62. J. Hanna, F. Karimi, J. Morris, and S. Almasy, "Police: Austin Bomber Left 25-Minute Confession Video on Phone," CNN, August 31, 2018, https://www.cnn .com/2018/03/21/us/austin-explosions/index.html.

9

Homeland vs. National vs. Practical Intelligence

In this chapter we look at the process of incorporating homeland security into national security, the application of national security concepts within homeland security, and how the two can and should complement each other. National security deals fundamentally with grand-scheme international relations and gathers, processes, and disseminates intelligence to those who need to know what is happening around the world. Rarely does it directly or indirectly inform homeland security. Yet it should.

When there is a major natural disaster in central sub-Saharan Africa, most people in the United States simply ignore the event. National intelligence agencies can't really see any impact on the country. So, why should homeland security even have a concern about the disaster? Because primarily impoverished countries or those with tropical jungle involvement tend to have large disease outbreaks following disasters of any type. The people with passports and current visas simply hop on aircraft and fly to Europe or the United States where they will be "safe" from the disease outbreaks, similar to what happened recently with the coronavirus pandemic. Rich people simply left areas where the virus was prevalent. Unfortunately, in today's world of high-speed international air transportation, an infected person may leave their country, arrive in the United States, and never show signs of any disease until after they are already here and have interacted with many people.

The classic example is Thomas Eric Duncan of Monrovia, Liberia. On September 15, 2014, he helped a neighbor in Monrovia get to a hospital where Ebola patients were being treated. Four days later he boarded a flight to Brussels, Belgium, and lied on his forms about having been exposed to an Ebola-infected person. Once in Belgium, he transferred to a United Airlines flight to the United States, arrived at Dulles, transferred to another flight, and arrived in Dallas at 7:01 p.m. on September 20, 2014. Duncan stayed with his partner and her five children in very close contact in a small apartment in the Vickery Meadow neighborhood of Dallas.

Four after that, on September 24, 2014, he started to experience symptoms. He went to the Texas Health Presbyterian Hospital at 10:37 p.m. on September 25. The nurse at the triage station never asked about international travel even though they had signs on the counters telling patients to tell the nurse if they had been out of the country. Duncan was sent home in the early morning of September 26. By the next morning Thomas Duncan had developed full-blown Ebola and was highly contagious and extremely sick. He arrived by ambulance at the same hospital at 10:07 a.m. A doctor found he had been in Liberia, and Duncan was immediately tested for Ebola. The confirmation didn't come back until September 30, when he was officially isolated and treatment started. He died at 7:51 a.m. on October 8, 2014. But not before infecting two of his treatment nurses, Nina Pham and Amber Joy Vinson.

Vinson, even though she had been treating an Ebola patient and reported having a fever, decided to take a Frontier Airlines flight to Cleveland to spend a weekend in Tallmadge and Akron, Ohio. She returned to Dallas (on another flight) on October 13, and when she reported to work on October 15, she was immediately isolated and tested for Ebola. The result was positive.

Although Vinson and Duncan fortunately didn't infect anybody during their transportation, Duncan did infect two nurses operating under the stringent guidelines of the CDC, in an isolation facility, with the best of infectious disease protections. Considering the numbers of people who were exposed to Ebola en route and over the weekend by Duncan, as well as by Vinson, why wasn't there a greater outbreak or a pandemic? The CDC doesn't offer much to explain this other than that the conditions on the aircraft were not conducive to spreading the disease. Aircraft tend to be air-conditioned and that could be a factor as Ebola is a tropical disease usually transmitted in hot and humid environments. Another factor is that while nobody knows the infectious time frame for

Ebola, it is transmitted through contact with infected bodily fluids including blood, tears, saliva, or sperm.

National security agencies, which knew about and were tracking the Ebola outbreak in Liberia, should have also been tracking each and every person attempting to enter the United States after having been in the affected country. Duncan should have been stopped and closely interrogated in Brussels before ever being allowed onto a US-bound aircraft. He wasn't, because nobody in the national security intelligence complex bothered to identify international passengers originating from the involved countries and report them to the Transportation Security Agency, Department of Homeland Security, and Customs and Border Protection for additional screening before allowing them into the country at an overseas screening point or a port of entry.

Worse, within the United States a highly trained nurse, who had the very first signs of infection, and knew what she was doing, decided to travel and potentially infect hundreds of people on the flights she took for a weekend vacation. Why didn't Texas Health Presbyterian Hospital provide a list of all the people working with Duncan to DHS so that their travel could be monitored and perhaps prevented?

This incident shows one of the reasons why national security and homeland security agencies must communicate and share intelligence. The world is much too close by air travel to allow potential pandemic disasters to happen just because two different intelligence organizations refuse to talk with each other. Instead of always looking for criminal or terrorist connections as their primary functions, a more practical approach to the concept of what intelligence is, and the application of that information, should be implemented.

Unrestricted Warfare

In the 1990s, two colonels of the People's Liberation Army of China, Qiao Liang and Wang Xiangsui, published an article in a military journal in which they addressed the strategies that militarily and politically disadvantaged nations might apply in order to successfully attack a geopolitical superpower such as the United States.[1] Since US military doctrine and the national security apparatus are led by technology, Qiao and Wang proposed that it was US dependence upon technology that created a crucial weakness. This opened a blind spot with regard to alternative forms of warfare that could be exploited by less advantaged nations.

As such, the traditional mentality that offensive action is limited to military measures was no longer adequate given the range of contemporary threats and the rising costs of traditional warfare. Thus, Qiao and Wang suggested the use of significant alternatives to direct confrontation with a world-class military power. They proposed the use of international policy, economic warfare, a focus on the target country's digital infrastructure and networks, and the use of terrorism. By utilizing these recommendations, even a relatively insignificant state can theoretically incapacitate a far more powerful enemy.

More than two decades later you see this scenario playing out across the world as China moves into the position of a preeminent industrial and economic power. Around the globe there are efforts to involve other countries in China's Belt and Road Initiative. The development of 5G technology, an ongoing race between China and the United States, is at the point where tariffs, import restrictions, and blacklisting of agencies and manufacturers have become the norm in the battle to win the leadership position for the technological future. Whoever develops and deploys the first fully functional 5G networks will have a significant economic and tactical advantage over other countries. The 5G networks mean much more than faster internet. It also means much faster interactions between computers of all types—5G is about three times faster than 4G systems.[2] Verizon estimates that their networks will operate at speeds up to 200 times faster when they change to 5G.[3] Initially this means that billions of devices and sensors of all types, from home devices to manufacturing, and from automated vehicles, 3D printing, and technology-enhanced healthcare services to robotics, will all operate faster as their connectivity speeds increase. In a simple sense, a surgeon at a computer in New York could operate on an injured soldier in Afghanistan via a medical robot with very little lag time between commands and actions.

The United States and China are in an ongoing trade war (international politics and economic warfare) that no president prior to Trump even considered addressing. Chinese-made computer chips permeate the industrial and military complexes of the entire world, and almost nobody has an idea what hidden code or firmware might be embedded in these microprocessors. Similar chips are in every appliance and nearly every vehicle used in Europe, Africa, Asia, South and North America, and Australia.

If you work for a homeland security agency, where you are tracking illegal migrants, money launderers, MS-13 members, and so forth, do you know how reliable your radios, computers, cameras, ground and airborne sensors are? Do you know if the chips in all those components are made in the United States or by a Chinese company? Can the chips even be swapped out or do you have to purchase all new equipment if they suddenly stop working? And should they suddenly stop working, what would be the impact on the security of the country, the aviation industry, trains, trucking, harbors, international shipping, ports of entry, and borders? If you remember, on September 11, 2001, one of the first actions was to ground all aircraft over or en route to the United States. Another was to close all border crossings into and out of the country. Almost immediately, all factories in the United States were shut down because they all operate on a just-in-time delivery system from their suppliers, nearly all of whom are outside of the country.

The future isn't necessarily China's navy going head to head with a US aircraft carrier battle group. It is (much more likely) being able to turn off the lights in every home in the country using simple computer code. We've already seen multiple tests of these abilities. In 2017, 147 million people were affected by the Equifax breach.[4] Three billion Yahoo email accounts were compromised in 2013 and 2014, but the company didn't tell their customers until 2017.[5] In 2013 and 2014 the Home Depot and Target corporation payment systems were breached, resulting in over 100 million credit card accounts being affected. This hit over 56 million Home Depot and 40 million Target customers.[6] The country of Estonia was attacked by Russia and essentially had its entire infrastructure, electronics, and banking shut down in 2007 over the removal of a World War II bronze sculpture of a Soviet soldier.[7] In July 2009 over 100,000 computers in South Korea and the United States, including in the White House, the South Korean National Assembly, the Pentagon, and media outlets, were hit in three waves of attacks likely carried out by the North Koreans.[8]

It's worse than just personal and government information systems being attacked. On February 28, 2018, GitHub, a popular developer platform, was slammed with a targeted distributed denial of service (DDoS) attack that clocked at 1.35 terabits per second.[9] Over a thousand different autonomous systems across tens of thousands of unique end points simultaneously hit the company. While you may not have heard of many of these attacks, and likely were never really very concerned about them, there was an attack that impacted just about everybody in Europe and the United States—the 2016 botnet cyberattack against the Dyn corporation. This was a DDoS on October 21, 2016, that involved the use of tens of millions of devices that comprise what is called the Internet of Things, from printers to baby monitors, all infected by the Mirai malware.[10] To date, nobody has provided a confirmed claim to the attack that shut down all communications, cell phones, internet, Twitter, and so forth across the eastern US seaboard and nearly all of western Europe.

If such efforts can cause this much distraction and damage, imagine what a full-blown cyberattack by any country with a cyber command military component could cause. Yet, once again, the national security intelligence apparatus, the private internet security providers, and the Department of Defense Cyber Command aren't talking to the homeland security people to share information, intelligence, and efforts to harden the systems used within national borders by the agencies responsible for keeping the country secure.

Colonels Qiao and Wang proposed this type of warfare over twenty years ago. Yet the world and particularly the United States are still unprepared to deal with the impact and effects and won't communicate the threats between or even within agencies.

Practical Intelligence

Intelligence comes in all forms and through all types of organizations and sources. The significant difference is in how all that information is processed and employed. If the intelligence is collected and retained in a single agency with the intent of developing a prosecutorial case that can be taken to court, then the ability to act upon that information in any type of proactive way is nearly impossible. If the intelligence is used to make plans to deploy forces in combat, to develop logistics needs to support deployed military forces, or to develop new weapons and defense systems to defeat enemy weapons, then it is being used proactively, but it is rarely actionable on an immediate basis.

Practical intelligence can be defined as data from any and all sources that can be acted upon to prevent or mitigate a negative outcome. Within the IC this would be referred to as actionable intelligence. As an example, let's say you are the owner of stock in the General Electric corporation. You read an article about a new electrical generation system that can be installed in every home and apartment and as a primary supply for every business across the country. This product is in production and is available for a relatively low cost compared to the usual lifetime of electric bills that most homes and businesses have to pay. What does that tell you about your General Electric stock? Since GE is a major supplier of electrical generation equipment, either they get into this new business, buy this business, or ignore this business. If they do either of the first two, it is likely that the value of your GE stock will go up. If they ignore the business, then the value of your GE stock will probably go down, at some point. This is practical intelligence that anybody can act upon, and you have to decide what to do with it when it comes to your investment just as GE has to decide what to do with it as it concerns its future business sustainability and profitability.

Here is another example. You work for a local sheriff's office in Waco, Texas. A motorcycle club (MC) member gives you a call and tells you that there will be a meeting between the Bandidos MC and the Cossacks MC along with a couple of other groups to act as mediators in their discussions. This is going to happen at a local restaurant on Sunday in the early afternoon. You now have actionable intelligence. Do you arrange a police presence to ensure the peace, or do you set up a police ambush to contain any potential violence after the meeting starts?

Tough question and even tougher decision. Yet this actually happened. On May 17, 2015, nine bikers were killed and another eighteen were wounded in a shootout.[11] The shootout was not between the MC members. Police lying in ambush had previous orders to deal with any incident as an active-shooter situation, and the police opened fire on the bikers leaving the restaurant when a fistfight broke out. All of the shots that killed or wounded people were fired by the police! While 177 MC individuals were arrested, none were ever convicted and only one of them went to trial. No police officer has ever been charged with any crime or misconduct.

This is an example of practical intelligence that was badly handled and the response poorly planned. The police agencies involved dealt with the information they received as actionable intelligence that they needed to act upon, not as practical intelligence that could be used to better interact with and monitor the meeting between two motorcycle clubs that are often involved in drug trafficking. The response should not have been just the local Waco police and a handful of Texas State Troopers. It should have involved the county emergency manager, city manager/mayor, county judge (the most powerful person in the county), and the Department of Homeland Security. There should have been an advance effort to offer a safe and secure location for the MC groups to meet to address their interclub dispute. Competent medical care should have been standing by. And if the police were to be involved at all, it should not have been in an ambush setup with authority to open fire at any time and under any conditions. This type of activity based on information is an example of what makes practical intelligence different from actionable intelligence.

The availability of practical intelligence requires that the persons in receipt of it be competent to examine, evaluate, and plan for the best possible outcome. It should never be used in a reactionary manner, as is actionable intelligence. Instead, practical intelligence should be used to enhance a planned outcome. Keep in mind that in the emergency management world, a fundamental component of homeland security, you can regularly see that some agencies take the information they receive and use it to plan for specific outcomes, to mitigate the effects of weather and natural disasters, and to prevent terrorists from carrying out their attacks.

Sharing Intelligence

There is an international intelligence-sharing alliance comprised of Australia, Canada, New Zealand, the United Kingdom, and the United States. This is commonly called the Five Eyes group and it was created through the UKUSA Agreement (Treaty) in 1946, a secret treaty between the United States and the United Kingdom that was later expanded to include the other three countries. The treaty was so secret that even the Australian prime minister was unaware that his country was part of the intelligence-sharing organization until 1973. It wasn't until 2010 that the full text of the treaty was finally revealed to the public.

These countries share signals and human intelligence through the ECHELON program, which collects private and commercial communications as well as military and diplomatic signals traffic. This is mass surveillance and industrial espionage on a global scale. Each country has a set of specific regions that it is responsible for monitoring, and the collected information is shared across all the countries.

Five Eyes is a surveillance arrangement comprised of the US National Security Agency, the UK Government Communications Headquarters, the Australian Signals Directorate, Canada's Communications Security Establishment, and New Zealand's Government Communications Security Bureau. Five Eyes is not a centrally organized entity but rather a coalition of affiliated independent intelligence agencies. It is the most enduring and comprehensive intelligence alliance in the world, and is uniquely situated to handle the challenges brought by globalization. Primarily a signals intelligence (SIGINT) organization, Five Eyes does not conduct covert operations but complements each nation's respective national intelligence capability with extensive coverage on a global scale.

Australia monitors South Asia and East Asia while New Zealand monitors Southeast Asia and the western Pacific. Canada's geographical proximity to Russia allows for considerable monitoring of that country as well as the interior of China. The United States focuses on the Middle East, China, Russia, the Caribbean, and Africa. The UK monitors Europe, European Russia, the Middle East, and Hong Kong. You'll note that none of the Five Eyes countries has responsibility for South America. Nothing in the available Five Eyes responsibilities data indicates that any particular country is responsible for South American nations.

Among the Five Eyes countries, in the UK the Security Service (MI5) handles security intelligence while the Secret Intelligence Service (SIS, or MI6) handles human intelligence. In the United States, MI5's counterpart is the FBI while MI6's counterpart is the CIA. Australia has their Security Intelligence Organization carry the security intelligence functions while the Secret Intelligence Service handles the human intelligence functions. The countries of Canada and New Zealand have a single intelligence service each that handles both security and human intelligence.

Over the years the system has been expanded to include the Nine Eyes and Fourteen Eyes. Nine Eyes include the Five Eyes countries plus Denmark, France, the Netherlands, and Norway. Fourteen Eyes consist of the Nine Eyes countries plus Germany, Belgium, Italy, Spain, and Sweden. The official name of the Fourteen Eyes countries is SIGINT Seniors Europe, and it is primarily concerned with the coordination and exchange of military signals intelligence among its members.

In the Pacific region, the countries of Singapore and South Korea are also tied into this system for intelligence sharing. Germany wants to become part of the Five Eyes group while France is being specifically excluded by its own choice and the fact that it regularly spies on the United States and UK. All these countries spy on each other's citizens, and through this exchange of information, intelligence organizations are receiving intelligence data on their citizens even when prohibited by their own laws. For example, *Der Spiegel* noted that

> No one is safe from this mass spying—at least almost no one. Only one handpicked group of nations is excluded—countries that the NSA has defined as close friends, or "2nd party," as one internal document indicates. They include the UK, Australia, Canada and New Zealand. A document classified as "top secret" states that, "The NSA does NOT

target its 2nd party partners, nor request that 2nd parties do anything
that is inherently illegal for NSA to do."[12]

For all other countries, including the group of around thirty nations
that are considered to be third-party partners, however, this protection
does not apply. "We can, and often do, target the signals of most 3rd
party foreign partners," the NSA boasts in an internal presentation.[13]

Additionally, over eighty global corporations share intelligence information with the Five Eyes group through partnerships with the National
Security Agency. The volume of data and human intelligence gathered
and dispersed is amazing, running into the billions of terabytes. Parsing
through these data to get to practical intelligence that can be acted upon is
not only difficult, but nearly impossible. Therefore, the NSA runs a series
of algorithms in its computers looking for trends and data spikes to focus
upon. How does this become actionable for the homeland security enterprise? That's a secret the authors don't yet have access to. Yet the process
of evaluation and dissemination is routinely seen in the aftermath of a disaster or terrorist attack when within hours everything that can be known
about the perpetrators is broadcast all around the world.

Hunting for WMD

One advantage of the Five/Nine/Fourteen Eyes programs is that the data
gathered can be used to inform the hunt for weapons of mass destruction, or WMD. In the United States this is a primary function of the
DHS and the Customs and Border Protection units at ports of entry
across the United States as well as overseas.

According to DHS, "The United States faces a rising danger from
terrorists and rogue states seeking to use weapons of mass destruction.
A weapon of mass destruction is a nuclear, radiological, chemical, biological, or other device that is intended to harm a large number of people. The Department of Homeland Security works every day to prevent
terrorists and other threat actors from using these weapons to harm
Americans."[14] To accomplish this task in an ever changing world where
the threat from terrorism is constantly evolving, the DHS "must evolve
as well in order to stay ahead of the enemy." DHS attempts to analyze
existing defenses and determine potential improvements.

Through careful coordination with officials at all levels of government, DHS has increased the prevention and response capabilities of

public safety personnel across the United States. This is accomplished through training, exercises, and other support to operational partners. The department also collects and analyzes forensic evidence from WMD attacks in order to identify the perpetrators. The ability to determine who is responsible for an attack is critical to preventing follow-on attacks and to reduce proliferation of WMD, their delivery systems, and related materials to and from states and nonstate actors of concern. One method of accomplishing this is through the Proliferation Security Initiative (PSI).

From the CBP website:

> CBP participation in the PSI provides the United States Government (USG) with expertise on Customs matters and the full range of CBP enforcement programs, including targeting and analysis, automation tools, technology, detention and inspection, intelligence and information-sharing, industry outreach, as well as methods to halt proliferation networks through post-interdiction activities. CBP actively supports the PSI through its Operational Experts Group (OEG) meetings, exercises, workshops and other capacity building activities.

This is practical intelligence in action! The information may not be actionable, but it clearly defines and directs the planning and consolidated actions of multiple DHS agencies.

> CBP maintains a Proliferation Security Initiative Directive, which places its Office of International Affairs (INA) as the primary policy and programmatic lead for CBP contributions to the PSI. The overall INA approach to engagement in the PSI includes:
>
> - coordination and consultation with appropriate CBP offices and subject matter experts;
> - engagement in the development of USG policy through coordination with interagency partners;
> - regular participation in international PSI activities; and
> - analysis of where international training, technical assistance, and capacity building may be enhanced to include strategic interdiction goals.
>
> Notably, since the establishment of the PSI's Critical Capabilities and Practices (CCP) effort—CBP has been a key international contributor to a number of CCP "tools" and "resources" that can help international partners improve their capacities to meet the PSI Statement of Interdiction Principles. . . .
>
> CBP is just one entity involved in the global effort to counter the proliferation. CBP works with interagency partners in the United

States, as well as international Customs administrations around the globe.[15]

Cargo Security and Examinations

From the CBP website:

> Each year, more than 11 million maritime containers arrive at our seaports. At land borders, another 11 million arrive by truck and 2.7 million by rail. We are responsible for knowing what is inside, whether it poses a risk to the American people, and ensuring that all proper revenues are collected. Working with the trade community, programs like the Container Security Initiative and the Customs Trade Partnership Against Terrorism help to increase security and safeguard the world's trade industry.[16]

Container Security Initiative

From the CBP website:

> As the single, unified border agency of the United States, U.S. Customs and Border Protection's (CBP) mission is extraordinarily important to the protection of America and the American people. In the aftermath of the terrorist attacks on September 11, 2001, U.S. Customs Service began developing antiterrorism programs to help secure the United States. Within months of these attacks, U.S. Customs Service had created the Container Security Initiative (CSI).
>
> CSI addresses the threat to border security and global trade posed by the potential for terrorist use of a maritime container to deliver a weapon. CSI proposes a security regime to ensure all containers that pose a potential risk for terrorism are identified and inspected at foreign ports before they are placed on vessels destined for the United States. CBP has stationed teams of U.S. CBP Officers in foreign locations to work together with the host foreign government counterparts. Their mission is to target and prescreen containers and to develop additional investigative leads related to the terrorist threat to cargo destined to the United States.
>
> The three core elements of CSI are:
>
> - Identify high-risk containers. CBP uses automated targeting tools to identify containers that pose a potential risk for terrorism, based on advance information and strategic intelligence.
> - Prescreen and evaluate containers before they are shipped. Containers are screened as early in the supply chain as possible, generally at the port of departure.

- Use technology to prescreen high-risk containers to ensure that screening can be done rapidly without slowing down the movement of trade. This technology includes large-scale X-ray and gamma ray machines and radiation detection devices.

Through CSI, CBP officers work with host customs administrations to establish security criteria for identifying high-risk containers. Those administrations use non-intrusive inspection (NII) and radiation detection technology to screen high-risk containers before they are shipped to U.S. ports.

Announced in January 2002, CSI has made great strides since its inception. A significant number of customs administrations have committed to joining CSI and operate at various stages of implementation. CSI is now operational at ports in North America, Europe, Asia, Africa, the Middle East, and Latin and Central America. CBP's 58 operational CSI ports now prescreen over 80 percent of all maritime containerized cargo imported into the United States.[17]

The success of this continuing operation is due to the Customs Trade Partnership Against Terrorism (CTPAT).

From the CBP website:

CTPAT is but one layer in U.S. Customs and Border Protection's (CBP) multi-layered cargo enforcement strategy. Through this program, CBP works with the trade community to strengthen international supply chains and improve United States border security. CTPAT is a voluntary public-private sector partnership program which recognizes that CBP can provide the highest level of cargo security only through close cooperation with the principle stakeholders of the international supply chain such as importers, carriers, consolidators, licensed customs brokers, and manufacturers. The Security and Accountability for Every Port Act of 2006 provided a statutory framework for the CTPAT program and imposes strict program oversight requirements.

A Growing Partnership

From its inception in November 2001, CTPAT continued to grow. Today, more than 11,400 certified partners, spanning the gamut of the trade community, have been accepted into the program. The partners include U.S. importers/exporters, U.S./Canada highway carriers; U.S./Mexico highway carriers; rail and sea carriers; licensed U.S. Customs brokers; U.S. marine port authority/terminal operators; U.S. freight consolidators; ocean transportation intermediaries and non-operating common carriers; Mexican and Canadian manufacturers; and Mexican long-haul carriers, all of whom account for over 52 percent (by value) of cargo imported into the U.S.

How CTPAT Works

When an entity joins CTPAT, an agreement is made to work with CBP to protect the supply chain, identify security gaps, and implement specific security measures and best practices. Applicants must address a broad range of security topics and present security profiles that list action plans to align security throughout the supply chain.

[As a result] CTPAT members are considered to be of low risk, and are therefore less likely to be examined at a U.S. port of entry.

CTPAT Benefits

CTPAT Partners enjoy a variety of benefits, including taking an active role in working closer with the U.S. Government in its war against terrorism. As they do this, Partners are able to better identify their own security vulnerabilities and take corrective actions to mitigate risks. Some of the benefits of the program include:

- Reduced number of CBP examinations
- Front of the line inspections
- Possible exemption from Stratified Exams
- Shorter wait times at the border
- Assignment of a Supply Chain Security Specialist to the company
- Access to the Free and Secure Trade (FAST) Lanes at the land borders
- Access to the CTPAT web-based Portal system and a library of training materials
- Possibility of enjoying additional benefits by being recognized as a trusted trade Partner by foreign Customs administrations that have signed Mutual Recognition with the United States
- Eligibility for other U.S. Government pilot programs, such as the Food and Drug Administration's Secure Supply Chain program
- Business resumption priority following a natural disaster or terrorist attack
- Importer eligibility to participate in the Importer Self-Assessment Program (ISA)
- Priority consideration at CBP's industry-focused Centers of Excellence and Expertise

How Do I Become a Partner? Join CTPAT Now

Participation in CTPAT is voluntary and there are no costs associated with joining the program. Moreover, a company does not need an intermediary in order to apply to the program and work with CBP; the application process is easy and it is done online. The first step is for the company to review the CTPAT Minimum Security Criteria for their business entity to determine eligibility for the program. The second step is for the company to submit a basic application via the CTPAT Portal system and to agree to voluntarily participate. The third step is for the company to complete a supply chain security profile. The security profile explains how the company is meeting CTPAT's minimum security criteria. In order to do this, the company should have already conducted a risk assessment. Upon satisfactory completion of the application and supply chain security profile, the applicant company is assigned a CTPAT Supply Chain Security Specialist to review the submitted materials and to provide program guidance on an on-going basis. The CTPAT program will then have up to 90 days to certify the company into the program or to reject the application. If certified, the company will be validated within a year of certification.[18]

Custom and Border Protection

From the CBP website:

Historically, cargo entering the United States from any foreign territory has been subject to physical examination by the U.S. Government to verify that it complies with U.S. laws and regulations. After September 11, 2001, a new combined organization of Border Patrol, the Immigration and Naturalization Service, Agriculture Inspection, and the U.S. Customs Service became Customs and Border Protection (CBP) in the Department of Homeland Security. . . .

The CBP antiterrorism mission is not limited to the physical examination of cargo when it arrives in U.S. ports. CBP is also using intelligence from a number of sources to identify high-risk shipments in order to concentrate its inspectional resources on them. For example, under bilateral agreements as part of the Container Security Initiative, CBP inspectors work in nearly 20 foreign ports to help ensure the security of U.S.-bound cargo before it disembarks.

In addition, under the Trade Act of 2002, CBP will issue regulations providing for advanced electronic submission of cargo information for security purposes. . . .

An important part of the CBP mission remains the facilitation of legitimate trade. In addition to its own regulations, CBP enforces over 400 laws on behalf of over 40 other U.S. Government agencies. A large number of these import restrictions and requirements are designed to protect the American people from dangerous and illegal goods. CBP has undertaken a number of initiatives, such as the use of non-intrusive inspection technology, to increase its ability to examine cargo effectively without slowing the flow of trade, which plays a significant part in the U.S. economy.[19]

From a CBP fact sheet:

In October 2010, the global counter-terrorism community disrupted an attempt by al-Qaeda in Yemen to conceal and ship explosive devices in cargo onboard U.S.-bound aircraft. Five days after the attempted attack, U.S. Customs and Border Protection (CBP) and the

Transportation Security Administration (TSA) began meeting with industry partners to better understand business practices and to collectively develop a mechanism to collect cargo data as soon as possible in the supply chain.

The result of this public/private cooperation was the Air Cargo Advance Screening (ACAS) pilot, which allowed CBP and TSA to use advance information from air carriers and other stakeholders to identify and intercept high-risk shipments in a pre-loading timeline. The two agencies formed a joint targeting operation at a centralized location (CBP's National Targeting Center), which allowed easy collaboration between Department of Homeland Security (DHS) components. The targeting operation uses CBP's Automated Targeting System and other available intelligence to identify packages that pose a possible security threat. [Once again, here is an example of practical intelligence driving interorganizational planning and action without necessitating immediate actionable intelligence to drive a response.]

The ACAS pilot operated for more than seven years, as CBP continued to collaborate with industry partners and the international community to develop viable and effective regulatory requirements.

ACAS is now a requirement. As a program, it enhances the security of the aircraft and passengers on U.S.-bound flights by providing an additional layer to DHS's robust risk-based layered security strategy. ACAS risk assessments identify and prevent the loading of high-risk air cargo that could pose a risk to the aircraft during flight.

The ACAS data elements:

- Shipper Name and Address—individual name or name of business and a valid street address with city/province, country and postal code
- Consignee Name and Address—individual name or name of business and a valid street address with city/province, country and postal code
- Cargo Description—generic cargo descriptions should be avoided
- Total Quantity—based on the smallest external packing unit
- Total Weight—total weight of cargo expressed in pounds or kilograms
- Air Waybill Number[20]

Applying Practical Intelligence

While readers can go to pretty much any of the DHS, FBI, Department of Justice, or state law enforcement agency websites and get the current results of their efforts to interdict contraband, arrest criminals and terrorists, and generally report data that pat themselves on the back, one of the best indicators and demonstrations of practical intelligence are the results of operations conducted by CBP's Air and Marine Operations (AMO) organization.

From the CBP website:

> With approximately 1,800 federal agents and mission support personnel, 240 aircraft, and 300 marine vessels operating throughout the United States, Puerto Rico, and U.S. Virgin Islands, AMO conducts its mission in the air and maritime environments at and beyond the border, and within the nation's interior.
>
> AMO interdicts unlawful people and cargo approaching U.S. borders, investigates criminal networks and provides domain awareness in the air and maritime environments, and responds to contingencies and national taskings. [One can frequently see their aircraft and boats following hurricanes. Sometimes a person can watch a news feed that shows them tracking and capturing semisubmersible cocaine vessels.]
>
> In Fiscal Year 2020, AMO agents seized or disrupted 285,976 pounds of narcotics, seized $51.5 million, contributed to the apprehensions of 47,813 individuals and rescued 184 persons.[21]

Another instance of practical intelligence being applied by a government entity happened in New Orleans, Louisiana, when the US Computer Emergency Response Team (US-CERT) provided a continuously updated list of current threats from all sources. This included software vulnerabilities as well as information on cyberattacks and their outcomes. The newly elected political leadership of New Orleans took this information to heart and started to listen to their information technology personnel to make important decisions concerning the security of the city computer systems. Rather than look at potential events through a political window, they saw that it was better to prepare for and respond to cyberattacks than to ignore the real dangers such attacks posed to the community overall.

As early as 2013, the Conference of US Mayors recognized that cybersecurity was a critical public safety issue, and referenced it in a nice statement accepted by the conference attendees. However, it appeared to not be translated into actions by the mayors and administrators of most US cities—of any size. Political sound words are not an effective deterrence against cyberattacks. Fewer than half of all US municipalities have cybersecurity insurance to offset expenses incurred during and after an attack. According to the *New York Times,* ransomware used to have a low rate of return, about 2.9 percent in 2012. By 2018 that rate was nearly 50 percent.[22] It was becoming profitable to hack and attack municipalities.

Usually it is less expensive to pay ransom than to have to go through the process of recovery and restoration of data as well as replacement of vulnerable and damaged hardware. If you cannot stop the attacks, then when it happens you have to be ready to either pay up the requested ransom or suffer the long-term financial (and political reputation) consequences that will arise when the attack becomes public. In 2015 and 2016, several healthcare facilities, a public transit system in Northern California, a fire department in Ohio, and other locations suffered debilitating attacks by hackers.

In early 2018, the Colorado Department of Transportation was hit. Fortunately, they maintained a complete off-site backup of their data. While restoration took weeks, they didn't have to directly address the issue of ransom. Unfortunately, it wasn't until later that it was discovered that the hackers had placed a number of hidden tracking and corruption programs in the system that could be activated later, wreaking havoc on the recovered IT systems.

Then, in March 2018 the city of Atlanta, Georgia, was attacked. The ransom was only $51,000 in Bitcoin—a pittance to a city so large. Yet a decision had to be made: pay up and get the system released (if the hackers were actually honest about it) or shut down and start over, rebuilding the entire municipality IT system. That ultimately cost over $17 million, immeasurable downtime, and a loss of reputation that can't be calculated. Big cities still didn't learn. In early 2019, the City of Baltimore was attacked and shutdown. By August 2019 twenty-two small cities and municipalities across Texas were attacked through a common provider of IT management systems for smaller communities. They were attacked by use of older attack systems such as Sodinokibi or possibly by Ryuk. Sodinokibi is so old it has been retired by hackers after bringing in probably billions in ransom, while Ryuk had forced Jackson County, Georgia, to fork over $400,000 in ransom just a few months earlier. On October 2, 2019, the FBI issued a high-impact cyberattack warning in response to attacks on state and local government targets. The FBI warning included health organizations, industrial companies, and the transportation sectors.

Addressing these types of continuing attacks requires not only the sharing of intelligence across different levels of government and business, but more importantly cooperation and action based on solid planning and available intelligence, accompanied by a political will or corporate mentality that is willing to recognize that the world is changing rapidly, much faster than can be addressed through traditional long-range planning and budgeting. New Orleans is an excellent example of how to apply the intelligence available from all sources as well as planning to respond effectively across the community to a major disruption. Leadership was aware and prepared. Just a month earlier the Louisiana school district computers had been taken down by ransomware—the second time in six months.

At 5 a.m. on December 13, 2019, New Orleans came under cyberattack. By 11 a.m. the city IT department had recognized and identified the attack and gave the order for all employees to power down all computers and disconnect from Wi-Fi. All the city servers were also powered down and employees were told to unplug any personal devices from the city system. Shortly after that, Mayor LaToya Cantrell declared a state of emergency due to the ransomware attack and filed with the civil district court the necessary papers to give police and public safety personnel extraordinary powers citywide. Thanks to system compartmentation, the 911 call system was not affected. Public safety cameras were still operating and recording, even though the Real-Time Crime Center (a centralized pattern-identity system used by law enforcement and emergency first responders) computers had been powered down.

The New Orleans declaration of a disaster and state of emergency warranted the use of all extraordinary measures appropriate to ensure public health, safety, welfare, and convenience. The superintendent of police was directed to take command and exercise control of all peace and police officers within the city. The city directed the commandeering of all available resources within the city, and of all boards and agencies, for the purposes of performing or facilitating emergency services. The declaration authorized the director of the city's Office of Homeland Security and Emergency Preparedness to "undertake any activity authorized by law which he deems necessary and appropriate in response to this declaration, and all city agencies are hereby authorized to take any actions directed by" the emergency manager necessary to respond to the emergency. This included the commandeering or utilization of any private property if necessary.

The response of New Orleans management to the ransomware attack was somewhat panned in the media as being overly reactive and beyond what was necessary to address the actual issue. However, when compared to the hundreds of millions of dollars that other communities have been forced to pay to hackers, the complete replacement and rebuilding of IT systems across communities, and the subjection of unprotected systems to repetitive attacks, it seems at least one major municipality in the United States has finally realized that cyberattack is a real issue and threat to the safety and security of their community. This can be traced back directly to the sharing of practical intelligence between multiple agencies and an awareness by city functionaries, even at a low level, to what's happening worldwide in their field of expertise.

Practical Intelligence and Counterterrorism in the Homeland

In 2018, the DHS asked the Homeland Security Operational Analysis Center, operated by the RAND Corporation, to examine the current state of terrorism prevention in the United States and to develop policy options based on their analysis. The complete report was published in 2019.[23] Major findings included gaps/shortfalls in national terrorism prevention efforts stemming from limited programmatic focus and resource investment, but also as a result of sustained opposition that tried to constrain or halt efforts toward countering violent extremism (CVE).[24] While there were some identified successes, including community education, public-private partnerships, and development of local capacity to intervene with individuals at risk of radicalization toward violence, most of those interviewed in the study were concerned whether these successes could be sustained over a longer period.

The United States started to focus on radicalization and mobilization to violence shortly after the September 11, 2001, attacks. Significant US activity related to CVE didn't start until after the 2009 attack by Major Hasan Nidal at Ft. Hood and the attempted Times Square bombing in 2010. Prevention of terrorism and radicalization toward extremism requires more than just investigating and incarcerating individuals suspected of planning or directly supporting violence. Yet the entire domestic intelligence function is organized around just that—investigation, prosecution, and conviction—often after the fact.

CVE is difficult to accomplish because of the perceived interference in constitutionally protected rights. The reason is that CVE focuses on activities that occur before any crime has been committed. Identifying those potentially subject to extremism as well as taking actions to interdict are all based on potential future activities that might appear to be threats. The very effort by law enforcement to implement CVE is often viewed as government overreach and interference along with the possible targeting of minority populations for extraordinary surveillance just because of their religion or ethnicity. All of these have been deter-mined to be unconstitutional by state and federal courts.

Overall the study found that there is a large menu of actions avail-able to support effective and practical federal policies and intervention options. One is for the federal government to provide credible informa-tion, including sharing of best practices and tools, to organizations seek-ing to implement terrorism prevention efforts. Another of the major findings was that the federal government could play a key role in data gathering and analysis by providing situational awareness into public views and concerns and national intervention capacity. This concept includes improved research supporting improved measurement and evaluation capabilities, program sustainability, and risk assessment. This study found, essentially, that development, evaluation, and distri-bution of practical intelligence was an important factor in CVE.[25] This was a finding of the 9/11 Commission Report in 2002! Two decades later it was still a major issue that had yet to be effectively addressed within the homeland security enterprise.

The outcome of the study is that while the four traditional federal security-focused agencies—DHS, DOJ, FBI, and the National Coun-terterrorism Center—play the most central roles in CVE, it is the involvement of agencies down to the local level, including nongovern-mental organizations, where the best results are found. Practical intel-ligence shows that it takes engagement at the local level of the affected communities for CVE to be successful. Additionally, intervention requires access to capabilities for mental health services, employment assistance, and other capacities maintained by nonprofit and service organizations. While some successful efforts are connected to govern-ment through multidisciplinary teams, including social service providers and police, others have been designed to explicitly separate from government (law enforcement in particular) the actions and out-comes in an effort to address potential threats while maintaining indi-vidual rights.

Conclusion

There are differences between actionable intelligence within the national security apparatus, homeland security intelligence, and practi-cal intelligence—notably, what data are collected and how the data are used and applied. Often, when it comes to practical intelligence most agencies simply don't use what is available to them. The problem stems fundamentally from the long history (of some agencies) of using gathered data to conduct prosecutions in court. It takes a mind-set change to look at intelligence data as a means to be proactive in planning and execution so as to minimize the overall impact of an event, or to mitigate any possible negative outcomes.

Practical intelligence is important for the homeland security enterprise to succeed, from evaluation and analysis of potential internal threats stemming from extremism, and the tracking and identifying of funding sources, to the identification of causes contributing to mass migrations in both directions across the US-Mexico border. This will become more evident in the next chapter with a detailed examination of how FEMA functions from the aspect of using all available intelligence resources to prepare for, respond to, and recover from disasters.

Notes

1. Qiao Liang and Wang Xiangsui, "Unrestricted Warfare" (Beijing: People's Liberation Army Literature and Arts Publishing House, 1999).

2. Brian O'Connell, "What Is 5G and What Does It Mean for Me in 2019?," *The Street*, February 25, 2019.

3. Ibid.

4. Federal Trade Commission, "Equifax Data Breach Settlement," January 2020, https://www.ftc.gov/enforcement/cases-proceedings/refunds/equifax-data -breach-settlement.

5. Lily Newman, "Yahoo's 2013 Email Hack Actually Compromised Three Billion Accounts," *Wired*, November 3, 2017, https://www.wired.com/story/yahoo -breach-three-billion-accounts/.

6. Kate Vinton, "With 56 Million Cards Compromised, Home Depot's Breach Is Bigger Than Target's," *Forbes*, September 18, 2014, https://www.forbes.com /sites/katevinton/2014/09/18/with-56-million-cards-compromised-home-depots -breach-is-bigger-than-targets/#45b321ff3e74.

7. Joshua Davis, "Hackers Take Down the Most Wired Country in Europe," *Wired*, August 21, 2007, https://www.wired.com/2007/08/ff-estonia/.

8. Matthew Weaver, "Cyber Attackers Target South Korea and US," *Guardian*, July 8, 2009, https://www.theguardian.com/world/2009/jul/08/south-korea-cyber -attack.

9. Lily Newman, "GitHub Survived the Biggest DDoS Attack Ever Recorded," *Wired*, March 1, 2018, https://www.wired.com/story/github-ddos-memcached/.

10. Nicky Woolf, "DDoS Attack That Disrupted Internet Was Largest of Its Kind in History, Experts Say," *Guardian*, October 26, 2016, https://www.theguardian .com/technology/2016/oct/26/ddos-attack-dyn-mirai-botnet.

11. Martin Pengelly, "Texas Biker Gang Shooting; Nine Dead and 18 Wounded at Restaurant in Waco," *Guardian*, May 18, 2015, https://www.theguardian /us-new /2015/may/17/biker-gang-shooting-waco-texas.

12. "Five Eyes," *Der Spiegel*, July 1, 2013.

13. Alfred McCoy, *In the Shadows of the American Century: The Rise and Decline of U.S. Global Power* (Chicago: Haymarket Books, 2017).

14. DHS, "Weapons of Mass Destruction," https://www.dhs.gov/topic/weapons-mass-destruction.

15. CBP, "Proliferation Security Initiative," https://www.cbp.gov/border-security/international-initiatives/proliferation.

16. CBP, "Cargo and Security Examinations," https://www.cbp.gov/border-security/ports-entry/cargo-security.

17. CBP, "CSI: Container Security Initiative," https://www.cbp.gov/border-security/ports-entry/cargo-security/csi/csi-brief.

18. CBP, "C-TPAT: Customs-Trade Partnership Against Terrorism," https://www.cbp.gov/border-security/ports-entry/cargo-security/ctpat.

19. CBP, "Cargo Examination," https://www.cbp.gov/border-security/ports-entry/cargo-security/examination.

20. CBP, "Air Cargo Advance Screening (ACAS)," https://www.cbp.gov/sites/default/files/assets/documents/2018-Jun/ACAS%20Fact%20Sheet%20060518A%20FINAL.pdf.

21. CBP, "AMO in Action," https://www.cbp.gov/newsroom/stats/cbp-enforcement-statistics/air-and-marine-operations-statistics-fiscal-year-2021.

22. Nathaniel Popper, "Ransomware Attacks Grow, Crippling Cities and Businesses," *New York Times,* February 9, 2020, https://www.nytimes.com/2020/02/09/technology/ransomware-attacks.html.

23. Brian A. Jackson, Ashley L. Rhoades, Jordan R. Reimer, Natasha Lander, Katherine Costello, and Sina Beaghley, *Practical Terrorism Prevention* (Santa Monica, CA: RAND Corporation with the Homeland Security Operational Analysis Center, 2019).

24. Ibid.

25. Ibid.

10

Making the System Work

When the term *systems approach* first comes up in conversation the speaker and listener are often thinking of business and economic applications of general system theory. For the purposes of this chapter we define a system as a cohesive combination of interrelated and interdependent parts, bounded by space and time, influenced by its environment, defined by its structure and purpose, and expressed through its functioning.

The Federal Emergency Management Agency (FEMA) is an excellent example of a government agency that is forced, by the environment within which it functions, to apply a systems approach to its proper functioning. Without the additional resources of multiple other agencies and a wide variety of intelligence inputs, FEMA would be useless. Thus, when considering the intelligence employed by FEMA, it depends on a system of agencies working together to produce an essential outcome. Those agencies exist outside of the Department of Homeland Security.

FEMA has no intelligence-gathering or prosecuting capability or function. It is totally dependent upon intelligence gathered and provided by other agencies. FEMA, as a component of the Department of Homeland Security, has no impact or control over the budgets and assets of the Department of the Interior, Department of Commerce, or Department of State and, therefore, as the key agency responsible for national preparedness, prevention (of terrorism), response, recovery, and mitigation, it is totally dependent upon other, separately funded and managed federal agencies for all of the actionable intelligence upon which it must act. This is a very difficult position for any federal agency, particularly one as important as FEMA.

Since most of the disasters seen in the United States are weather related, the first mentioned intelligence-gathering agency is the National Oceanic and Atmospheric Administration (NOAA), and its subordinate component, the National Weather Service (NWS). These are part of the Department of Commerce, and you probably know about them because your local news broadcasts use these resources for their predictions and to keep you updated on severe storms.

The Weather Channel, AccuWeather, and other popular sources of weather information are *not* part of the government, do not have their own intelligence-gathering systems or equipment, and are just as dependent upon NOAA and the NWS for information as are your local news broadcasters.

National Oceanic and Atmospheric Administration

NOAA's roots go back more than 200 years.[1] It is the US environmental intelligence agency. The nation's first civilian scientific agency, the National Geodetic Survey, was established in 1807 by President Thomas Jefferson to provide nautical charts to the maritime community for safe passage into US ports and along the extensive US coastline.[2] The Weather Bureau, the country's first agency dedicated to the atmospheric sciences, was founded in 1870 and, one year later, the US Commission of Fish and Fisheries was created, the first US conservation agency.

With the creation of NOAA in 1970, the culture of scientific accuracy, service to protect life and property, and stewardship of resources of these three agencies were brought together. "The year 2020 marks two monumental anniversaries within the weather, water, and climate community: NOAA celebrates 50 years since its founding, as the National Weather Service celebrates 150 years saving lives, protecting property, and enhancing the nation's economy!"[3]

National Weather Service

From the NWS Heritage fact sheet:

> The NWS of today and tomorrow was built on a 150-year-old foundation of science and service. Over time, advances in science, tech-

nology, and engineering have accelerated our understanding of the natural world, continually allowing us to better predict weather, water, and climate events.

As the needs of society have changed, so has the NWS. However, the fundamental mission has not: save lives, protect property, and enhance the nation's economy. From the very beginning, this has been the agency's fundamental focus. Furthermore, while the NWS jobs of today are vastly changed from those 150 years ago and in-between, our staff's dedication to meet the mission continues to be one of our biggest strengths.

Throughout its history, the NWS has continually evolved, driven by:

- Advances in science, technology, and engineering that have accelerated our understanding of the natural world, leading to better predictions of weather, water, and climate events.
- National and Global Economic Transitions, including the shift from agrarian to industrial economies, the growth of aviation, World Wars, internationalization, and the continual push-pull between serving public vs. commercial needs.
- Catalyzing Events, e.g., 1888 Blizzards, 1900 Galveston Hurricane, 1938 Long Island Express Hurricane, 1974 Super Outbreak of Tornadoes, and the 2011 Super Outbreak of Tornadoes in the Southeast that led to today's overarching goal to Build a Weather-Ready Nation and focus on providing Impact-based Decision Support Services.[4]

The National Weather Service provides water, climate, and weather data, forecasts, and warnings for the protection of life and property as well as support of the national economy with the vision of creating a weather-ready nation. Being weather-ready means that society is prepared for and responds to water, climate, and weather-dependent events in a timely manner.

The intelligence produced through the process of providing the nation's water, climate, and weather data, forecasts, and warnings requires a diversified organization. The massive amount of highly localized data produced by the NWS is of extreme importance to FEMA's ability to identify, prepare, and deploy response and recovery teams in the face of severe weather events. As you read through the following information on the NWS and its various components, keep in mind that everything they produce is a source of intelligence for FEMA.

NWS employees at local weather forecast offices, river forecast centers, center weather service units, and national centers receive this information and work to support all aspects of keeping the public safe from weather, water, and climate hazards and meeting the NWS mission to protect lives and property.[5] The local weather forecast offices are responsible for issuing warnings, advisories, statements, and short-term forecasts for their local county warning area. This includes emergency management, the media, aviation community, and other customers twenty-four hours a day, 365 days a year. Weather forecasters prepare digital forecasts, warnings, advisories and watches, aviation forecasts, and river forecasts and warnings. They monitor weather observations, provide public service, and program/monitor broadcasts over eleven NOAA Weather Radio–All Hazards Stations. They also collect and disseminate river and rainfall data, administer the Cooperative Weather Observer Program, and prepare local climate data reports.

National Weather Service Headquarters coordinates programs directly related to weather forecasting and warnings to ensure the effectiveness of weather services and that climate, water, and weather warnings and forecasts are provided to industry, government, and the general public in a timely manner. The NWS Headquarters also ensures funding is available to support regional requirements, manages information technology resources, and ensures a coordinated NOAA program of weather-related activities across line offices.

The six NWS regional offices manage all scientific and operational hydrologic, oceanographic, and meteorological programs of the region including observing weather services, forecasting, networks, and climatology and hydrology. They monitor these on a full-time basis and adjust resources as needed to provide the most effective weather and warning services possible.

The National Weather Service Headquarters and six regional headquarters operate to provide weather- and tsunami-related forecasts to the country and several other nations. Some headquarters provide more information to the public than do others, and this leads to some variance in how much information is provided on each region.

Eastern Region

The Eastern Region is headquartered in Bohemia, New York, and covers all of New England, south to New York, Pennsylvania, New Jersey, West Virginia and Virginia, Ohio, Maryland, Delaware, North and South Carolina, parts of eastern Tennessee and Kentucky, and Washington, DC.[6]

Southern Region

The Southern Region is headquartered in Ft. Worth, Texas, and covers Texas, Oklahoma, New Mexico, Louisiana, Arkansas, Mississippi,

Tennessee, Georgia, Alabama, and Florida, the Commonwealth of Puerto Rico, and the US Virgin Islands in the eastern Caribbean.[7] Seventy-seven million people reside in this area, with more than 150 million visitors annually. In addition, the Southern Region has coastal responsibilities that include major areas of the Gulf of Mexico, the Caribbean, and the area of the Atlantic Ocean that borders both Florida and Georgia.

The Southern Region has almost 1,000 field employees working in thirty-two forecast offices, four river forecast centers, the Space-flight Meteorology Group, seven center weather service units, the FAA Academy, and Southern Region headquarters.[8] The headquarters provides both administrative and operational support to its field offices and manages the region's programs, staffing, scientific enhancements, and an annual budget of nearly $110 million.[9] In addition to other duties, the Southern Region staff oversee technological developments and manage meteorological, climatological, hydrological, and tsunami activities.

Central Region

The headquarters for the Central Region is located in Kansas City, Missouri. From there they provide weather information concerning eastern Montana, Colorado, Wyoming, North and South Dakota, Kansas, Nebraska, Missouri, Minnesota, Iowa, Wisconsin, Illinois, Michigan, Indiana and Ohio, Tennessee, and Kentucky as well as some of West Virginia.[10]

Western Region

The Western Region is headquartered in Salt Lake City, Utah. They cover Washington, Oregon, Arizona, Nevada, California, Utah, Idaho, Wyoming, Montana, Colorado, and New Mexico.[11] You'll note that across the Rocky Mountains, the Southern, Central, and Western Regions provide weather coverage.

Alaska Region

Headquartered in Anchorage, the Alaska region is the second largest in the nation. It covers all of Alaska out to the end of the Aleutian Islands and above the Arctic Circle.[12] The area is so large that it is broken into five sections that can then be zoomed-in to provide local information.

Pacific Region

By far the largest weather forecasting region in the world, the Pacific Region is headquartered in Honolulu, Hawaii.[13] The region spans a distance larger than the continental United States reaching from Hawaii to Guam to Micronesia and across the equator to the islands of American Samoa. Each island location of the Pacific Region maintains a different indigenous culture including Hawaiian, Samoan, Chamorro, Marshallese, Pohnpeian, Chuukese, Yapese, and Palauan.[14] The diverse nature of distance, location, and cultures provides unique challenges along with a great depth of strength through cultural diversity.

The Pacific Region also provides tsunami bulletins across the basin through the Pacific Tsunami Warning Center while the International Tsunami Information Center mitigates tsunami hazards by improving tsunami preparedness for all Pacific Ocean nations.[15]

Starting just west of the International Dateline there is a weather service office (WSO) on Majuro island in the Marshall Islands. They operate surface and upper air observing programs and generate local forecasts and warnings. Originally started as a Weather Bureau airways station in 1955, upper air observations were taken once a day until 1958. At that time upper air observations were increased to four times daily to support the nuclear weapons testing of the Department of the Navy at Eniwetok Atoll.

Farther west lie the Federated States of Micronesia. The NWS maintains WSOs on three islands, Pohnpei, Chuuk, and Yap. All three of these offices were once US Navy weather stations, but they were ceded to the Weather Bureau in 1951. Within the Federated States of Micronesia are 607 islands spanning an area of 1,700 square miles. The 106,000 residents are frequented by heavy monsoon-type rains and many typhoons each year.

Continuing west, the Republic of Palau has over 300 volcanic and raised coral islands and atolls with the highest being 720 feet above sea level. The NWS in the republic of Palau started at the Koror Weather Bureau Office after taking over duties from the US Navy in July 1951. The area gets approximately 150 inches of annual rainfall. Palau isn't officially a part of the United States but instead is a presidential republic that freely associates with the United States, which provides funding, defense, and access to social services. The country uses the US dollar as its currency, and a significant portion of their gross national product is derived from foreign aid.

About 6,000 miles southwest of California is the island of Guam, a US territory and the location of major US Air Force and Navy installations. Naval Air Station Guam hosted the weather organization and forecasting agents up until the station was closed. The NWS office was then moved to the Guam International Airport from which it issues advisories, watches, and warnings for Guam, the Republic of Palau, the Federated States of Micronesia, the Commonwealth of the Northern Marianas, and the Republic of the Marshall Islands.

Moving south from Guam is the weather service office on the island of Pago Pago in American Samoa. Located about 2,577 miles south of Hawaii, WSO Pago Pago supports the weather reports and tropical cyclone warning responsibilities for US islands in the Southern Hemisphere. Unlike the other NWS offices across the Pacific and United States, all of the employees at WSO Pago Pago are native Samoans.

The International Tsunami Information Center

From the UNESCO website:

> The International Tsunami Information Centre (ITIC) was established . . . in November 1965 by the Intergovernmental Oceanographic Commission (IOC) of the United Nations Educational, Scientific and Cultural Organization (UNESCO). . . . [NOAA] provides the Director and office staff in Honolulu, Hawaii. . . . ITIC's mandate and functions in support of Member States of the Intergovernmental Coordination Group for the Pacific Tsunami Warning and Mitigation System (ICG/PTWS, formerly ITSU) were approved by IOC Resolution X-23 (1977). ITIC maintains . . . relationships with scientific research and academic organizations, civil defense agencies, and the general public in order to carry out its mission to mitigate the hazards associated with tsunamis by improving tsunami preparedness for all Pacific Ocean nations. ITIC is also assisting in the development and implementation of tsunami warning and mitigation systems globally (IOC Resolutions XXIII-12, 13, and 14 (Indian, Caribbean, and Mediterranean respectively, 2005).
>
> The ITIC's responsibilities include:
>
> - monitoring . . . tsunami warning activities in the Pacific and other oceans and recommending improvements in communications, data networks, acquisition and processing, tsunami forecasting methods, and information dissemination;
> - bringing to [the public] information on tsunami warning systems, on the affairs of IOC and ITIC, and on how to become active participants in the ICG/PTWS;

- assisting [the public] in the establishment of national and regional warning systems, and the reduction of tsunami risk through comprehensive mitigation programmes.[16]

ITIC also acts as a clearinghouse for event data collection as well as the development of educational and preparedness materials. ITIC's reach is both domestic and international.

Internationally, ITIC provides mitigation support outreach and training to countries participating in the Tsunami and Coastal Hazards Warning System for the Caribbean and Adjacent Regions and the Pacific Tsunami Warning and Mitigation System. During tsunami events, ITIC provides remote real-time support to countries as needed.

ITIC supports the US National Tsunami Hazard Mitigation Program, which includes twenty-eight coastal states, territories, and commonwealths, and the US Geological Society (USGS), NOAA, and FEMA as the participating US federal agencies. ITIC also supports Hawaii and the Pacific states of Guam, American Samoa, and the Northern Mariana Islands. During warning events, ITIC provides in-person support to the Hawaii Emergency Management Agency Emergency Operations Center.

The Pacific Tsunami Warning Center

"Tsunami warnings began in the United States with Thomas Jaggar's (founder of the Hawaiian Volcano Observatory (HVO)) attempt to warn the Hilo harbormaster of the possibility of a tsunami generated by the 1923 Kamchatka earthquake. His warning was not taken seriously, and at least one fisherman was killed."[17]

As a result of the 1960 earthquake and tsunami that devastated Chile, many people in Hawaii and possibly as many as 200 people in Japan were killed. Pacific nations

> decided to coordinate efforts to prevent such loss of life from ever occurring again in the Pacific Basin due to destructive . . . tsunamis. Under the . . . United Nations, the Intergovernmental Oceanographic Commission (IOC) established the Intergovernmental Coordination Group for the Pacific Tsunami Warning System (ICG/PTWS) in 1968. The U.S. offered the 'Ewa Beach center as the operational headquarters for the Pacific Tsunami Warning System, and the facility was re named [sic] the Pacific Tsunami Warning Center.
>
> PTWC issued tsunami warnings to Alaska until 1967 when the West Coast & Alaska Tsunami Warning Center (WCATWC) was established in response to the 1964 Alaskan earthquake and tsunami.

> In 1982, the WCATWC area of responsibility was enlarged to include the issuing of tsunami warnings to California, Oregon, Washington, and British Columbia for potential tsunamigenic earthquakes. . . . PTWC continued to issue tsunami warnings to these areas for Pacific-wide tsunamigenic sources until 1996 when that responsibility was also given to the WCATWC.[18]

After the Kalapana earthquake and tsunami on Hawaii's Big Island in 1975, PTWC began issuing official tsunami warnings to the state of Hawaii. PTWC also began issuing local tsunami warnings to Puerto Rico and the US Virgin Islands, but in June 2007 NTWC assumed that responsibility. Since the Indian Ocean tsunami in 2004, PTWC has taken on additional areas of responsibility including the South China Sea, Caribbean Sea, the Indian Ocean, and Puerto Rico and US Virgin Islands (until June 2007). PTWC's staff size increased from eight to fifteen people as a result of the Indian Ocean tsunami, and it now staffs the center 24/7.

The National Tsunami Warning Center

Following the great Alaskan earthquake that occurred in Prince William Sound on March 27, 1964, Congress provided funds in 1965 to construct two new observatories and establish a tsunami warning system in Alaska.[19]

> The first observatory constructed was at the U.S. Naval Station on Adak Island . . . in the Central Aleutians. The City of Palmer, in the Matanuska Valley 42 miles northeast of Anchorage, was selected as the site for the primary observatory due to its proximity to bedrock for instrumentation and to communications facilities. Construction of the observatory installations . . . was completed in the summer of 1967. With the dedication of the Palmer Observatory on September 2, 1967, the Alaska Regional Tsunami Warning System (ARTWS) became operational.[20]

Tsunami warning responsibility for Alaska was originally shared by the two observatories located at Adak and Sitka. Sitka and Fairbanks were the only two seismic stations operating in Alaska in 1964 prior to the Prince William Sound earthquake. Unfortunately, Adak and Sitka were limited to issuing a tsunami warning for seismic events occurring within 300 miles of their locations. After the Palmer Observatory became operational in 1967, the responsibility to provide tsunami warning services for Alaska was transferred from the Adak and Sitka observatories to the observatory in Palmer.[21] Sitka and Adak observatories were eventually closed in the early 1990s, although the seismic instrumentation in both locations is still maintained.

The National Weather Service took control of the Palmer Observatory in 1973 and changed its name to the Alaska Tsunami Warning Center (ATWC). In 1982, the ATWC's area of responsibility was increased to include the issuing of tsunami warnings to Washington, Oregon, California, and British Columbia for potential tsunamigenic earthquakes occurring in their coastal areas. The responsibility was again expanded in 1996 to include all Pacific-wide tsunamigenic sources that could affect the Washington, Oregon, California, British Columbia, and Alaska coasts, and the name was changed to the West Coast/Alaska Tsunami Warning Center (WCATWC). The name was changed again on October 1, 2013, to the National Tsunami Warning Center (NTWC).

A new NTWC building was constructed close to the original building in 2003. This new facility provides upgraded power and communications capability, as well as office space for the center staff.[22]

After the 2004 Indian Ocean tsunami, the NTWC expanded its warning area to the US and Canadian Atlantic coasts, the US Gulf coast, the Virgin Islands, and Puerto Rico.

National Centers for Environmental Prediction

The National Centers for Environmental Prediction (NCEP) delivers data-driven environmental predictions. NCEP creates accurate, timely, and reliable forecasts and warnings for the protection of American lives and property.[23] NCEP is the starting point for nearly every weather forecast in the country. NCEP responsibilities include the following:

- Create weather, ocean, climate, space, and environmental hazard products
- Supervise improvements to the NCEP model
- Support the research and development of new or enhanced models to operations
- Develop meteorological software applications
- Manage communication and products to and from the NCEP centers and customers[24]

NOAA's advanced Weather and Climate Operational Supercomputing Systems are located in Orlando, Florida, and Reston, Virginia, and consist of both IBM and Cray component computers.

The NCEP manages nine centers:

- The Aviation Weather Center provides aviation warnings for pilots and forecasts of hazardous flight conditions at all levels within domestic and international air space.
- The Climate Prediction Center monitors and forecasts short-term climate fluctuations.
- The Environmental Modeling Center develops numerical climate, hydrological, weather, and ocean data through a broad program in partnership with the scientific community.
- The National Hurricane Center provides forecasts of the movement and strength of tropical weather systems and issues watches and warnings for the United States.
- The NCEP Central Operations executes the operational suite of numerical analysis programs and forecast models and prepares NCEP products for dissemination.
- The Ocean Prediction Center issues weather warnings and forecasts for the Atlantic and Pacific Oceans north of 30 degrees.
- The Space Weather Prediction Center provides space weather alerts and warnings for disturbances.
- The Storm Prediction Center provides tornado and severe weather watches and warnings for the contiguous United States.
- The Weather Prediction Center provides nationwide analysis and forecast guidance.[25]

River Forecasting Centers

Timely and accurate flood warnings and river forecasts are critical to saving lives and property. The thirteen river forecasting centers (RFCs) monitor the nation's waterways to minimize loss of life and property damage from flooding. RFCs produce flood forecasts, river and water information used for recreation, reservoir operations, navigation, and water supply planning. The National Water Center (NWC) is the primary location for water forecast operations. It supports the existing regional RFCs with a national center focused on water information and services to the nation. The NWC also supports research efforts and collaboration across federal water science and management agencies.[26]

Center Weather Service Units

Center weather service units (CWSUs) provide accurate and timely weather information to the FAA and pilots contributing to the safest and most efficient use of the nation's National Airspace System. There are eighty-four NWS meteorologists dispersed throughout twenty-one CWSUs, which are co-located within air route traffic control centers. CWSU meteorologists perform briefings to air traffic controllers and are vital in helping FAA personnel safely and efficiently route traffic. Other functions include producing and disseminating a short-term weather forecast (lasting up to two hours) on how weather is impacting aviation and a medium-range forecast product (two to twelve hours) used for planning purposes.

Consolidated Appropriations Act of 2021 for NOAA

On December 27, 2020, the Consolidated Appropriations Act, 2021 (Pub.L.116-260) for FY 2021 was signed into law by President Trump. This provides a total of $5.65 billion for NOAA, including $4.10 billion for NOAA Operations, Research and Facilities and $1.55 billion in Procurement, Acquisition and Construction.[27] Fortunately, these funds are higher than those in fiscal year 2020, which is a positive trend.

FEMA has no budget to spend on acquisition of intelligence information from another federal agency. It is all funded by tax dollars, so why should FEMA and other government entities have to pay NOAA for the data they collect? The same problem exists with the general public and their local media outlets that provide up-to-date weather information and warnings. It is the citizens' tax dollars that fund NOAA; therefore, you have already paid for the product they produce.

However, if a business wants detailed forecasts so that it can plan the cross-country delivery routes of trains and trucks, then perhaps it should purchase that information, particularly if it is using tax loopholes to reduce its business tax burdens. The same goes for airlines. And for corporate entities such as Weather Central, The Weather Channel, and AccuWeather, all of which make millions of dollars each year broadcasting information we, as taxpayers, paid for. So, let's look at the overall NOAA budget approved by the president for 2021.

The Office of Oceanic and Atmospheric Research (OAR) is a division of NOAA, and is also referred to as NOAA Research. The only sections of OAR that did not receive as much or more in fiscal year 2021 were the Joint Technology Transfer Initiative (allocated $13.0 million, a decrease of $2 million from fiscal year 2020), and the National Oceanographic Partnership Program ($3.0 million, a decrease of $2.0

million). All other sections of OAR were allocated as much or more than the previous year.[28]

From the NOAA website:

> [NOAA's Office of the Chief Financial Officer] OCFO provides significant value to society through careful budgeting, robust internal controls and financial management as well as strong accountability for our performance and "return on investment" to the American people. NOAA's budget reflects a thoughtful balance of priorities that are thoroughly justified to advance the Administration's vision for the Nation. Once enacted, the OCFO ensures the budget is executed in accordance with congressional direction, taxpayer dollars are appropriately and lawfully spent, and waste, fraud and abuse are eliminated. The OCFO is also a good steward of taxpayer funds through accurate financial systems. Due in no small measure to these effective management practices, NOAA is able to detail in the reports . . . the enormous benefit the agency contributes to the economy and in keeping Americans out of harm's way.[29]

For example, in the June 2018 publication, *NOAA by the Numbers: NOAA's Value to the Nation*, it states, "NOAA's research and forecasts lead to reduced damage from storms and other natural hazards. The agency provides information that helps businesses make decisions and allows key industries like transportation and agriculture to operate more efficiently. NOAA's management programs for oceans and coastal areas help enhance both the current and future productivity of these economically vital resources."[30]

NOAA contributes value to the economy in two basic ways: by providing information that people use to influence decisions, and by managing, or helping to manage, natural resources that are valuable. Understanding the economic worth created by NOAA involves asking how the value of resources is enhanced through NOAA management.

Much of the valuable information created by NOAA is "operational" in nature, including the full range of weather information together with ocean conditions and forecast information. The information is considered operational because it is utilized for actual operational planning and execution. It is relevant, timely intelligence, used by people in a range of situations and environments to improve decision-making. It is used to make critical decisions about preparing for weather- and climate-related activities.

Operational information is worth a great deal only when it is both timely and accurate. Timeliness means that the information gets to organizations and people soon enough to ensure an appropriate response. Accuracy means the information is correct, or correct to within a reasonable margin of error. The value of the information lies in how much it improves economic or social outcomes for either the organization or individual, or both. Thus, the value or worth of information also depends on the following:

- The ability to use the information to make a better decision and to act upon the information (regardless of the precision or timeliness, information has no practical value if there is no way to act);
- The perceptions of the users (do they trust the information enough and have the ability to act upon it?); and
- The potential economic and/or societal gain resulting from a relevant and timely decision.

It is unusual for a person not to check the weather at some point each day. Everybody uses the services NOAA provides. These include daily weather forecasts that support the country's nearly $4.6 trillion in annual economic activity generated by US seaports and disaster response. The gross domestic product (GDP) varies 3.4 percent from year to year due to weather; this equated to $485 billion in 2008 or $545 billion in 2016.[31] Businesses that are directly dependent on the oceans and Great Lakes resources contribute more than $350 billion to US GDP, supporting more employment than crop production, building construction, and telecommunications combined.[32]

A nationwide survey indicated that weather forecasts generate $31.5 billion annually in economic benefits to the country.[33] The total of all federal spending on meteorological operations and research was $3.4 billion, while an additional $1.7 billion ($1.9 billion in 2016) was spent on weather forecasting by the private sector, totaling $5.1 billion spent on public- and private-sector weather operations and research in 2009.[34] Based on the above numbers, the value provided by weather forecasts to households was 6.2 times the cost of producing them—a very good deal for the US citizen.

Imagine the expense if FEMA had to duplicate these spending efforts to conduct all of its assigned functions. Clearly, one of the unheralded successes in homeland security intelligence is the interactive and cooperative nature of the FEMA relationship with NOAA and the NWS. However, NOAA is just one federal agency that provides intelligence for FEMA.

US Geological Survey

The US Geological Survey was established with the passage of the Organic Act in 1879.[35] The main responsibilities of the agency were to map public lands, evaluate mineral resources, and examine geological structure. Over time, the mission expanded to include the research of environmental health, ecosystems, natural hazards, climate, and land use change. USGS provides detailed information about the natural hazards that threaten lives, the water, minerals, energy, and other natural resources the United States relies upon.

Core Science Systems

Core Science Systems (CSS) leads the US Geological Survey's mission as the primary civilian mapping agency for the country. CSS personnel conduct detailed surveys and develop high-quality, highly accurate hydrographic, geologic, topographic, and biogeographic data and maps. The maps allow precise planning for critical mineral assessments, energy development, mineral assessments, urban planning, flood prediction, infrastructure projects, emergency response, and hazard mitigation.

Ecosystems

The USGS Ecosystems mission area is the biological research arm of the Department of the Interior. This agency provides impartial research information and tools to the country's natural resource managers to manage species and priority ecosystems. This work is done within the broader mission of the USGS to serve the nation with science that advances understanding of natural resources.

Energy and Minerals

The Energy and Minerals mission area conducts research and assessments that focus on the quantity, quality, and location of energy and mineral resources, including the economic and environmental effects of resource extraction and use. Geologic studies are done in an impartial manner and performed in collaboration with energy and mineral experts.

Environmental Health

The Toxic Substances Hydrology and Contaminant Biology Programs work to assess and differentiate threats related to environmental contaminant and pathogen exposures that can cause actual health risks. Specialized teams of geologists, chemists, hydrologists, biologists, and geographers work together in the field and laboratories across the United States.

Land Resources

Experts at Land Resources work to understand how land use affects natural resources, livelihoods, and communities. Science plays an essential role in helping people understand the local to global implications of change, anticipate the effects, and reduce the risks associated with decisionmaking in a changing environment.

Natural Hazards

Natural hazards threaten lives and livelihoods and result in billions of dollars in damage every year in this country. USGS works with many agencies to assess, monitor, and conduct research on a wide range of natural hazards so that citizens and policymakers have the necessary knowledge and understanding they need to enhance preparedness, response, and resilience. This is another very important component of the intelligence that FEMA depends upon.

Water Resources

Basic information about water is fundamental to local and national economic well-being, protection of life and property, and effective management of US water resources. The USGS works with partners to assess, monitor, conduct research, and disseminate information on a wide range of water resources and conditions including streamflow, water quality, groundwater, and water use and availability.

Emergency Management

USGS has its own emergency management functions, separate and distinct from FEMA. These include providing oversight, direction, and support to USGS managers in responding to major hazard events and ensuring that the USGS is able to fulfill its mission under all circumstances.[36] They also provide support to certain National Response Framework emergency support functions. Among these are the USGS ShakeAlert Earthquake Early Warning System and the use of streamgages.

USGS ShakeAlert Earthquake Early Warning System. Wherever people live with the risk of earthquakes, there is a desire for an early warning system. Following a magnitude 6.8 earthquake on the Hayward Fault in California in 1868, the *San Francisco Daily Evening Bulletin* published an editorial proposing an early warning system. Calls echoing that desire continued throughout the twentieth century in countries as far off as Italy, Iran, Japan, and Mexico.

In the United States, USGS geophysicist Tom Heaton proposed the first serious earthquake warning system in 1985.[37] Dr. Heaton's insight was ahead of its time, but the technology available in 1985 was not adequate for the system he wanted.

After the 1989 Loma Prieta earthquake, other USGS scientists used some of Heaton's imaginative ideas to try to safeguard the lives of rescue workers in the San Francisco Bay Area. The intense shaking from the Loma Prieta earthquake collapsed a 1.6-mile (2.5-kilometer) section of the Nimitz Freeway (referred to as the Cypress Structure) along I-880 through Oakland.[38] As first responders worked to free people trapped in the rubble of the freeway, the risk of damaging aftershocks injuring the workers became apparent. So, USGS scientists set up a temporary radio aftershock warning system that sent alerts to the workers whenever there was a significant aftershock. During its six months of operation, the system sent warnings for twelve earthquakes greater than magnitude 3.7.

An earthquake early warning system requires a widespread network of seismometers. In the United States, the first regional seismic networks were begun by research universities such as the University of California at Berkeley, Caltech, and the University of Washington. These regional networks and others were later coordinated by the Advanced National Seismic System in 2000.

Around 2000, seismometers went from analog to digital, which allowed them to log data much faster and more accurately. Also, high-bandwidth data communications had become more common, allowing seismic stations to quickly transmit more data across greater distances.

In 2006, USGS, the University of California–Berkeley, Caltech, the Southern California Earthquake Center, and the Swiss Federal Institute of Technology in Zurich formed a partnership to create standards for what would constitute ShakeAlert, America's earthquake early warning system. These standards included specifications for what kinds of data analysis would be needed to recognize that an alert was required, what kind of seismic equipment would be needed, and how best to distribute alerts to users quickly so they could take protective actions.

After all, earthquake early warning is similar to the requirements of good intelligence: timely, relevant, and critical information, disseminated to the people who need it in time for action to be taken. In addition to those basic requirements, early warning of an earthquake also requires direct information about the degree of hazard people may face within a short time frame. In addition, they must also be given specific instructions about what protective actions they must take, and possibly where to go, in order to be safe.

The key for organizations was to develop digitized techniques to identify potentially damaging earthquakes quickly enough to notify people potentially in danger prior to quake-related shaking reaching them. That capability also required possibly upgrading and increasing the density of equipment in existing seismic sensor networks, as well as improving the information technology infrastructure to more accurately estimate ground shaking intensity at the user's location.

The speed of the warning is extremely important for people to get alerts before shaking arrives at their location. Testing of earthquake early warning systems has indicated that the amount of warning time is dependent on the proximity of seismic stations to the earthquake, the distance of a user from the epicenter, and how one receives the alert. Thus, the public and other end users may receive an alert before, during, or after shaking arrives at their location.

In 2012, the Pacific Northwest Seismic Network, an Advanced National Seismic System regional network operated by the USGS, the University of Oregon, and the University of Washington, joined the earthquake early warning efforts that began in California. Their goal was to extend the USGS ShakeAlert Earthquake Early Warning System across the US mainland Pacific Coast.

In 2018, USGS declared that the ShakeAlert system was ready to go and available to alert personnel via automated delivery to computers within organizations. The next phase was a test of public alerting in Los Angeles County using a cellphone app developed by the City of Los Angeles, which debuted in early 2019.

In parallel with the development of the technology to produce and deliver earthquake warnings, USGS and its partners are also studying how users react to alerts and how to best educate the public about the system's capabilities. The most technologically advanced warning system in the world is useless unless people know what to do in response to alerts.

USGS, its partners, and the nation's earthquake early warning capacity have come a long way since Loma Prieta in 1989. Dozens of organizations from the public and private sectors have partnered, hundreds of seismometers have been installed, thousands of quakes have been detected, and social science research on the best way to alert the public is underway.

Restoring streamgages. "There are approximately 8,300 USGS-operated streamgages across the country that measure water levels, streamflow, and rainfall."[39] Streamgages or gaging stations are locations used by environmental scientists to monitor and test bodies of water such as streams and rivers. These devices provide information on the water level surface elevation or "stage" and/or volumetric discharge or "flow" of water. Some topographical maps provide gaging station locations. Most streamgages are automated and use telemetry capabilities to transmit data to a central data-logging facility.

> Information provided through the USGS National Streamflow Network forms the scientific basis for decision-making related to protection of life and property from water-related hazards, such as floods; cost-effective management of freshwater that is safe and available for drinking, irrigation, energy, industry, recreation, and ecosystem health; and national, state, tribal, and local economic well-being. The USGS provides this data to federal, state, and local agencies, as well as to the public.
>
> For more than 125 years, the USGS has monitored flow in selected streams and rivers across the United States.[40]

In October 2018, about 14 percent of streamgages were offline due to an issue with the telemetry system that records and transmits data. The USGS identified and made its highest priority getting those inoperative gages back online in areas expected to receive significant rainfall over the next few days. The public was notified about affected streamgages at the local level. Gages in forty-three states were affected. The affected gages were back online on November 8, 2018.

Knowing the amount of water in a stream or river and how the water flow is changing is essential intelligence for FEMA. Without these data it would be impossible to effectively warn the public about imminent flooding, nor would the agency be able to deploy response and recovery teams to assist in the aftermath of significant flooding.

Volcano Hazards Program

From the USGS website:

> The mission of the USGS Volcano Hazards Program is to enhance public safety and minimize social and economic disruption from eruptions through delivery of effective forecasts, warnings, and information of volcano hazards. . . .
>
> The USGS Volcano Hazards Program (VHP) monitors and studies active and potentially active volcanoes, assesses their hazards, and conducts research . . . in order for the USGS to issue "timely warnings" of potential volcanic hazards to emergency-management professionals and the public. . . .
>
> Data collected by volcano-monitoring networks and extensive fieldwork surveys . . . help scientists interpret volcanic behavior, forecast eruptions . . . and provide situational awareness—information relating to eruptions and unrest. The most effective monitoring is achieved by applying a combination of techniques (seismic, geodetic, hydrological, and geochemical) via arrays of several instruments at single volcanoes on a continuous near-real-time basis. Airborne and satellite remote-sensing technology provide enhanced capabilities for detecting and tracking signs of unrest and eruption including gas emissions, topographic changes, ash clouds, and lava flows. . . .
>
> Hazard assessments are the foundation for effective hazard mitigation strategies.[41]

This is a clearly important intelligence source for FEMA. Knowing potential volcanic hazards helps scientists plan mitigation not only for the immediate area, but across the country concerning ashfall.

> VHP develops both long- and short-term volcano hazards assessments. Long-term assessments are based upon detailed geologic mapping and dating a volcano's deposits, which provide the record of past eruptions. Using the knowledge of past behavior, models of potential volcanic hazards (e.g. ash plumes and ashfall, lava-flow or lahar pathways and travel times) are created. Geologic and modeling data are integrated with high-resolution topographic mapping of the landscape and analyzed using the Geographic Information System (GIS) to develop comprehensive hazard-zone maps and assessments, which may include risk and vulnerability analysis and/or probabilistic recurrence information. These provide an essential basis for monitoring network design, long-term eruption forecasting, land-use planning, and short-term emergency planning. During an eruption, real-time

monitoring, observations, and hazards models are combined to evaluate the most likely hazards on a day-to-day basis, which feed into short-term hazards assessments. . . .

VHP scientists employ many different disciplines to investigate volcanic processes from the magma storage regions beneath volcanoes to eruption products on the surface and in the atmosphere. Geologic research provides a long-term view of volcanic behaviors and eruption intervals, which helps anticipate the most likely styles and frequency of activity in the future. Mathematical and physical models of volcanic processes help scientists interpret the data streams from volcano monitoring networks. Microscopic chemical and physical analysis of eruption products provides insight into the duration and location of magma storage and how it erupts from a volcano. Such fundamental research provides greater understanding of the physical behavior of volcanoes and how eruptions could impact communities and ecosystems. Research provides the scientific factual basis for delineating areas impacted during past eruptions, improving eruption forecasts and warnings, enabling quantitative hazard assessments, and bringing heightened awareness to volcanic risks. . . .

Preparation is key to staying safe and experiencing minimal impact during hazardous volcanic events. For communities and infrastructure at risk, VHP personnel work directly with Federal, State, and local officials, as well as industry, news media, and the public, to increase awareness of location-specific hazards and to participate in response planning activities well ahead of volcanic crises.

To be effective during a volcanic event, volcano-hazard information must be communicated quickly and accurately. VHP provides situational awareness by 1) issuing authoritative forecasts, warnings, and status updates of volcanic activity; 2) investigating and rectifying reports of unrest and eruption that are false or misleading; 3) providing access to volcanic information and real-time data to the public via websites, social media, and subscription services; 4) participating in targeted volcano-hazard education and planning activities.[42]

These are all utilized by FEMA to develop response, recovery, and mitigation plans and to prepare deployment teams for potential events.

US Army Corps of Engineers

The Army Corps of Engineers has a long history, from the very beginning of the country extending thirteen months before the signing of the Declaration of Independence in July 1776. The Continental Congress organized what was to become the Army Corps of Engineers on June 16, 1775, with a chief engineer and two assistants.

George Washington appointed the first engineer officers of the army on June 16, 1775, during the American Revolution, and engineers have served in combat in all subsequent American wars. The army established the Corps of Engineers as a separate, permanent branch on March 16, 1802, and gave the engineers responsibility for founding and operating the US Military Academy at West Point.

Since then, "the U.S. Army Corps of Engineers has responded to changing defense requirements and played an integral part in the development of the country. Throughout the 19th century, the Corps of Engineers built coastal fortifications, surveyed roads and canals, eliminated navigational hazards, explored and mapped the Western frontier, and constructed buildings and monuments in the Nation's capital."[43]

> From the beginning, many politicians wanted the Corps to contribute to both military construction and works "of a civil nature." Throughout the 19th century, the Corps supervised the construction of coastal fortifications and mapped much of the American West with the Corps of Topographical Engineers, which enjoyed a separate existence for 25 years (1838–1863). The Corps of Engineers also constructed lighthouses, helped develop jetties and piers for harbors, and carefully mapped the navigation channels.
>
> In the 20th century, the Corps became the lead federal flood control agency and significantly expanded its civil works activities, becoming among other things a major provider of hydroelectric energy. . . . Its role in responding to natural disasters also grew dramatically.[44]

In addition, the "Corps of Engineers is one of the nation's leading federal providers of outdoor recreation with more than 400 lake and river projects in 43 states."[45] These include over 2,500 recreation areas at 463 locations (primarily lakes) as well as leasing 1,800 sites to state or local parks and recreation authorities or private parties.

> Assigned the military construction mission in 1941, the Corps built facilities at home and abroad to support the U.S. Army and Air Force. During the Cold War, Army engineers managed construction programs for America's allies, including a massive effort in Saudi Arabia. In addition, the Corps of Engineers also completed large construction programs for federal agencies such as NASA and the postal service. The Corps also maintains a rigorous research and development program in support of its water resources, construction, and military activities.
>
> In the late 1960s, the Corps became a leading environmental preservation and restoration agency. It now carries out natural and cultural resource management programs at its water resources projects

and regulates activities in the Nation's wetlands. In addition, the Corps assists the military services in environmental management and restoration at former and current military installations.

When the Cold War ended, the Corps was poised to support the Army and the Nation in the new era. Army engineers supported 9/11 recovery efforts and currently play an important international role in the rapidly evolving Global War on Terrorism, including reconstruction in Iraq and Afghanistan.[46]

Multipurpose Waterway Development

From the US Army Corps of Engineers website:

> Neglected waterways, demands for hydropower throughout the country, and calls for irrigation projects in the West drew attention to the nation's water resources at the beginning of the 20th century. Multipurpose partisans advocated the application of scientific management to ensure efficient water use. This meant a program of basinwide development that would address all potential applications of the resource.
>
> Unlike the West, where irrigation became the focus of attention, the East was more concerned with hydropower development. Beginning in the early 1880s, when a plant in Appleton, Wisconsin, first used falling water to produce electricity, the construction of hydroelectric dams on the nation's waterways proliferated. These private dams threatened navigation and forced Congress, acting through the Corps of Engineers, to regulate dam construction. The Rivers and Harbors Acts of 1890 and 1899 required that dam sites and plans be approved by the secretary of war and the Corps of Engineers before construction. The General Dam Act of 1906 empowered the federal government to compel dam owners to construct, operate, and maintain navigation facilities without compensation whenever necessary at hydroelectric power sites.
>
> Private interests developed most power projects before World War I. The Corps of Engineers did install a power station substructure at Lock and Dam #1 on the upper Mississippi River. The government later leased the power facility to the Ford Motor Company. In 1919, the Corps began construction of Dam #2 later renamed Wilson Dam as a hydroelectric facility at Muscle Shoals on the Tennessee River. Support for the facility, which was intended to supply power for nitrate production, declined with the end of World War I, and its completion was threatened. However, by 1925 that project was substantially finished.
>
> President Franklin Roosevelt favored the development of federal hydropower projects to provide consumers with low-cost energy. During the New Deal, the Corps participated in three major hydroelectric power projects: Passamaquoddy Tidal Power Project in

Maine, Bonneville Dam on the Columbia River, and Fort Peck Dam on the Missouri River. In 1937, Congress created the Bonneville Power Administration to dispose of the power and set the rates for the power generated at Bonneville Dam.

Meanwhile, concern over flood control intensified. In 1912 [and 1913], two terrifying floods devastated the lower Mississippi Valley and showed the inadequacy of the levee system. Another flood came in 1916, and the first flood control act was passed the following year; it applied only to the Mississippi and Sacramento rivers. Still, the Mississippi River Commission and the Corps continued to depend on levees. That policy was finally changed in 1927, when one of the worst disasters in the nation's history hit the lower Mississippi. The flood was the result of high waters from throughout the Mississippi River's drainage area (41 percent of the continental United States) coming together and inundating the lower Mississippi Valley. Between 250 and 500 people were killed, over 16 million acres were flooded, and over 500,000 people were forced from their homes to refugee camps.

Clearly, depending on levees was not the answer. The chief of engineers, Major General Edgar Jadwin drew up a new plan requiring that the water be dispersed through controlled outlets and floodways as well as confined between levees. After lengthy debate, Congress approved this plan in the 1928 Flood Control Act and placed its implementation under the control of the Corps of Engineers. This act launched what today is called the Mississippi River and Tributaries Project. . . .

Floods continued elsewhere, especially on the Ohio River. Additionally, during the 1930s, there was the misery caused by the Great Depression. Responding to the twin needs for flood protection and work relief, Congress passed the 1936 Flood Control Act, one of the most important events in the history of the Corps of Engineers. For the first time, Congress declared that flood control was a proper activity of the federal government. The act put the Corps firmly into the reservoir construction business, despite earlier Corps' reservations about the effectiveness of reservoirs. It also established that a potential project's economic benefits must exceed its costs. Furthermore, the act specified the obligations that would have to be assumed by local interests before the Corps could begin certain projects.

The 1944 Flood Control Act signaled the victory of the multipurpose approach. It empowered the secretary of the interior to sell power produced at Corps and other federal projects. The act also authorized the gigantic multipurpose civil works project for the Missouri Basin commonly called the Pick-Sloan Plan. It amalgamated the plans for developing the Missouri Basin proposed by Major General Lewis Pick, formerly Missouri River Division engineer, and W. Glenn Sloan, the assistant regional director for the Bureau of Reclamation. In the ensuing years, the Corps built several huge dams on the main stem of the Missouri River. These dams were all multipurpose. They provided flood control, irrigation, navigation, water supply, hydropower, and recreation.

Following World [War] II, federal multipurpose projects expanded considerably. Congress authorized major systems involving hydroelectric power on the Columbia and Snake rivers in the Pacific Northwest, and the Missouri and the Arkansas rivers. The Eisenhower administration challenged some of these ambitious projects as costly federal burdens. However, overall federal power development continued to increase. By 1975, Corps projects the largest on the Columbia and Snake rivers, were producing 27 percent of the total U.S. hydropower and 4.4 percent of all electrical energy output.[47]

Responding to Natural Disasters

From the US Army Corps of Engineers website:

The Corps' role in responding to natural disasters has evolved since just after the Civil War. Direct federal participation in disaster relief began in 1865 when the federal government helped freed blacks survive flooding along the Mississippi. The Corps' first formal disaster relief mission was during the Mississippi Flood of 1882, when it supported Army Quartermaster Corps' efforts to rescue people and property. Army engineers played a critical role in responding to the Johnstown, Pennsylvania, flood of 1889 and the San Francisco earthquake of 1906.

In 1917, the Army reorganized its disaster relief responsibilities and assigned command and control during disaster situations to department or Corps area commanders. Following major flooding in 1937, the chief of engineers ordered all engineer districts to develop flood emergency plans.

In 1947, the Corps responded to an explosion of 2,400 tons of ammonium nitrate on board a ship docked in Texas City, Texas. Two years later, it handled its first major snow removal emergency [during] a massive blizzard on the Great Plains. By 1950, the Corps had established a reputation for responding quickly and effectively to disaster relief missions. Under the Federal Disaster Relief Act of 1950 the Corps continued to be the lead federal agency during flood disasters. Five years later, Congress passed Public Law 84 99 which improved the Corps' ability to fight floods. The law authorized an emergency fund of $15 million annually for flood emergency preparation, flood fighting and rescue operations, and repair or restoration of a flood control work.

During the 1960s the Corps responded to two powerful natural disasters: the Alaskan earthquake of 1964 and Hurricane Camille in 1969. The extensive damage caused by these events and Tropical Storm Agnes (1972) prompted Congress in 1974 to broaden federal responsibility for disaster assistance and assigning responsibility to federal agencies.

By the 1980s the Corps' mission had expanded from flood fighting to other hazards. Consequently, the Corps established an emergency management program. In 1988 the Robert T. Stafford Disaster Relief and Emergency Assistance Act authorized the Federal Emergency Management Agency to provide for all disasters, regardless of cause. . . .

Between 1989 and 1992, the Corps responded to the largest and most destructive oil spill in U.S. history in Prince William Sound in Alaska. It also responded to Hurricane Hugo, which caused major damage in the Virgin Islands and coast of the Carolinas, and to the Loma Prieta Earthquake in California. The 1990s brought even costlier natural disasters. Between 1992 and 1995 the Corps performed major repair and rehabilitation work in the wake of Hurricanes Andrew and Iniki, record flooding on the Mississippi and Missouri rivers, and the Northridge earthquake in California.[48]

The Corps works closely with FEMA in many natural disasters including floods, earthquakes, and volcanic eruptions. This is important information as the joint efforts of FEMA and the Corps are essential when addressing natural disasters and humanitarian relief efforts.

Figure 10.1 is a representation of how FEMA continuously responds to disasters. The FEMA disaster management cycle indicates preparation before the event, which includes both capacity building and pre-impact planning; the response to the disaster; and the recovery, which combines restoration and reconstruction, toward mitigating the event to the extent possible.

Under the Obama administration a fifth component was added to the disaster management cycle: prevention. This component only applies to acts of terrorism and includes the perspective of risk reduction.

If we revise the disaster management cycle so that it includes a variety of outside intelligence sources necessary to address disasters, one can see that the use of outside intelligence is essential from FEMA's perspective. For example, Figure 10.2 is a basic (not at all inclusive) example of some of the combined intelligence and response support required for a flood disaster.

A Systems Approach to Intelligence

FEMA is one of two homeland security agencies that operate using a systems approach to their operations. The other is the US Coast Guard. Other components of DHS are related to law enforcement and

Figure 10.1 The FEMA Disaster Management Cycle

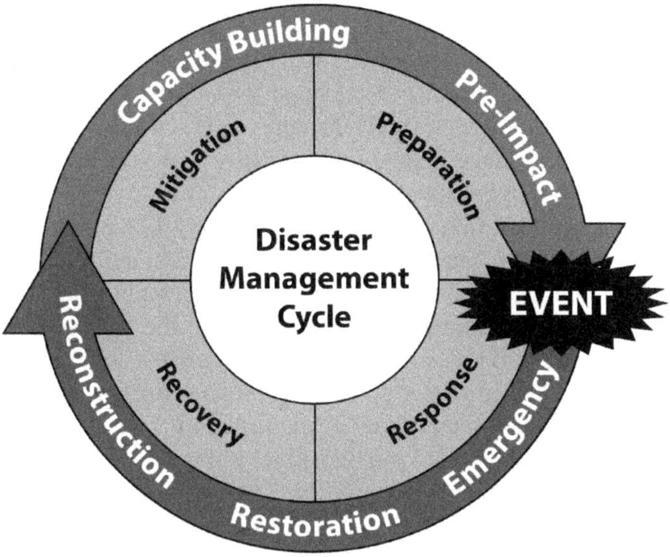

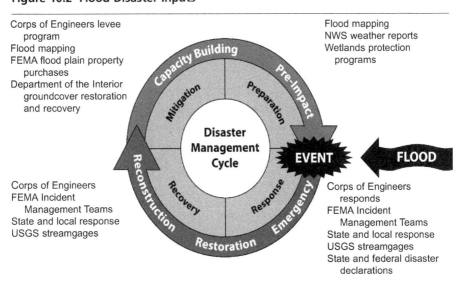

Capacity Building
Pre-Impact
Mitigation
Preparation
Disaster Management Cycle
EVENT
Reconstruction
Recovery
Response
Emergency
Restoration

Credit: James Phelps.

Figure 10.2 Flood Disaster Inputs

Corps of Engineers levee program
Flood mapping
FEMA flood plain property purchases
Department of the Interior groundcover restoration and recovery
Flood mapping
NWS weather reports
Wetlands protection programs
Capacity Building
Pre-Impact
Mitigation
Preparation
Disaster Management Cycle
EVENT
FLOOD
Reconstruction
Recovery
Response
Emergency
Restoration
Corps of Engineers
FEMA Incident Management Teams
State and local response
USGS streamgages
Corps of Engineers responds
FEMA Incident Management Teams
State and local response
USGS streamgages
State and federal disaster declarations

Credit: James Phelps.

immigration and do not apply a systems approach to their operations. This is their major failure.

Figure 10.3 shows that a system is a cohesive amalgam of interrelated and interdependent parts that are bounded by space and time. The environment influences the system. It is clearly defined by its structure and purpose and expressed through its functioning. In the case of the FEMA intelligence system, it is actually more than the sum of its parts because it expresses synergy and emergent behavior.

The FEMA intelligence system is also a learning system because it can adapt, grow, and engage with the environment that creates it. How well it adapts is dependent upon the management of the agency as well as the operations and funding provided to the data-contributing agencies. It has no direct impact on or involvement with the data producers but is wholly dependent upon them to carry out its functions.

Some might claim that FEMA failed in the case of Hurricane Katrina (2005), but the failures there were of political entities that operated the City of New Orleans and the State of Louisiana. The flooding of New Orleans was not the result of any actions taken by FEMA, but a direct result of the failure of several Army Corps of Engineers levees coupled with a failure of the Department of the Interior to properly maintain wetlands around the sea approaches to the city.

By and large the overall ability of FEMA to access and employ the intelligence gathered by numerous other agencies is highly successful. This creates an example of cooperation not seen in fusion centers, between law enforcement agencies at all levels of government, and especially not by the federal law enforcement, the FBI in particular.

Other government agencies with mandates to cooperate and share intelligence across disciplines could learn much from how FEMA operates. Doing so would significantly reduce the threat of terrorism and the failures of law enforcement responses to rapidly emerging threats, and improve the overall safety of the people of the United States.

Conclusion

A system is a cohesive combination of interrelated and interdependent parts, bounded by space and time, influenced by its environment, defined by its structure and purpose, and expressed through its functioning. The

Figure 10.3 The FEMA Intelligence System

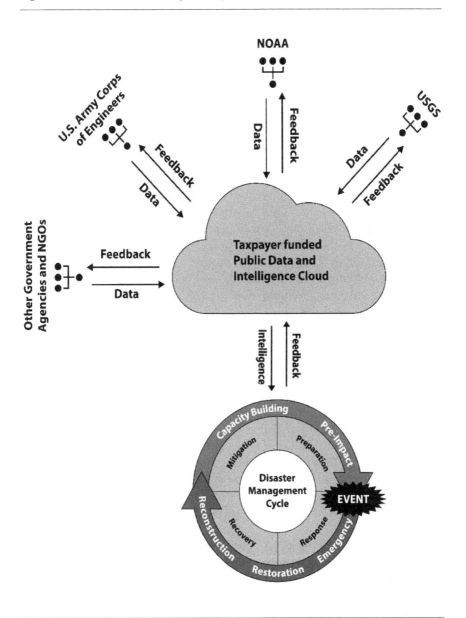

Credit: James Phelps.

most successful government agencies (and private ones), including FEMA, function as systems.

FEMA is essentially forced to adopt a systems approach to do its job. Agencies outside the DHS provide FEMA with the data it requires to function; it is completely dependent on data provided by other agencies.

Both NOAA and the National Weather Service are part of the agencies that provide FEMA with usable, timely intelligence—in this case, weather information. NOAA's roots go back over 200 years. The National Geodetic Survey, a forerunner to NOAA, was established in 1807 by President Thomas Jefferson to provide nautical charts to America's maritime community.

The Weather Bureau, the precursor to the NWS, was created in 1870, and was the first US agency dedicated to atmospheric science. Over time, advances in science, technology, and engineering have enhanced the ability of the NWS to predict weather, climate, and water events, but it has not altered its fundamental mission to protect lives and property and support the nation's economy.

Hazard warning systems include both earthquakes and tsunamis. The Alaska Regional Tsunami Warning Center became operational in 1967 with the dedication of the Palmer Observatory northeast of Anchorage, Alaska. Six years later in 1973 the NWS took control of Palmer and created the Alaskan Tsunami Warning Center.

The US Geological Survey was created in 1879, with the express purpose of mapping public lands and evaluating mineral resources and geological structure. In time, the mission of the agency expanded to include the research of environmental health, ecosystems, natural hazards, climate, and land use change.

Among the natural hazards the USGS has responsibility for are earthquakes. The first regional seismic network was begun by research universities and was brought together in the Advanced National Seismic System in 2000.

The US Army Corps of Engineers has a history longer than the United States. The Continental Congress organized what became the US Army Corps of Engineers on June 16, 1775. Since that date it has responded to both military and civilian needs and played an integral part in the development of the United States.

As shown in the figures in this chapter, FEMA utilizes a systems approach to collecting and analyzing information from various agencies, both within and outside the Department of Homeland Security.

Notes

1. NOAA, "Our History," https://www.noaa.gov/our-history.

2. Ibid.

3. NOAA, "National Weather Service Heritage" fact sheet, https://vlab.ncep
.noaa.gov/documents/5512867/8691878/Heritage-factsheet-FINAL.pdf/6fa0c189
-c591-17c8-9019-4dff61ce209c.

4. Ibid.

5. Ibid.

6. NWS, "NWS Eastern Region Bohemia, NY," https://www.weather.gov
/erh/#.

7. NWS, "Welcome to NWS Southern Region Headquarters," https://www
.weather.gov/srh/welcome.

8. Ibid.

9. Ibid.

10. NWS, "NWS Central Region Headquarters," https://www.weather.gov/crh/.

11. NWS, "NWS Western Region Headquarters," https://www.weather.gov
/wrh/#.

12. NWS, "Alaska Region HQ," https://www.weather.gov/arh/.

13. NWS, "Pacific Region Headquarters Honolulu, Hawaii," https://www
.weather.gov/prh/.

14. Ibid.

15. International Tsunami Information Center, "About ITIC," http://itic.ioc
-unesco.org/index.php?option=com_content&view=category&layout=blog&id
=1173&Itemid=1173.

16. Ibid.

17. Pacific Tsunami Warning Center, https://tsunami.gov/?page=history.

18. Ibid.

19. National Tsunami Warning Center, https://tsunami.gov/?page=history.

20. Ibid.

21. Ibid.

22. Ibid.

23. National Centers for Environmental Prediction, "Who We Are," https://
www.weather.gov/about/nws#:~:text=The%20National%20Centers%20for%20
Environmental,enhancement%20of%20the%20national%20economy.

24. NCEP, "NCEP Central Operations," nco.ncep.noaa.gov/about.shtml.

25. Ibid.

26. NWS, "We Are the National Weather Service," https://www.weather.gov
/about/nws.

27. Consolidated Appropriations Act of 2021 for NOAA, https://research
.noaa.gov/External-Affairs/Budget.

28. Ibid.

29. NOAA, "Value to Society," https://www.noaa.gov/organization/budget
-finance-performance/value-to-society.

30. *NOAA by the Numbers: NOAA's Value to the Nation* (Washington, DC:
NOAA, June 2018), p. 6, https://www.noaa.gov/sites/default/files/atoms/files
/NOAA-by-the-Numbers-Accessible-Version-Corrected-17-JUL-18%20%281
%29.pdf.

31. Jeffrey K. Lazo, "Economics of Weather," National Center for Atmospheric Research, 2011, https://www.wmo.int/pages/prog/dra/eur/documents/SEB %20Conferenc/presentations/RA6SEB_S1_Lazo_Economics_of_Weather.pdf.

32. Ibid.

33. Jeffrey K. Lazo, R. Morss, and J. Demuth, "300 Billion Served: Sources, Perceptions, Uses, and Values of Weather Forecasts," *Bulletin of the American Meteorological Society* 90, no. 6 (2009): 785–798.

34. Ibid.

35. US Geological Survey, https://www.usgs.gov.

36. USGS, "Emergency Management," https://www.usgs.gov/natural-hazards /emergency-management.

37. USGS, "ShakeAlert Earthquake Early Warning System," https://www.usgs .gov/news/usgs-shakealert-earthquake-early-warning-system.

38. California Department of Conservation, "The 1989 Loma Prieta Earthquake," https://www.conservation.ca.gov/cgs/earthquakes/loma-prieta.

39. USGS, "USGS Working to Restore Streamgages," https://www.usgs.gov /news/usgs-working-restore-streamgages.

40. Ibid.

41. USGS, "About the Volcano Hazards Program," https://www.usgs.gov /volcano-hazards/about.

42. Ibid.

43. US Army Corps of Engineers, https://www.sam.usace.army.mil/About /History/.

44. US Army Corps of Engineers, "A Brief History," https://www.usace .army.mil/about/history/brief-history-of-the-corps/introduction/.

45. US Army Corps of Engineers, "Recreation Overview," https://www.usace .army.mil/missions/civil-works/recreation.

46. US Army Corps of Engineers, "A Brief History," https://www.usace .army.mil/about/history/brief-history-of-the-corps/introduction/.

47. US Army Corps of Engineers, "Multipurpose Waterway Development," https:// www.usace.army.mil/About/History/Brief-History-of-the-Corps/Multipurpose -Waterway-Development/.

48. US Army Corps of Engineers, "Responding to Natural Disasters," https:// www.usace.army.mil/About/History/Brief-History-of-the-Corps/Responding-to -Natural-Disasters/.

11

The Future of Intelligence in Homeland Security

Our study of intelligence in homeland security opened with definitions and descriptions of early terrorist attacks and how they were addressed by the people, governments, and courts of the day. John Brown is still a classic example of a religious extremist with underlying political motives; Osama bin Laden is a more recent example. Although the actors change, terrorism as a tool for driving a political agenda does not.

After looking at the development of homeland security, how it operates today, and how the different components of the national effort to gather and disseminate intelligence function (or not), significant time was taken to consider the failures of intelligence, as well as the successes as demonstrated by FEMA. At the beginning of 2020, another major worldwide failure was added to the list of intelligence fiascos impacting not only the United States but every nation: Covid-19. The Chinese version of the CDC knew another pandemic was coming, the World Health Organization was expecting one, and the US CDC—by far the premier infectious disease organization in the world—knew about it as well. They were all planning to face one. Yet, politics, economics, globalization, and just plain denial by world leaders (and in particular the Chinese Communist Party) created a situation in which when Covid-19 made its debut, nobody reacted and many tried to suppress the information.

The Extreme Century

In *Book of Extremes*, Ted Lewis tells us that "the 21st Century is an age of rapid change, principally because the Internet connects everyone to everyone else, ideas and money flow like contagions, and innovation is progressing at an unparalleled pace."[1] In addition, the major change Lewis warns us about is that physical society will transition to virtual society, local concerns to global concerns, and individuals will become as powerful as traditional authorities. Not only is the new world more interconnected and more globalized, but with that interconnectedness the level of self-organized criticality becomes extreme to the point where minor events could result in major disruptions in supply chains and possibly societal collapse. From an intelligence perspective this is predictable, as are mass migrations, alterations in criminal organization operations, changes in terrorist perspectives and approaches, and the potential of nation-state-level conflicts as well as avoidance.

The Covid-19 outbreak is a good example of how the sensitive structure of the international globalized supply chain can be disrupted. The disease was completely foreseeable and easily predicted. Unfortunately, the dots were not connected, shared, or acted on promptly enough to prevent or reduce the terrible impact it has had not only on the United States but also globally.

In a similar way, the same lack of intelligence gathering, sharing, and analysis led to the 9/11 attacks in the United States and subsequent major terrorist attacks in London and Madrid. The failure of imagination of intelligence workers across multiple agencies led to the complete failure to predict, let alone understand, the Arab Spring and the subsequent multiple failures by the United States and European countries to either capitalize on or modify the outcomes.

Lewis warns us that although the twenty-first century will be the most exciting one mankind has ever experienced, it will also be the most dangerous. He uses the example of one person in a million who wants to do harm to others. Today, that one person has more power than ever to wreak havoc on society. What does one person in a million actually mean? It means that there are over 7,000 perpetrators today empowered to use the internet to cause financial and economic destruction, who might want to plant a bomb in a public park, take down a skyscraper, unleash a pandemic, or hold the entire world hostage to the threat of nuclear war—as have the past and present leaders of North Korea. This isn't counting regular hackers, homegrown terrorists, and just plain unstable fanatics. At the exact same time, societies around the world are freely giving up their privacy to unseen corporations, Big Data, and the all-seeing eyes of governments.

How does homeland security intelligence address such rapidly changing and emerging issues? Can the existing legacy systems based in bureaucracy and individual agency pride adjust to embrace the changing world? These questions are the ones that must be addressed today and in future efforts of the overall intelligence organizations that work inside and in conjunction with homeland security.

The existing Department of Homeland Security was thrown together, rapidly, in an attempt to placate the American public, "proving" that the government was willing to do whatever it takes to safeguard the United States and prevent another attack similar to what happened on September 11, 2001. The twenty-two agencies placed into the DHS were chosen in an ad hoc manner, but not so much for their ability to fight the war on terror as for political expediency. Most agencies had little or nothing to do with counterterrorism or cyberthreats. Each DHS secretary has since attempted to focus the agency in one direction or another, unsuccessfully. DHS is still trying to figure out what its focus is supposed to be.

As described in Chapter 10, FEMA is the best-connected user of practical passive intelligence within the DHS. The example provided by FEMA offers a model that can be used among all the agencies that make up DHS, particularly if the intelligence components of those agencies choose to break out of their traditional siloed paradigms.

Silo is a term that is used to describe self-interested and self-contained systems that don't respond to outside influences or share with outside organizations. Everybody has seen a silo either in person or in photos. Those are the tall circular towers you see next to barns on a farm. The wheat or corn collected from the fields is stored in these tall structures and then drawn out of the bottom as there is a need for the contents. In some parts of the country you can see lots of huge concrete silos all joined together in long lines, often two silos deep, where major rail junctions come together. The wheat, corn, silage, and other dried grains stored in these giant structures are where your bread, tortillas, corn chips, and flour for cookies and cakes come from. Yet these groups of silos (called grain elevators) are not actually interconnected. The contents of one are not intermixed and collected together with the contents of the others. Grain elevators are a good analogy of how intelligence within any given agency is siloed and not interchanged.

As in a grain elevator, each (intelligence) silo gets and keeps to itself the information that it collects. That information is moved up and down the silo, processed, and ultimately distributed to some end user. But one silo doesn't interact with the ones next to it or around it except (possibly indirectly) through the massive control and distribution head assembly that runs the logistics of the entire structure. This is an example of a fusion center (and how it theoretically is supposed to operate). Bits and pieces of the more important intelligence contained within the silo rise to the top, are shared through a common control and interchange apparatus, and then action is taken to address the intelligence if it is deemed important. When some piece of intelligence in a silo is ignored or not addressed properly, the entire structure can symbolically short-circuit—sort of like when the FBI missed connecting all the dots on the Tsarnaev brothers and the result was the Boston Marathon bombing of April 15, 2013.[2]

To fix problems associated with homeland security intelligence, it is important that the contents of preexisting silos are mixed together so that the key pieces can be viewed, evaluated, and acted upon by all. To do this it is important to go back to the FEMA approach to intelligence gathering and prosecution.

Breaking Silos

Instead of storing and processing the individual intelligence gathered by each office of each homeland security agency and allowing what is perceived to be the most important to rise to the top, sometimes being shared with the top of the agency itself, collect all the intelligence gathered by all the offices within an agency, along with all the intelligence from all the other DHS agencies, and mix it all up.

One example recommendation is related to the recent surge of Nicaraguan immigrants to the United States. Take the bits and pieces overheard during USBP interviews with MS-13 members and put them with US State Department data on changing economics in Nicaragua. Toss in the CIA country data on Nicaragua and its neighbors. Then add in what NOAA tells us about changing environmental conditions that are leading to a major drought across Central America. Question the coyotes of Los Zetas, Sinaloa, and other cartels apprehended by ICE to see what changes their organizations are planning to exploit. Combine this collection of information with some thinking outside of the box, and you get an outcome that indicates a possible major surge of Nicaraguan migrants moving north toward the US-Mexico border the following summer.

With such information, USBP and CBP could prepare for the onslaught of tens of thousands of Nicaraguans before they start the movement north. DHS, in conjunction with the US State Department, can propose economic aid packages that would reduce the need for the Nicaraguan people to look for refuge in the United States by addressing the upcoming impact of a major drought before it ever strikes.

Think this is a pie in the sky dream? It isn't. In 2009 and 2011 the authors proposed at international conferences in Turkey and Orlando, Florida, that when Venezuela ceased providing cheap oil and gasoline to other Central and South American socialist countries, there would be a sudden arrival of large numbers of economic migrants from those countries in certain USBP sectors along the US-Mexico border. Attendees at the conferences agreed with our analysis and predictions. The data and analysis were offered to USBP and CBP. Unfortunately, these agencies rejected the forecast and analysis because the authors were not government intelligence agents and analysts, but simple college professors. Our prediction was proven right in 2012 when the number of Nicaraguans apprehended along the US-Mexico border nearly doubled from the previous year (Table 11.1). All of the increase in apprehensions happened thirty days after President Nicolas Maduro of Venezuela stopped sending artificially low-priced subsidized oil to Nicaragua.

All of the intelligence needed to make that prediction was readily available and easy to find. Yet USBP, CBP, and ICE were all caught by surprise when large numbers of Nicaraguans started being apprehended illegally entering the United States. The numbers didn't just jump in 2012, but continued to increase annually through the election of President Trump in 2016.

The numbers were so overwhelming, added to the massive migration of Hondurans, El Salvadorans, and Guatemalans, that the US State Department under President Obama initiated a mission to actively interview people in those countries who were separated from family members (and in particular children apprehended in the United States illegally) so

Table 11.1 USBP Reported Apprehensions of Nicaraguans

	2009	2010	2011	2012	2013	2014	2015
Number apprehended	930	836	660	1,041	1,519	1,768	2,646

Source: Data from US Border Patrol via FOIA request, on file with James Phelps.

that those families could be reunited and resettled in the United States at the expense of American taxpayers and without basis in any immigration law. This was not so that the apprehended persons could be returned to their families in their countries of origin, but to reunite them as new immigrants to the United States.

Breaking the silo mentality among all the agencies involved across the homeland security enterprise requires a change in how people view and act upon intelligence. It requires a paradigm shift, or perhaps complete removal of the preexisting paradigms, for intelligence to succeed. It requires recognition at the political/policymaker level that a change is essential if homeland security intelligence is to be successful on a national scale.

Homeland Security Intelligence Analysis

The DHS Information Analysis and Infrastructure Protection Directorate (IAIP) was codified in law, 116 Stat. 2146, 6 U.S.C. Section 121(d)(1) and assigned to "access, receive, and analyze law enforcement information, intelligence information, and other information from agencies of the Federal Government, State and local government agencies, and private sector entities, and to integrate such information in order to (a) identify and access the nature and scope of terrorist threats; (b) detect and identify threats of terrorism against the U.S.; and (c) understand such threats in light of actual and potential vulnerabilities of the homeland."

The original intent of the IAIP was to perform an analytical function utilizing the products of other agencies, both data and finished reports, to provide current assessments of vulnerability, warnings of impending attacks, and recommendations for action at the state, federal, and local levels. However, when President Bush announced in 2003 his intention to create the Terrorist Threat Integration Center (TTIC), the new agency was tasked to undertake many of the tasks planned for the DHS informational analysis element. DHS, through the IAIP, was never intended to duplicate the intelligence collection efforts of the existing agencies within the intelligence community. The IAIP was originally given the authority to acquire and review information from law enforcement agencies, state and local government agencies, the members of the intelligence community, and unclassified public information (open source intelligence).

Unfortunately, the IAIP has not predicted any terrorist activity, investigated any potential terrorist activity, or provided any assistance in the investigation of and subsequent arrest or capture of any terrorism perpetrators over its life span. Since counterterrorism is a function of the FBI and the Terrorism Threat Integration Center is operated by the heads of the CIA, DOD, DHS, and FBI, the IAIP is essentially a redundant organization within DHS that provides little if any actionable intelligence. It is time to modify the responsibilities of the IAIP (renamed the Office of Intelligence and Analysis in 2005) as the actual threats to the homeland are much more diverse than terrorism. In addition, the DHS Intelligence and Analysis agency should protect the United States against threats related to mass migration, trends in Mexican drug cartel operations, homegrown terrorism threats, vulnerabilities in border and maritime security, organized crime groups that exploit and threaten national infrastructure, and potential environmental and natural disasters within the homeland that may affect homeland security concerns.

The authors propose several recommendations relative to the "new" Intelligence and Analysis agency. One is to limit the size of the agency to a maximum of 100 people, in order to create a fluid organizational structure that utilizes working groups from mixed backgrounds consisting of eight members each. Each working group would select their own spokesperson to provide reports from their section to the Intelligence and Analysis director. These group spokespersons are also the ones who interact with other groups to share their group analysis results. These spokespersons can ask the NGA representatives for geospatial support, the climatologists for weather and climate analyses and future climate predictions, and the USGS representatives for terrain mapping and analysis as needed to support analysis. Each working group would be assigned by the Intelligence and Analysis leader to look at specific concerns, relating to the above-mentioned threats. The groups themselves should be mixed and changed as needed to address changing concerns. No group should remain static in members assigned or intelligence analyzed as all types of intelligence can be interrelated across all venues being examined.

One of the new responsibilities of the Intelligence and Analysis agency would be to create homeland security intelligence estimates that can be shared across all agencies and offices. This is what the CIA and the NSA do when they produce National Intelligence Estimates of threats posed to US policies and national security. The difference is, instead of a generalized estimate that is submitted to policymakers at the cabinet level, an estimate would be directly submitted to the heads of all the agencies at the federal, state, territorial, and tribal levels with a determination made by the director of DHS as to whether the information is specific enough to require sharing it with governors of states that might be affected.

How would an improved Intelligence and Analysis agency function? Probably a lot like an OODA (observe, orient, decide, and act) loop with multiple inputs and outputs. It would request and accept data from all members of the DHS, as well as (among others) fusion centers, the ATF, the DEA, the US Army Corps of Engineers, the FBI (Organized Crime Reports), and the Centers for Disease Control, and it would work directly for and report directly to the director of DHS. The agency would have the authority to issue homeland security intelligence estimates directly to the heads of all homeland security agencies without the need for any approval by the director or any other political appointee. It would be up to the director to share estimates with the president and other cabinet directors, at their discretion. Homeland security intelligence estimates would be minimally classified, if at all possible at the Law Enforcement Sensitive level, so that there would not be restrictions related to sharing the information across fusion centers and with governors.

Incorporating the new Intelligence and Analysis agency within DHS allows for a high-level analytical group with direct access to actual raw intelligence data and criminal case data from across a wide range of homeland security–related organizations. From the smallest county sheriff to the largest metropolitan areas, from all the fusion centers, from the wide range of law enforcement agencies spread across states, territories, tribal partners, and the expanse of federal agencies, raw data would flow into an agency that theoretically could produce quality actionable intelligence to inform everybody dealing with threats to the homeland. From potential domestic terrorism, to post–natural disaster criminal activity, to threats posed by mass migrations, to changes in drug cartel shipping routes and methodologies, a single intelligence group would work to provide practical and actionable analysis to everybody involved in protecting the United States.

Conclusion

The twenty-first century opened with the terrorist attacks of 9/11. Since then the United States has been involved in wars in Afghanistan, Iraq, and Syria. The US military has been deployed to eighty nations on six continents to conduct counterterrorism operations. The highly porous border with Mexico is just beginning to be secured two decades into the century with the latest efforts being in response to the Covid-19 pandemic—President Trump sent US Army troops to help secure the border with Mexico. Drug cartels build submersibles to move tons of cocaine to beaches and backwater ports and inlets along the US coastline. Unmanned aerial vehicles are being flown by the air and marine branch of CBP to provide observation over the southern border. Hurricane Katrina devastated New Orleans in 2005, not because the storm struck the city, but because the levees and other infrastructure failed to keep the storm surge out. Homegrown terrorists, many whom the FBI knew about and dismissed, have shot people on military bases, attempted (sometimes successfully) to bomb military and civilian venues, and attacked nightclubs, workplaces, synagogues, churches, and concerts. And, let's not forget the impact of the DC snipers, or the havoc caused by the anthrax attacks.

Hackers (from within the United States and from other countries) have attacked US infrastructure causing massive damage to communications servers, shutting down cities and local governments across the country. They have attacked hospitals during a pandemic, stolen information from the Office of Personnel Management putting millions of Americans at risk of identity theft, as well as data from corporations across the country. And this is just the tip of the iceberg of cyberattacks. Everybody knows people who have been personally targeted and fleeced of hundreds or thousands of dollars by cybercriminals.

The United States has seen decades of extreme wildfires from California to Colorado, from Texas to Montana, many caused by arsonists. Often the extent being the result of poor forest and range management for politically charged reasons. The financial cost of these disasters cannot be completely calculated. Toss in multiple years of repetitive flooding across the central plains and along coastlines, and events such as Superstorm Sandy. Hurricane Katrina wasn't alone in the damage caused across vast swaths of the United States but just one of many storms that were predicted, but that people and governments failed to effectively prepare for and address or mitigate against.

As marijuana legalization has shifted across the country, drug cartels have shifted from MDMA (ecstasy) and cocaine to opioids supplied to them by Chinese manufacturers. As masses of humans moved north from failing Central American countries, the cartels took advantage and stole from the migrants, forced them to transport drugs, and turned them into brothel workers who moved from oil field to oil field and truck stop to truck stop all across Texas, New Mexico, Arizona, and California.

Protecting the homeland requires more than a focus on counterterrorism. It requires a holistic approach to the overall threats posed from a rapidly evolving myriad of origins, some known to law enforcement, others relatively unknown. Intelligence collection, analysis, and dissemination to those able to stop terrorism have to evolve as rapidly as the threats. The current domestic intelligence infrastructure in the United States is not only inadequate to do the job, it has become dysfunctional and counterproductive.

A century of extremes requires a whole new approach to practical intelligence that can be acted upon from the smallest county sheriff along the border with Mexico to the highest levels of government policymakers. The current system is broken. It's time that changes to homeland security intelligence be as extreme as the century that spawned the concept of a secure homeland.

Notes

1. Ted Lewis, *Book of Extremes: Why the 21st Century Isn't Like the 20th Century* (New York: Springer, 2014), p. 165.

2. Joan Vennochi, "FBI's Repeated Failures," *Boston Globe*, April 17, 2014, https://www.bostonglobe.com/opinion/editorials/2014/04/16/fbi-must-answer-for -poor-job-marathon-bombing-investigation/pKoEQXdjAZ3KSEI7WQ6JrN /story.html.

Acronyms

ACC	American Chemistry Council
ANSP	Ammonium Nitrate Security Program
ATF	Bureau of Alcohol, Tobacco, Firearms and Explosives
BAU+	business as usual plus
BCA	benefit-cost analysis
BSA	Bank Secrecy Act
BTS	Border and Transportation Security
CBP	US Customs and Border Protection
CDC	Centers for Disease Control and Prevention
CDL	commercial driver's license
CERCLA	Comprehensive Environmental Response, Compensation, and Liability Act
CETC	Current and Emerging Threats Center
CFATS	Chemical Facility Anti-Terrorism Standards
CI	counterintelligence
CIA	Central Intelligence Agency
CIMC	Counterintelligence Mission Center
CINT	chief intelligence officer (DHS)
CISA	Cybersecurity and Infrastructure Security Agency
COAG	Council of Australian Governments
COINTELPRO	Counterintelligence Program
CT	counterterrorism
CTMC	Counterterrorism Mission Center
CTPAT	Customs Trade Partnership Against Terrorism
CVE	countering violent extremism
CWMD	Countering Weapons of Mass Destruction Office

CYMC	Cyber Mission Center
DA	Department of the Army
DCI	director of Central Intelligence
DEA	Drug Enforcement Administration
DHS	US Department of Homeland Security
DOC	US Department of Commerce
DOD	US Department of Defense
DOJ	US Department of Justice
DOL	US Department of Labor
DOT	US Department of Transportation
DTO	drug trafficking organization
EAP	emergency action plan
EC	European Commission
ECTF	Electronic Crimes Task Force
ELINT	electronic intelligence
EPA	US Environmental Protection Agency
EPCRA	Emergency Planning and Community Right-to-Know Act
ERD	Explosives Regulatory Division
ESMC	Economic Security Mission Center
EU	European Union
FAA	Federal Aviation Administration
FALN	Fuerzas Armadas de Liberación Nacional
FARC	Fuerzas Armadas Revolucionarias de Colombia
FBI	Federal Bureau of Investigation
FDA	US Food and Drug Administration
FEMA	Federal Emergency Management Agency
FHWA	Federal Highway Administration
FIE	foreign intelligence entities
FIG	Field Intelligence Group
FLETC	Federal Law Enforcement Training Center
FOD	Field Operations Division
FRA	Federal Railroad Administration
FSB	Russian Federal Security Service
FTA	Federal Transit Administration
GEOINT	geospatial intelligence
GPS	global positioning system
HHS	Health and Human Services
HITEC	Homeland Identities, Targeting and Exploitation Center
HME	homemade explosive
HRT	Hostage Rescue Team
HSIN	Homeland Security Information Network
HUMINT	human intelligence
I&A	Office of Intelligence and Analysis
IATA	International Air Transport Association
IC	intelligence community
ICE	US Immigration and Customs Enforcement
IED	improvised explosive device
IME	Institute of Makers of Explosives

IMINT	image intelligence
IRTPA	Intelligence Reform and Terrorism Prevention Act
ISIS	Islamic State of Iraq and Syria
JTTF	Joint Terrorism Task Force
KKK	Ku Klux Klan
KSP	Known Shipper Program
MARAD	Maritime Administration
MASINT	measurement and signature intelligence
MSHA	Mine Safety and Health Administration
MTSA	Maritime Transportation Security Act
NACD	National Association of Chemical Distributors
NCCIC	National Cybersecurity and Communications Integration Center
NCEP	National Centers for Environmental Prediction
NCSC	National Counterintelligence and Security Center
NCTC	National Counterterrorism Center
NFPA	National Fire Protection Association
NHTSA	National Highway Traffic Safety Administration
NIE	National Intelligence Estimate
NIEM	National Information Exchange Model
NIH	National Institutes of Health
NNSA	National Nuclear Security Agency
NOAA	National Oceanic and Atmospheric Administration
NRMC	National Risk Management Center
NRO	National Reconnaissance Office
NSA	National Security Agency
NSC	National Security Council
NSI	Nationwide SAR Initiative
NTL	National Transit Library
NTWC	National Tsunami Warning Center
NWC	National Water Center
NWS	National Weather Service
OAR	Oceanic and Atmospheric Research
OCC	Office of the Comptroller of the Currency
OFAC	Office of Foreign Assets Control
OIG	Office of Inspector General
OMB	Office of Management and Budget
OSHA	Occupational Safety and Health Administration
OSINT	open-source intelligence
PBIED	person-borne improvised explosive device
PGS	Programme Global Shield
PHMSA	Pipeline and Hazardous Materials Safety Administration
PIRA	Provisional Irish Republican Army
PPD	Presidential Policy Directive
PPF	powder, paste, and flake
PSI	Proliferation Security Initiative
QHSR	Quadrennial Homeland Security Review
SAR	Suspicious Activity Reporting

SCP	Standing Committee on Precursors
SDR	SAR Data Repository
SIGINT	signals intelligence
SLTT	state, local, tribal, and territorial
SOCMA	Society of Chemical Manufacturers and Affiliates
TOCMC	Transnational Organized Crime Mission Center
TSA	Transportation Security Administration
TSCA	Toxic Substances Control Act
TTIC	Terrorist Threat Integration Center
TWIC	Transportation Workers Identification Credential
UAS	unmanned aerial system
UAV	unmanned aerial vehicle
UFF	United Freedom Front
UN	United Nations
UNODC	United Nations Office on Drugs and Crime
UPS	United Parcel Service
USBDC	US Bomb Data Center
USBP	US Border Patrol
USCIS	US Citizenship and Immigration Service
USGS	US Geological Survey
USPS	US Postal Service
USSS	US Secret Service
VBIED	vehicle-borne improvised explosive device
WHO	World Health Organization
WMD	weapons of mass destruction

Bibliography

Agren, David. "Mexico Maelstrom: How the Drug Violence Got So Bad." *The Guardian*, December 26, 2017.

Anti-Defamation League. *A Dark and Constant Rage: 25 Years of Right-Wing Terrorism in the United States.* New York: ADL, 2017.

Ashcroft, John. Testimony Before the 9/11 Commission, April 2004.

Bargent, J. "2014: A Record Year for Disappearances in Mexico." InSight Crime, November 20, 2014.

Beittel, June S. "Mexico: Organized Crime and Drug Trafficking Organizations." CRS Report No. R41576. Washington, DC: Congressional Research Service, updated July 28, 2020. https://fas.org/sgp/crs/row/R41576.pdf.

Bellavita, Christopher. "Changing Homeland Security: What Is Homeland Security?" *Homeland Security Affairs* 4, Article 1 (June 2008). https://www.hsaj .org/articles/118.

Bowden, Mark. *Killing Pablo: The Hunt for the World's Greatest Outlaw.* New York: Atlantic Monthly Press, 2001.

Bush, George W. *The Department of Homeland Security.* June 2002. https://www .dhs.gov/xlibrary/assets/book.pdf.

Calderón, Laura, Octavio Rodríguez Ferreira, and David A. Shirk. "Drug Violence in Mexico: Data and Analysis Through 2017." Justice in Mexico Special Report, University of San Diego, Dept. of Political Science and International Relations, April 2018.

California Department of Conservation. "The 1989 Loma Prieta Earthquake." https://www.conservation.ca.gov/cgs/earthquakes/loma-prieta.

Carton, Evan. *Patriotic Treason.* New York: Simon and Schuster, 2006.

Centers for Disease Control and Prevention WONDER database. "Mortality." 2018.

Chalk, Peter. "Profiles of Mexico's Seven Major Trafficking Organizations." *CTC Sentinel*, January 2012.

Clarke, Colin P. "ISIS Is So Desperate It's Turning to the Drug Trade." *The Rand Blog,* July 25, 2017.

Clarke, Richard. *Against All Enemies: Inside America's War on Terror.* New York: Free Press, 2004.

Cole v. Young, 351 US 536 (US 1956).

Corcoran, Patrick. "Mexico Has 80 Drug Cartels: Attorney General." InSight Crime, December 20, 2012.

Dahl, Erik J. *Intelligence and Surprise Attack: Failure and Success from Pearl Harbor to 9/11 and Beyond.* Washington, DC: Georgetown University Press, 2013.

Davis, Joshua. "Hackers Take Down the Most Wired Country in Europe." *Wired,* August 21, 2007.

Department of Homeland Security. "Counterintelligence Activities (Summary)." July 29, 2010. https://www.oig.dhs.gov/assets/Mgmt/OIG_10-97_Jul10.pdf.

Department of Homeland Security. "Customs-Trade Partnership Against Terrorism (C-TPAT)." February 14, 2013. https://www.dhs.gov/publication/customs-trade -partnership-against-terrorism-c-tpat.

Department of Homeland Security. "Department Six-Point Agenda." https://www .dhs.gov/department-six-point-agenda.

Department of Homeland Security. *DHS Risk Lexicon: 2010 Edition.* Washington, DC: DHS, 2010.

Department of Homeland Security. "Nationwide SAR Initiative (NSI), NSI Partners." https://www.dhs.gov/nationwide-sar-initiative-nsi/nsi-partners#.

Department of Homeland Security. *The Office of Intelligence and Analysis Strategic Plan for FY 2020–2024.* https://www.dhs.gov/blog/2020/01/29/office -intelligence-and-analysis-strategic-plan-fy-2020-2024.

Department of Homeland Security. "Weapons of Mass Destruction." https://www.dhs.gov/topic/weapons-mass-destruction.

Der Spiegel. "Five Eyes." July 1, 2013.

De Witt, Robert. *The Life, Trial and Execution of Capt. John Brown: Being a Full Account of the Attempted Insurrection at Harper's Ferry, VA.* Charleston: Bibliolife DBA, 2011.

Drug Enforcement Administration. *2017 National Drug Threat Assessment.* https://www.dea.gov/docs/DIR-040-17_2017-NDTA.pdf.

Drug Enforcement Administration. *Cartels and Gangs in Chicago.* 2017. https://www.dea.gov/docs/DIR-013-17%20Cartel%20and%20Gangs%20in %20Chicago%20-%20Unclassified.pdf.

Dudley, S., D. Bonello, J. López-Aranda, M. Moreno, T. Clavel, B. Kjelstad, and J. Restrepo. *Mexico's Role in the Deadly Rise of Fentanyl.* Washington, DC: Wilson Center, Mexico Institute, 2019.

Duenas, V. "Recalibrating the U.S. Strategy for the War on Drugs." Carnegie Council for Ethics in International Affairs, 2017.

Executive Order 12333. National Archives, United States Intelligence Activities, Federal Register.

Federal Bureau of Investigation. "COINTELPRO." https://vault.fbi.gov/cointel-pro.

Federal Bureau of Investigation. "Domestic Terrorism in the Post-9/11 Era." September 7, 2009.

Federal Bureau of Investigation. "First Strike: Global Terror in America." https://archives.fbi.gov/archives/news/stories/2008/february/tradebom_022608.

Federal Bureau of Investigation. "Unabomber." FBI Famous Cases and Criminals. https://www.fbi.gov/history/famous-cases/unabomber.

Federal Bureau of Investigation. "What We Investigate, Counterintelligence." https://www.fbi.gov/investigate/counterintelligence.

Federal Trade Commission. "Equifax Data Breach Settlement." January 2020. https://www.ftc.gov/enforcement/cases-proceedings/refunds/equifax-data-breach-settlement.

Fisher, S., and P. J. McDonnell. "Mexico Sent in the Army to Fight the Drug War, Many Question the Toll on Society and the Army Itself." *Los Angeles Times*, June 18, 2018.

Fleming, Thomas. *American Chronicles*. Boston: New Word City, 2016.

Geraghty, Jim. "Politically Motivated Violence Is on the Rise." *National Review*, April 24, 2018.

Gerra, G., V. Poznyak, S. Saxena, N. Volko, and UNODC-WHO Informal International Scientific Network. "Drug Use Disorders: Impact of a Public Health Rather Than a Criminal Justice Approach." *World Psychiatry* 16, no. 2 (2017): 213–214.

Gonzalez, F. E. "Mexico's Drug Wars Get Brutal." *Current History*, February 2009.

Gornick, Vivian. *Emma Goldman: Revolution as a Way of Life.* New Haven: Yale University Press, 2011.

Hanna, J., F. Karimi, J. Morris, and S. Almasy. "Police: Austin Bomber Left 25-Minute Confession Video on Phone." CNN, August 31, 2018.

History.com editors. "Boston Marathon Bombing." March 28, 2014. https://www.history.com/topics/21st-century/boston-marathon-bombings.

Hoffman, Bruce. *Inside Terrorism*, 3rd ed. New York: Columbia University Press, 2017.

Horwitz, Tony. *Midnight Rising: John Brown and the Raid That Sparked the Civil War.* New York: Henry Holt, 2011.

IBISWorld. "Pharmaceutical Manufacturing Industry in China: Industry Market Research Report." September 2018. https://www.ibisworld.com/industry-trends/international/china-market-research-reports/manufacturing/pharmaceutical/pharmaceutical-manufacturing.html.

Inserra, David, and Ceara Casterline. "Here's How Bad the TSA Is Failing Airport Security. It's Time for Privatization." The Heritage Foundation, November 20, 2017.

Jackson, Brian, Ashley Rhoades, Jordan Reimer, Natasha Lander, Katherine Costello, and Sina Beaghley. "Practical Terrorism Prevention." Homeland Security Operational Analysis Center, Rand Corporation, 2019.

Jackson, Richard. *Writing the War on Terrorism: Language, Politics and Counter-Terrorism.* Manchester, UK: Manchester University Press, 2005.

Jones, Thai. "Why the Bloodiest Labor Battle in U.S. History Matters Today." *The Nation*, April 21, 2014.

Justice News. "Attorney General Sessions Announces New Indictments in International Fentanyl Case." April 27, 2018. https://www.justice.gov/opa/speech/attorney-general-sessions-announces-new-indictments-international-fentanyl-case.

Katz v. U.S., 389 U.S. 347, 1967.

Kilgannon, Corey, and Joseph Goldstein. "Sayfullo Saipov, the Suspect in the New York Terror Attack." *New York Times*, October 31, 2017.

Kreiter, M. "What Happened to Dzhokhar Tsarnaev? Update on Boston Marathon Bomber Sentenced to Death." *International Business Times*, April 16, 2017. https://www.ibtimes.com/what-happened-dzhokhar-tsarnaev-update-boston-marathon-bomber-sentenced-death-2526052.

Kross, Peter. "The Venona Project." HistoryNet. n.d. https://www.historynet.com/the-venona-project.htm.

Lawrence, Bruce. *Messages to the World: The Statements of Osama bin Laden.* New York: Verso Books, 2005.

Lazo, Jeffrey K. "Economics of Weather." National Center for Atmospheric Research, 2011.

Lazo, Jeffrey K., R. Morss, and J. Demuth. "300 Billion Served: Sources, Perceptions, Uses, and Values of Weather Forecasts." *Bulletin of the American Meteorological Society* 90, no. 6 (2009): 785–798.

Lewis, T. G. *Book of Extremes: Why the 21st Century Isn't Like the 20th Century.* New York: Springer, 2014.

Liang, Qiao, and Wang Xiangsui. "Unrestricted Warfare." Beijing: People's Liberation Army Literature and Arts Publishing House, 1999.

Lowenthal, Mark M. *Intelligence: From Secrets to Policy,* 7th ed. Thousand Oaks: Sage, 2017.

Madsen, F. G. "International Narcotics Law Enforcement: A Study in Irrationality." *Journal of International Affairs* 66, no. 1 (Fall/Winter 2012): 123–141.

Marrin, Albert. *A Volcano Beneath the Snow: John Brown's War Against Slavery.* New York: Alfred A. Knopf, 2014.

Marshall, Everett. *The Complete Life of William McKinley and the Story of His Assassination.* Chicago: Historical Press, 1901.

Martin, C. A. *Understanding Terrorism: Challenges, Perspectives, and Issues.* Los Angeles: Sage, 2009.

McCoy, Alfred. *In the Shadows of the American Century: The Rise and Decline of U.S. Global Power.* Chicago: Haymarket Books, 2017.

McDonnell, P. J., and C. Sanchez. "A Mother Who Dug in a Mexican Mass Grave to Find the 'Disappeared' Finally Learns Her Son's Fate." *Los Angeles Times,* March 20, 2017.

Meserve, J. "Sources: Staged Cyberattack Reveals Vulnerability in Power Grid." CNN, September 26, 2007.

Metropoulos, E. J., and J. Platt. "Global Cyber Terrorism Incidents on the Rise." Marsh & McLennan *Insights,* 2018. https://www.mmc.com/insights/publications/2018/nov/global-cyber-terrorism-incidents-on-the-rise.html.

Miller, Scott. *The President and the Assassin*: *McKinley, Terror and Empire at the Dawn of the American Century.* New York: Random House, 2013.

National Commission on Terrorist Attacks upon the United States. *9/11 Commission Report.* New York: Norton, 2004.

Newman, Lily. "GitHub Survived the Biggest DDoS Attack Ever Recorded." *Wired,* March 1, 2018.

Newman, Lily. "Yahoo's 2013 Email Hack Actually Compromised Three Billion Accounts." *Wired,* November 3, 2017.

O'Connell, Brian. "What Is 5G and What Does It Mean for Me in 2019?" *TheStreet,* February 25, 2019.

Office of the Director of National Intelligence. *National Counterintelligence Strategy: 2020–2022.* Washington, DC: National Counterintelligence and Security Center, 2020. https://www.dni.gov/files/NCSC/documents/features/20200205-National_CI_Strategy_2020_2022.pdf.

Olmstead v. United States (277 U.S. 438), 1928.

Patton, William W. "John Brown's Body." *Chicago Tribune,* December 16, 1861.

Pegram, Thomas. *One Hundred Percent American: The Rebirth and Decline of the Ku Klux Klan in the 1920s.* Chicago: Ivan R. Dee, 2011.

Pengelly, Martin. "Texas Biker Gang Shooting; Nine Dead and 18 Wounded at Restaurant in Waco." *The Guardian,* May 18, 2015.

Phelps, James R., Jeffrey Dailey, and Monica Koenigsberg. *Border Security.* 2nd ed. Durham, NC: Carolina Academic Press, 2018.

Popper, Nathaniel. "Ransomware Attacks Grow, Crippling Cities and Businesses." *New York Times*, February 9, 2020.

Presidential Daily Briefing. "Bin Ladin Determined to Strike in US." August 6, 2001. https://fas.org/irp/cia/product/pdb080601.pdf.

Riesenfeld, C. L. "Mexico Cartels Recruiting US Border Agents: Inspector General." InSight Crime, April 16, 2015.

Robertson, Campbell, Christopher Mele, and Sabrina Tavernise. "11 Killed in Synagogue Massacre; Suspect Charged with 29 Counts." *New York Times*, October 27, 2018.

Romo, Vanessa. "FBI Finds No Motive in Las Vegas Shooting, Closes Investigation." NPR, January 29, 2019.

Rose, S. E. F. *The Ku Klux Klan or Invisible Empire.* New Orleans: Graham, 1914.

Schiller, D., and J. Pinkerton. "Agents Feared Mexican Drug Cartel Attack on Border Dam." *Houston Chronicle*, June 2, 2010.

Stewart, S. "The Hasan Case: Overt Clues and Tactical Challenges." STRATFOR: *Security Weekly*, November 11, 2009.

Tromblay, Darren. *Spying: Assessing US Domestic Intelligence Since 9/11.* Boulder: Lynne Rienner, 2019.

United Nations Office on Drugs and Crime. *Afghanistan Opium Survey 2017: Cultivation and Production.* Vienna: UNODC, 2017.

United Nations Office on Drugs and Crime. *The Drug Problem and Organized Crime, Illicit Financial Flows, Corruption and Terrorism.* Vienna: UNODC, 2017.

United Nations Office on Drugs and Crime. *World Drug Report 2019.* Vienna: UNODC, 2019.

United States v. Salameh, 152 F.3d 88, 107-108 2d Cir. 1998.

United States v. Yousef, No. S12 93 CR 180 (KTD) (S.D. N.Y.), Oct 22, 1997, (transcript).

Usborne, David. "America Faces a New Wave of Homegrown Political Violence and Terrorism if Its Divisions Continue." *The Independent*, June 24, 2017.

US Congress. "Our Nation's Transportation and Core Infrastructure: Hearings Before the House Committee on Public Works and Transportation." 1991.

US Department of Justice. "Attorney General Sessions Announces New Indictments in International Fentanyl Case." April 27, 2018. https://www.justice.gov/opa/speech/attorney-general-sessions-announces-new-indictments-international-fentanyl-case.

US Department of Justice. *Fusion Center Guidelines: Developing and Sharing Information and Intelligence in a New Era.* Washington, DC: DOJ Office of Justice Programs, 2006.

US Department of State, Bureau of International Narcotics and Law Enforcement Affairs. "2014 International Narcotics Control Strategy Report (INCSR)." March 2014. https://www.state.gov/j/inl/rls/nrcrpt/2014/vol1/index.htm.

US Department of the Treasury. *2018 National Money Laundering Risk Assessment.* Washington, DC: Dept. of the Treasury, 2018. https://home.treasury.gov/system/files/136/2018NMLRA_12-18.pdf.

US Department of the Treasury. "Treasury Sanctions Chinese Fentanyl Trafficker Jian Zhang." April 27, 2018. https://home.treasury.gov/news/press-releases/sm0372.

US Drug Enforcement Administration. "National Forensic Laboratory Information System: Year 2016 Annual Report." 2017. http://www.nflis.deadiversion.usdoj .gov/DesktopModules/ReportDownloads/Reports/NFLIS2016AR_Rev2018.pdf.

US Drug Enforcement Administration. "National Forensic Laboratory Information System: NFLIS-Drug Annual Report 2017." 2018. http://www.nflis.deadiversion .usdoj.gov/DesktopModules/ReportDownloads/Reports/NFLIS-Drug -AR2017.pdf.

US Government Accounting Office. *2017 Annual Report: Additional Opportunities to Reduce Fragmentation, Overlap, and Duplication and Achieve Other Financial Benefits*. GAO-17-491SP. Washington, DC: GAO, April 26, 2017.

US Intelligence Careers. "How Intelligence Works." https://www.intelligence careers.gov/icintelligence.html.

Van Cleave, M. K. "What Is Counterintelligence? A Guide to Thinking and Teaching About CI." *Journal of U.S. Intelligence Studies* 20, no. 2 (Fall/Winter 2013): 58.

Vennochi, Joan. "FBI's Repeated Failures." *Boston Globe*, April 17, 2014. https://www.bostonglobe.com/opinion/editorials/2014/04/16/fbi-must-answer -for-poor-job-marathon-bombing-investigation/pKoEQXdjAZ3KSEI7WQ6JrN /story.html.

Vinton, Kate. "With 56 Million Cards Compromised, Home Depot's Breach Is Bigger Than Target's." *Forbes*, September 18, 2014.

Weaver, Matthew. "Cyber Attackers Target South Korea and US." *The Guardian*, July 8, 2009.

Whittaker, David. *Terrorism: Under the Global Threat,* 2nd ed. New York: Routledge, 2013.

Woolf, Nicky. "DDoS Attack That Disrupted Internet Was Largest of Its Kind in History, Experts Say." *The Guardian*, October 26, 2016.

Index

About the Book

Since the September 11 terrorist attacks—considered one of the worst intelligence failures in US history—the many agencies that constitute the homeland security enterprise have aggressively developed their intelligence capabilities and activities. Jeffrey Dailey and James Phelps provide a comprehensive introduction to the nature of intelligence—its structures, roles, and missions—in the context of homeland security.

This accessible text:

- Covers the full gamut of agencies involved in homeland security
- Tackles difficult ethical issues
- Discusses specific threats—ranging from drug trafficking and money laundering to bioterrorism and the challenges of Covid-19—and how they are dealt with by the intelligence community
- Looks at how intelligence for national security can be applied to domestic security
- Addresses the realities of intelligence sharing among federal, state, and local organizations

Enriched with numerous case studies of both successes and failures, the book has been carefully designed to meet the needs of students focusing on homeland security, intelligence, criminal justice, policing, security management, and related fields.

Jeffrey Douglas Dailey is associate professor in the Department of Security Studies and Criminal Justice at Angelo State University. **James Robert Phelps** created one of the nationally top-10-ranked programs in border and homeland security at Angelo State University. He is now on the adjunct graduate faculty at Aurora University and NOVA Southeastern University.